Film Festivals

The last decade has witnessed an explosion of interest in film festivals, with the field growing to a position of prominence within the space of a few short years. *Film Festivals: History, Theory, Method, Practice* represents a major addition to the literature on this topic, offering an authoritative and comprehensive introduction to the area. With a combination of chapters specifically examining history, theory, method, and practice, it offers a clear structure and systematic approach for the study of film festivals.

Offering a collection of essays written by an international range of established scholars, it discusses well-known film festivals in Europe, North America, and Asia, but equally devotes attention to the diverse range of smaller and/or specialized events that take place around the globe. It provides essential knowledge on the origin and development of film festivals, discusses the use of theory to study festivals, explores the methods of ethnographic and archival research, and looks closely at the professional practice of programming and film funding. Each part, moreover, is introduced by the editors, and all chapters include useful suggestions for further reading.

This will be an essential textbook for students studying film festivals as part of their film, media, and cultural studies courses, as well as a strong research tool for scholars who wish to familiarize themselves with this burgeoning field.

Marijke de Valck is Associate Professor in the Department of Media and Culture Studies at Utrecht University. She is a well-known specialist in film festival studies and author of *Film Festivals: From European Geopolitics to Global Cinephilia* (2007). She co-founded the Film Festival Research Network and is co-editor of the book series *Framing Film Festivals*.

Brendan Kredell is Assistant Professor of Cinema Studies at Oakland University. His research focuses on media and urban studies, an area in which he has published widely. He received a Fulbright fellowship for his work on culture-led urban redevelopment and the Toronto International Film Festival.

Skadi Loist is a lecturer and postdoctoral researcher at the Institute for Media Research of the University of Rostock. She co-founded the Film Festival Research Network and serves as member of the Steering Committee of NECS. Her research interests include film festivals, queer cinema, and media industries. She has worked with the Hamburg International Queer Film Festival since 2002.

Film Festivals

History, Theory, Method, Practice

Edited by Marijke de Valck,
Brendan Kredell and Skadi Loist

Routledge
Taylor & Francis Group

LONDON AND NEW YORK

First published 2016
by Routledge
2 Park Square, Milton Park, Abingdon, Oxon OX14 4RN

and by Routledge
711 Third Avenue, New York, NY 10017

Routledge is an imprint of the Taylor & Francis Group, an informa business

© 2016 Marijke de Valck, Brendan Kredell and Skadi Loist

British Library Cataloguing-in-Publication Data
A catalogue record for this book is available from the British Library

Library of Congress Cataloging-in-Publication Data
A catalog record for this book has been requested

ISBN: 978-0-415-71246-0 (hbk)
ISBN: 978-0-415-71247-7 (pbk)
ISBN: 978-1-315-63716-7 (ebk)

Typeset in Bembo
by Wearset Ltd, Boldon, Tyne and Wear

Contents

Illustrations

Figures

Table

Contributors

Diane Burgess teaches Arts Studies in Research and Writing at the University of British Columbia. She received her PhD in Communication from Simon Fraser University. Her research and publications focus on international film festivals, national cultural policy, and the discursive construction of festival circuits. From 2000 to 2005, she was the Canadian Images Programmer for the Vancouver International Film Festival.

Liz Czach is Associate Professor in the Department of English and Film Studies at the University of Alberta in Edmonton, Canada. She researches and publishes on home movies and amateur film, Canadian and Quebec film, and film festivals. She was a film programmer at the Toronto International Film Festival from 1995 to 2005.

Marijke de Valck is Associate Professor in the Department of Media and Culture Studies at Utrecht University. She is a specialist on film festival studies and author of *Film Festivals: From European Geopolitics to Global Cinephilia* (Amsterdam University Press 2007). She co-founded the Film Festival Research Network and is co-editor of the book series *Framing Film Festivals* for Palgrave Macmillan.

Tamara L. Falicov is Associate Professor and Chair of the Department of Film and Media Studies at the University of Kansas. She specializes in Latin American film industries. She is co-editor of the book series *Framing Film Festivals* for Palgrave Macmillan.

Janet Harbord is Professor of Film at Queen Mary, University of London. Her work crosses the disciplines of film studies, art history, visual culture, cultural studies, and anthropology. Her publications include *The Evolution of Film* (Polity 2007), *Simon Starling* (Phaidon 2012), and a book about Giorgio Agamben and film archaeology, *Ex-centric Cinema* (Bloomsbury Academic 2016).

Dina Iordanova is Professor of Film and Director of the Institute for Global Cinema and Creative Cultures (IGCCC) at the University of St Andrews in Scotland. She has published extensively on film festivals, and, through her engagement with festival-related projects, advanced development of the field. She has often been a guest and served on juries at festivals around the globe.

Brendan Kredell is Assistant Professor of Cinema Studies at Oakland University. His research focuses on media and urban studies, an area in which he has published widely. He received a Fulbright fellowship for his work on culture-led urban redevelopment and the Toronto International Film Festival.

Toby Lee is an artist and scholar working across video, installation, drawing, and text. She holds a PhD in Anthropology and Film and Visual Studies from Harvard University, and is Assistant Professor of Cinema Studies at NYU's Tisch School of the Arts.

Skadi Loist is a lecturer and postdoctoral researcher at the Institute for Media Research of the University of Rostock. She is co-founder of the Film Festival Research Network and serves on the Steering Committee of NECS. She has worked with the Hamburg International Queer Film Festival since 2002. Her research interests include film festivals, queer cinema, and media industries.

Dorota Ostrowska is Senior Lecturer in Film and Modern Media at Birkbeck College, University of London. Her research covers European media studies, film festivals, and the history of film and media production. She is working on the cultural history of the Cannes film festival. Her publications include *Reading the French New Wave: Critics, Writers and Art Cinema in France* (2008).

Roya Rastegar is the Director of Film Programming of the Los Angeles Film Festival. She received her PhD from the University of California, Santa Cruz. Since 2005 she has engaged in curatorial work across film and art. She participated in the programming of a range of festivals, including Tribeca, Sundance, and the Santa Cruz Woman of Color Film Festival.

Julian Stringer is Associate Professor in Film and Television Studies at the University of Nottingham. He has published widely on film festivals, East Asian cinema, Hollywood, and transnational filmmaking. He edited *Movie Blockbusters* (Routledge 2003), and co-edited *New Korean Cinema* (Edinburgh University Press 2005), and *Japanese Cinema* (Routledge 2015). His monograph on film festivals will appear with Palgrave Macmillan.

Cindy Hing-Yuk Wong is Professor of Communication in the Department of Media Culture at the College of Staten Island, City University of New York. Her work has dealt with film festivals, grassroots media, and transnational and diasporic media. She is author of *Film Festivals: Culture, People, and Power on the Global Screen* (Rutgers 2011) and co-author of *Global Hong Kong* (Routledge 2005).

Ger Zielinski was a FQRSC postdoctoral research fellow at the Tisch School of the Arts at New York University and then served as an Assistant Professor of Cultural Studies at Trent University. He received his PhD from McGill University where he wrote his dissertation on the cultural politics of queer film festivals. His research interests include new media aesthetics, cinematic cities, and transnational underground cinemas. Zielinski is co-founder of the Film and Media Festivals Scholarly Interest Group at SCMS.

Foreword

The film festival and film culture's transnational essence

Dina Iordanova

Back in 1937, Rattana Pestonji, a young Parsi man from Bangkok who had just graduated in London, sent a short film he had made to the Amateur Cine Competition in Glasgow.[1] Before long, a letter arrived notifying the first-time director that *Tang*—the story of a young Thai girl—had won the Hitchcock award for Debut Film. It was this prize, purportedly awarded after some involvement from Alfred Hitchcock himself, which was to determine Pestonji's subsequent path in life. He promptly dropped the career his family had charted out for him and went on to establish the first Thai film studio, Hanuman, making scores of films through the 1950s and 1960s. Today, he is hailed as Thai cinema's first master and is a source of inspiration for younger generations. Had the festival in Glasgow not provided him with opportunity and given the initial impetus to his work, the then-aspiring Asian filmmaker would perhaps have become an engineer.

Even so, little is known today about this transnational dimension of the festival in Glasgow, and almost nothing about the defining role it played on the cinematic processes of faraway Thailand, a country with seemingly little connection to Scotland. The few people who have studied and published on the Amateur Cine Competition have examined it according to a self-contained national cinematic framework. They recount details of the local venues, of the local political struggles, and of the involvement of local film-makers, such as Norman McLaren or John Grierson. The international connections and exchanges of the festival are not part of their investigations, and this is typical. When they are studied at all, film festivals are most often explored as domestic phenomena with exclusive significance for the given national cinema. The general dominance of national frameworks over the study of film culture has stifled the emergent study of film festivals for too long.

And then there is the privileged relationship that persists between film studies and just one of its disciplinary strands, textual analysis. To analyze film merely as text is to leave unexplored most of the actual context of a film's reception, and this is where the festival plays a role in reality. Still, wherever the approach to film is textual, the film festival does not appear to be afforded any particular relevance.

Yet another "traditional" academic framework that marginalizes the film festival is the study of film as industry. Because it focuses along three main lines of inquiry—production, distribution, and exhibition—it still does not have a clear place for the film festival, which is a phenomenon that straddles elements of all three areas (Iordanova 2015).

In fact, it is the dominance of textual analysis, national frameworks, and industry studies that has significantly delayed a turning of attention to the film festival as a phenomenon that best reveals film culture's transnational essence.

★★★

The examination of film festivals undertaken in this volume is not just concerned with chronicling awards and filling in gaps in film history. And it is not just about reiterating the extent to which we are still ignorant of the cinematic interactions that come to light once we begin scrutinizing exchanges in the context of festivals. The study of festivals is key to the study of film as an art form, one that has important transnational and social dimensions, rather than, as it still currently is, an agglomeration of national cinemas or texts. Studying film festivals is an endeavor to bring out a more complex *transnational* narrative that permits comprehension of the full dynamics of cinema's evolution as a global art form.

As we have noted, it is not that festivals have not been written about over the years. In fact, film magazines are full of festival reports and reviews. Eminent film commentators and scholars—from Dilys Powell in 1947, to Andre Bazin in 1955, and Thomas Elsaesser in 1969—have explored some of the unique features displayed by film festivals over the decades. The typical festival review, however, consists of a short introductory discussion of the festival's venues and sidebars and then draws focus on the films that are presented at that particular edition of the festival. And it is often just the focus on the films that remains in the annals. Overriding attention is directed toward transitory critical content while the specifics of the more durable container, the festival, remain overlooked and unanalyzed. Occasional voices have called for a more consistent investigation of festivals, but even this is a tacit admission that no previous investigation has materialized, even where intended (Willemen 1998).

What is important today is to ensure that the film festival is studied as a phenomenon complete in itself, emptied of *specific* content (the films remain intrinsic, but they can be any films), independent of particular national cinema frameworks (though admitting of their and other cultural concerns), and separate from film industry considerations (as industry is just one of a festival's many stakeholders).

Why is this necessary? Because if the overarching considerations related to texts, national film traditions, and industry networks are allowed to predominate, then the investigation of film festivals on and in their own terms will keep disappearing and dissolving. Recognition needs to be given to the emergence of the film festival as a hub of exchange in its own right and of the consequent seconding of text, tradition, and industry by film festival studies to its own purposes.

Under guidance, and not without some luck, the study of film festivals has gradually emancipated itself from the more traditional approaches that have kept the festival phenomenon in the shadows. Recent attention to studies in film culture is finally permitting a proper emphasis on the key importance of the film festival in the transnational infrastructure of cinematic art.

The turn toward a cultural framework is part of a wider trend among exhibition-based events. For example, museum and gallery studies, a discipline formerly preoccupied with institutions and infrastructure, has flourished and proliferated in recent years as a powerful and popular sub-discipline within art history. The study of film festivals is closely related to branches of cultural sociology that deal with lively networks (Latour), flow (Castells), production of taste (Bourdieu), places of conviviality (Oldenburg), or the economies of prestige (English). And it encompasses not only the study of the films screened, but also a host of other disciplinary approaches that keep the public sphere in focus: cultural policy, cultural diplomacy, translation. More and more, one recognizes that the films have become but one of the many elements that make up a festival, and that such aspects as the celebrity attendance, the gossip, the party, the red carpet, the glamour, the venues, the sponsors, the audiences, the journalists, and so on are also of intrinsic importance and must be studied in a balanced manner. It is the nature of the specific relationships between a festival's various stakeholders that largely determines the social standing of a festival within the public sphere; what will be its selection of films; what will be the relative importance of those films in the general context of the event; which filmmakers will be invited; what concurrent events there will be; the social program; the dress code; the accommodation and meals schedule; the marketing; the media coverage sought; and so on. It is the idiosyncratic combination of all these elements that gives a festival its unique profile and creates what Daniel Dayan (2000) would term that festival's "narrative." This volume attempts to give due attention to all these elements.

★★★

The global reach of film is enabled by its unique and inherently transnational infrastructure. And, as the place where the various cinemas come together, film festivals are the most important branch in this infrastructure, but also the most overlooked one.

From its outset the large film festival has been the very antithesis of an enclosed national cinema. Such a festival brings together works from all over the world—and the more it manages to do so, the more respected it is. In that, the film festival has always been the site where the inherently transnational character of cinematic art reveals itself most glaringly. If it were not for the festival recognition and awards that bring important and nascent film-makers to the attention of international audiences—filmmakers often under-appreciated in their own countries—how would we know and cherish the oeuvre of some of the greatest Japanese or Iranian directors today?

Film festivals are places for transnational encounters and exchanges, as well as nodes in more general transnational infrastructures, both cultural and com-mercial (Iordanova 2011). That, from early on, global commercial players capitalized on the festival circuit is true not only for those in the West who congregated at Cannes and Berlin, but also for players farther afield. Major Asian diasporic film producers, such as Shaw Brothers, recognized the festival circuit as a key node of a distribution set-up that would transcend national borders. Commonly believed to exemplify "the cosmopolitan and boundary-crossing business culture of diasporic Chinese capitalists" (Fu 2008: 3), Shaw Brothers made use of film festivals, both within Asia and internationally, as part of a well-planned business strategy.[2] The film festival, as Abé Markus Nornes remarks, "is a scene of power," a contested gathering of global indus-try players (2007: 65).

Film festivals are inherently transnational in that no matter what the inten-tion of the festival is—and even where a festival is launched with a nationalist agenda in mind—the diverse content that is being showcased effectively undermines and counter-balances nationalist tendencies. While many important international film festivals have, as one of their chief objectives, to showcase recent "national" output (Canadian at Toronto, South Korean at Busan, German at Berlinale), even so, these national agendas remain subordi-nate and predictably lost in the shadow of the transnational.

Today, the filmmaking and circulation processes are marked by a "new localism" that manifests itself in terms of dynamic regional production and distribution networks (within Asia, within Europe, or the Americas) and in a seemingly interminable proliferation of festivals. Film festivals appear to be in direct competition with each other—witness the case of Busan and Hong Kong, or the "bidding war" among three lavish Gulf festivals, or the venera-ble A-list category fests of Europe—while nonetheless attending to the same project of raising cinema's transnational profile. There is no better place than a film festival to witness the transnational dynamics of cinema coming into full light. It is a context that allows for an elegantly diplomatic handling of divergent nationalist agendas that may lurk below the surface, but which are soon dropped in favor of "accelerated transnational cultural flows" (Iwabuchi 2002: 19) that open up to wider supranational exchanges.

★★★

The fledgling field of festival studies is only about a decade old now. But we have gone a long way toward recognizing and exploring the important role of film festivals in all these processes. Venturing into work dedicated to film festivals at first felt like taking a stroll in the desert—not only wasn't there much out there to see, but there seemed to be no one particularly engaged with the subject matter either. Today, I am delighted by how our knowledge and understanding of film festivals grows richer and deeper every year, and how the festival world is opening itself up to our insights.

The emergence of multiple festival case histories necessitates the emergence of new narratives that recount and account for the dynamics of global film culture. This book is another important addition to a range of studies that have appeared in recent years, tracing explicit and implicit factors that enable the circulation of cinema; this includes monographs such as Janet Harbord's *Film Cultures* (2002), Abé Markus Nornes's *Cinema Babel* (2007), Charles Acland's *Screen Traffic* (2003), Marijke de Valck's *Film Festivals* (2007), Brian Larkin's *Signal and Noise* (2008), Cindy Wong's *Film Festivals* (2011), or Ramon Lobato's *Shadow Economies of Cinema* (2012), as well as Mark Shiel and Tony Fitzmaurice's edited volume on *Cinema and the City* (2001), Julian Stringer's on *Movie Blockbusters* (2003), Rosalind Galt and Karl Schoonover's on *Global Art Cinema* (2010), and my own attempt to bring together important writing on festivals in *The Film Festival Reader* (2013).[3]

The theoretical framework that will underwrite future studies becomes more defined here, accommodating important contributions from theoreticians such as Bourdieu, Habermas, and Hansen, and considering important aspects of the festival, such as cultural legitimization, industrial aspects, audiences, and cultural mediation. It places the film festival firmly within the tradition of the study of film culture and fully recognizes its important role as part of a global public sphere.

Notes

1 Pestonji (1908–1970) was 29 at the time; the film *Tang* also won an award at the New York World Film Festival in 1939. The Glasgow Amateur Film Festival had been in existence since 1933 (Washbrook 2009).
2 Run Run Shaw was one of the founders of the Asia-Pacific Film Festival in 1954; Shaw Brothers also engaged extensively with such established film festivals as Cannes and San Francisco, which they used, with varying success, as part of a concerted effort to capitalize on diasporic cinema cultures and construct a wider marketplace for their prodigious output (Fu 2008: 9, 11).
3 This list could and should be much longer and would also include numerous other volumes: on concrete festivals (e.g., SooJeong Ahn's examination of *The Pusan International Film Festival 1996–2005*), on festival programming (Jeff Ruoff's volume *Coming Soon to a Festival Near You*), on festival management (Alex Fischer's *Sustainable Projections*), as well as the important series of six *Film Festival Yearbooks* (2009–2014).

References

Acland, C. (2003) *Screen Traffic: Movies, Multiplexes and Global Culture*. Durham, NC and London: Duke University Press.

Ahn, S. (2011) *The Pusan International Film Festival, South Korean Cinema and Globalisation*, Hong Kong: Hong Kong University Press.

Bazin, A. (2009 [1955]) "The Festival Viewed as a Religious Order," in R. Porton (ed.) *Dekalog 03: On Film Festivals*, London: Wallflower, pp. 13–20.

Bourdieu, P. (2010 [1979]) *Distinction: A Social Critique of the Judgement of Taste*, Abingdon and New York: Routledge.

Castells, M. (2009 [2000]) *The Rise of the Network Society: Information Age: Economy, Society and Culture*, Vol. 1, Hoboken, NJ: Wiley-Blackwell.

Dayan, D. (2013 [2000]) "Looking for Sundance: The Social Construction of a Film Festival," in D. Iordanova (ed.) *The Film Festival Reader*, St Andrews: St Andrews Film Studies, pp. 45–59.

De Valck, M. (2007) *Film Festivals: From European Geopolitics to Global Cinephilia*, Amsterdam: Amsterdam University Press.

Elsaesser, T. (1969) "Letter from Venice," *The Brighton Film Review*, November 13.

English, J. (2008) *Economy of Prestige: Prizes, Awards and the Circulation of Cultural Value*, Cambridge, MA: Harvard University Press.

Fischer, A. (2012) *Sustainable Projections: Concepts in Film Festival Management*, St Andrews: St Andrews Film Studies.

Fu, P. (2008) "Introduction: The Shaw Brothers Diasporic Cinema," in P. Fu (ed.) *China Forever: The Shaw Brothers and Diasporic Cinema*, Urbana-Champaign, IL: University of Illinois Press, pp. 1–27.

Galt, R. and K. Schoonover (eds.) (2010) *Global Art Cinema: New Theories and Histories*, Oxford: Oxford University Press.

Harbord, J. (2002) *Film Cultures*, London: Sage.

Iordanova, D. (2011) "East Asia and Film Festivals: Transnational Clusters for Creativity and Commerce," in D. Iordanova and R. Cheung (eds.) *Film Festival Yearbook 3: Film Festivals and East Asia*, St Andrews: St Andrews Film Studies, pp. 1–37.

Iordanova, D. (ed.) (2013) *The Film Festival Reader*, St Andrews: St Andrews Film Studies.

Iordanova, D. (2015) "The Film Festival as an Industry Node," *Media Industries*, 1(3), pp. 7–11.

Iwabuchi, K. (2002) *Recentering Globalization: Popular Culture and Japanese Transnationalism*, Durham, NC and London: Duke University Press.

Larkin, B. (2008) *Signal and Noise: Media, Infrastructure, and Urban Culture in Nigeria*, Durham, NC and London: Duke University Press.

Latour, B. (2007) *Reassembling the Social: An Introduction to Actor-Network-Theory*, Oxford: Oxford University Press.

Lobato, R. (2012) *Shadow Economies of Cinema: Mapping Informal Film Distribution*, London: BFI.

Nornes, A. M. (2007) *Cinema Babel: Translating Global Cinema*, Minneapolis, MN: University of Minnesota Press.

Oldenburg, R. (2001) *Celebrating the Third Place: Inspiring Stories About the Great Good Places at the Heart of Our Communities*, Boston, MA: Da Capo Press.

Powell, D. (1947) "The Importance of International Film Festivals," *The Penguin Film Review*, 3, pp. 59–61.

Ruoff, J. (ed.) *Coming Soon to a Festival Near You: Programming Film Festivals*, St Andrews: St Andrews Film Studies.

Shiel, M. and T. Fitzmaurice (eds.) (2001) *Cinema and the City: Film and Urban Societies in a Global Context*, Oxford: Wiley-Blackwell.

Stringer, J. (ed.) (2003) *Movie Blockbusters*, London and New York: Routledge.

Washbrook, R. (2009) "Innovation on a Shoestring: The Films and Filmmakers of the Scottish Amateur Film Festival," in I. Craven (ed.) *Movies on a Home Ground: Explorations in Amateur Cinema*, Newcastle upon Tyne: Cambridge Scholars Publishing, pp. 36–65.

Willemen, P. (1998) "Introduction," in P. Willemen and J. Pines (eds.) *The Essential Framework: Essays in Cultural Studies and Film Theory*, London: EpiGraph, pp. 1–7.

Wong, C. H.-Y. (2011) *Film Festivals: Culture, People, and Power on the Global Screen*, New Brunswick, NJ: Rutgers University Press.

Acknowledgments

We've been lucky to work with Natalie Foster and Sheni Kruger at Routledge; from the seed of an idea through to an in-blossom manuscript, their encouragement, patience, and guidance enabled this book to grow into what you have before you today.

The success of a collection like this is judged on the strength of its contributions, and in this regard we're extremely fortunate to have collaborated with the world's leading scholars on film festivals. They have each given generously of their time and ideas, and we only hope the book does justice to their work.

We've drawn inspiration for this project from our own experiences in the classroom, where our students' keen insights and probing questions helped to define what the goals of a book like this should be. Thanks go to all of our former and current colleagues at our home institutions: the University of Amsterdam and Utrecht University, the University of Calgary and Oakland University, and the Universities of Hamburg and Rostock. Their support and assistance was invaluable. A special thanks goes to the University of Amsterdam and the Amsterdam Centre for Globalisation Studies, whose generosity enabled a valuable face-to-face meeting halfway through our cross-Atlantic collaboration.

In addition, we would like to acknowledge the many fruitful conversations with colleagues in the research and festival community as part of the Film Festival Research Network; it was in this context that the need and potential of a textbook was first discussed.

Most of all, thanks to our friends, partners, and families, for everything you do.

Introduction

What is a film festival? How to study festivals and why you should

Marijke de Valck

There are distinct images that come to mind when the term "film festival" is used: red carpets, open-air screenings, paparazzi, a bustling crowd that fills the theaters and dominates the public spaces that are temporarily taken over by the festival event. This iconic film festival imagery renders a feeling of glamour, celebration, happening, and community. It conveys a multilayered message about film festivals as sites of power, being able to bestow prestige on the films and filmmakers that were selected for the event; as sites of leisure, where public and professionals alike are courted to indulge themselves; and also as events that are relevant for society, that matter in the lives of people visiting them, offering a social environment where one can feel part of a community. These are events capable of generating daily news, of carrying the promise of larger impact and of making history and social change. To ask what a film festival *is*, then, appears to be a trick question that hopes to fool its audience into thinking it can be answered readily with a clear definition. But fixed definitions do little to advance our understanding of film festivals. What are needed instead are frames that can be utilized to expose the different mechanisms operating within and through festivals, as well as parameters that allow us to differentiate between them. In this introduction we will discuss how to go about studying film festivals, but first we will tackle the important issue of diversity and difference within the film festival phenomenon.

Distinguishing film festivals

Every day of the year somewhere in the world, one or more film festivals take place. There are big international film festivals that generate an abundance of media coverage. These are the events that have created the prevailing film festival imagery of red carpets, buzz, and stars. In terms of numbers, however, they only constitute a fraction of the total amount of film festival events taking place annually. In fact, film festivals come in many sizes and flavors. Next to the major and well-known film festivals stand a multitude of medium-sized, small, and tiny festival events. A lovely example of a small film festival is Pluk de Nacht Open Air Film Festival, which was started by four friends in Amsterdam back in 2003.[1] The concept of the festival is to screen films that are not available in Dutch movie theaters, and to do so in the attractive mix of an urban summertime outdoor location and social setting. Long before the night begins to fall and the movie starts (which is around 9 PM Amsterdam summer time), people flock to the festival site to secure a good seat (either brought or rented). They bring drinks or snacks with them and hang out with friends. No red carpet or stars, not even an admission fee; just a celebration of the night and of cinema, made possible by a lot of volunteer work. Clearly, Pluk de Nacht belongs to a different breed than the professional organization of the International Documentary Film Festival Amsterdam (1988), Amsterdam's best-known festival, which turns the city into a meeting place and trade hub for documentary filmmaking each autumn. In order to unravel the potpourri of film festivals that exist we will begin by looking at some key parameters that shape festivals.

Size is one of the most obvious elements of distinction. Typically the number of films shown, the visitor count, and organizing budget correlate; they grow or decrease in size together, the latter being less common. The obsession with growth is one of the oldest criticisms leveled at festivals: the idea that bigger is necessarily better has been recurrently challenged, in particular by film critics who assessed various events as too unwieldy to navigate. The criticism persists, and is confirmed by existing hierarchical relations, as the most powerful film festivals are without exception of considerable size. For new festivals, too, it is growth that typically marks success and grants access to greater resources and fosters increased organizational sustainability. Failure to acquire such critical mass, on the other hand, is often a harbinger of doom for smaller festivals. Size, in other words, may be an indication of maturity. Most young events start small and need time to prove themselves and gain weight. The success of Pluk de Nacht—which promotes itself as the largest open-air film festival of the Netherlands[2]—is, for example, visible in its expansion to other Dutch cities, like Arnhem (since 2013), The Hague (2013–2014), and Utrecht (since 2014). Notable exceptions to this rule are the dozen or so film festivals that have been launched as well-funded mega-events from their inception, such as the international film festivals in Busan [previously Pusan] (1996) and Beijing (2011) in Asia; Tribeca (2002) in North America; Dubai (2004) and Abu Dhabi (2007) in the Middle East; and Rome (2006) in Europe. In all these cases governments and private sponsors have invested substantially and structurally in the events, often also establishing new film funds and film markets, in a bid for power in global and regional film industry scenes.[3]

Another parameter to consider is festivals' outreach. Major film festivals as a rule advertise themselves as "international" events, meaning they cater not only to local or national audiences, but specifically aim to attract international visitors and guests. To stage an international film festival involves additional services, like subtitling films in globally spoken languages (usually English or French); operating industry and press offices; organizing industry and press screenings; and facilitating video booths, networking opportunities, and social events. Such services require substantial funding, and as a result, international film festivals are more dependent on a variety of stakeholders backing up the event financially. Many film festivals, however, are quite content reaching local audiences. In the case of Pluk de Nacht this local audience includes the large student, international, and expat communities living in Amsterdam; nearly all films screened are either English-language or presented with English subtitles. In this way, festivals with a local outreach may also have a clear international dimension. Apart from obvious locations like cosmopolitan cities, one can stumble upon such festivals in smaller towns that promote the event of a film festival to enhance the attraction of the location as a tourist destination. For example, the Portuguese island of Madeira, a paradise for advanced surfers seeking big waves, has hosted the Madeira Island Surf Film Festival (MadSwell) since 2013 in the municipal theater and on the beaches of the capital city, Funchal. In similar vein there are film festivals about climbing organized in mountainous regions (e.g., the Mountain Film Festival Aysen in Patagonia, Chile), wine or food-themed festivals in rural areas known for their vineyards or gourmet local foods (such as the Napa Valley Film Festival, held in the four villages of Napa, Yountville, St. Helena, and Calistoga in California), and archaeology film festivals near excavation sites (e.g., the International Archaeology Film Festival in Split, Croatia). In addition to local residents, all these festivals target international audiences who visit the town or region for other primary purposes. This marks a key difference from the norm-setting, major international film festivals, which have distributors, buyers, sales agents, and sponsors as their primary interest groups (Peranson 2008: 39). For these groups, tourism or leisurely exploration of the host city/region are ancillary attractions.

When discussing film festivals' outreach one should not only consider the way in which festivals differ in their appeal to international, national, and local audiences, but also take note that certain festivals target specific communities or demographic groups. Good examples are LGBT and queer film festivals, Jewish film festivals, women's film festivals, and festivals aiming at particular ethnic communities (such as the Asian American International Film Festival discussed by Cindy Hing-Yuk Wong in Chapter 5). This category of events can also be referred to as "identity-based festivals" because the thematic selection of films programmed for these festivals is made with explicit interest in engaging identity questions and representational issues that concern specific communities and groups. There is substantial research and literature available on such festivals, and the annotated bibliography found on the website of the Film Festival Research Network[4] (www.filmfestivalresearch. org) constitutes a good starting point for exploration of the material.

Another avenue into one's exploration of film festivals is to take the films as starting point for comparison and differentiation. Beside general events, which screen all types of film, many festivals choose to focus on one genre. Such specialized or thematic events may span the complete spectrum of high- to low-brow culture; cover niche, cross-over and mainstream tastes; and cater to professionals as well as general publics. Probably the best-known genre-based festivals are the ones for documentary. In addition, there are well-developed sub-circuits focusing on popular genres like horror, fantasy, and sci-fi, but also niche fests for silent and archival film. Other examples of genre-based film festivals include animation, short films, experimental cinema, and student films.

It may not always be crystal clear, however, if a festival should be understood on the basis of its outreach or its selection of films, as the two tend to be interrelated. The Bucheon International Fantasy Film Festivals (1996) in South Korea, for example, targets the local fan communities of fantasy film, broadly defined as "all that we cannot experience in the real world"[5]—which includes horror, sci-fi, suspense, and action films. So, is it outreach or the selection of films that defines this event at heart? The fest's title and abbreviation (BiFan) are ambiguous.[6] And what about the Galway African Film Festival (2008), a festival in Ireland that screens African cinema? Like many festivals that focus on national or regional film production such thematic interest is spurred by the wish to advance understanding of certain (film) cultures, but often goes hand in hand with the aim of reaching local ethnic communities. In the case of LGBT and queer festivals, adversely, one is prone to assume that due to their historical roots in activist counterculture the identity of the audience will take prominence, and that the selection of films is typically guided by curatorial ideas about possible reception. This crucially means that films that do not explicitly address a queer theme are also considered for selection, for the embedding in the context of a LGBT festival can bring out submerged, queer readings of texts that reflect or arouse the community's experience and/or imagination (Loist 2012).

In this way, it is the core activity of programming that bridges the parameters of outreach and film. The question each festival has to ask itself is which parameter should lead the self-positioning of the festival. Back in the 1970s and 1980s Hubert Bals, the charismatic programmer and founder of the International Film Festival Rotterdam (1972), believed one should *always* start with the films, and then proceed by trying to find an audience for each film (De Valck 2012). In the context of today's festival world, this position appears outdated and rather dogmatic. As Roya Rastegar shows in Chapter 10, many festivals will accomplish the demanding task of programming by going back and forth between films, outreach considerations and practical limitations; combining an assessment of films in their own right with ideas about audiences' needs and expectations, the framing effect of program labels, as well as an eye for the overall consistency and balance within a given festival's edition. The umbrella term of activist film festivals—including human rights film festivals, so-called radical or subversive film festivals, disability film festivals, eco or green film festivals, etc.—offers particularly interesting cases to study the practice of thematic programming with explicit outreach aims. Such festivals address a diverse palette of social issues—injustices, inequalities, discrimination, environmental hazards, etc.—through the medium of film in the hope of spreading awareness of problems, correcting false beliefs, countering misrepresentations, and ultimately contributing to better and more just societies.

Again, it is worthwhile to reiterate that when it comes to festivals, descriptive terms should not be taken as exclusive identifiers. Identity-based and activist—or what we may call "social concern" festivals[7]—can easily overlap. Queer film festivals, for instance, can be very activist in set-up, mobilizing LGBTQ communities to stand up for their rights. The broader label of activist film festivals includes events that solicit attention for a range of social concerns (e.g., human rights or the effects of global warming) that may or may not intersect with a particular community's needs, and the term can help to focus our attention on the type of critical questions that are relevant to raise with regard to a particular fest.

Finally, it is becoming increasingly relevant to look at the variety of ways in which films may be screened at festivals. With the near-global turn to digital filmmaking and post-production, and the conversion of movie theaters to digital, many festivals followed and nowadays only screen films in DCP format. For some film festivals, however, projection in analogue formats is part of the attraction. The San Francisco Silent Film Festival (1992) narrates on its website how its founders, Melissa Chittick and Stephen Salmons, "wanted to share their love of early cinema with the world and [...] knew that presenting silent films as they are meant to be seen—in beautiful prints on a big screen with live musical accompaniment—could thrill modern audiences."[8] This quote underlines that it is not only the technological format that is being preserved at archival festivals, but also the cultural projection tradition, the *dispositif*,[9] which is in the case of silent film to be shown with live musical accompaniment (Fossati 2011: 248).

The *dispositif* of contemporary film festivals can be argued to be in transition as well. In its classic execution the festival *dispositif* makes use of the black box (theatrical projection) and/or open-air screenings, thus revolving around reception set for immersion (big screens are preferred) and shared experience (packed theaters or public spaces are strived after). Many festivals, however, are comfortable breaking with these traditional settings. The International Film Festival Rotterdam, for example, is known for experimenting with alternative projections, starting with the well-received Exploding Cinema programs in 1996—exploring the options of CD-ROM and other exiting new digital media of the time—and continuing with programs on a variety of platforms (televisions, monitors, and iPods) and locations (such as urban screens, hotel rooms, and churches). Even if the classic festival settings continue to dominate, a new generation of film festivals is dawning: festivals that take place online, focus on films shot with mobile phones[10] or tablets, and experiment with interaction and virtual reality.

Framing film festivals

Now that we have looked beyond the dominant imagery of film festivals and brought the diversity and difference between events into the limelight, the next challenge poses itself. If the festival world indeed is a potpourri of events, how do you go about studying them? If there is no encompassing definition for film festivals, how can one know what elements beckon scrutiny? While it is clear that there is no one-size-fits-all approach for film festivals, it is certainly feasible to design appropriate, effective, and rigorous research set-ups for any film festival, even if you are a newcomer to the field of film festival studies. Typically, the path toward a solid research design follows five steps:

1   **Familiarize yourself with existing film festival history and research.**
    Film festivals are an established part of the global cultural field. There have been turning points in the development of the organizational structure of film festivals, and other crucial moments that continue to resonate in contemporary practices. In addition, many individual happenings and events have influenced what went into the general annals of film history. Basic knowledge of film festival history is a prerequisite for anyone interested in studying film festivals. The academic study of these events, moreover, has taken flight since the 2000s, and by familiarizing oneself with existing literature, the researcher will be able to adapt her or his own design to contribute to existing debates, delve into un(der)explored topics, or, possibly, counter widely accepted frames. Without aiming to be exhaustive, this book provides a good starting point and broad introduction to the study of film festivals, with chapters clustered in sections on history, theory, method, and practice.

2   **Get to know your case study/ies.**
    Given the fact that film festivals come in many sizes and flavors, a lot of the existing work on film festivals is case-study based. It is crucial that any project that involves the study of one or more festivals begins with the collection of factual information and a thorough description of its case(s). What is the size of the festival? When was it founded? Is it an international or local event? Does it target a professional audience, the general public, specific communities or a mix? Are there other outreach considerations that stand out? Is there a thematic focus in selection of films, or an explicit curatorial mission? In what way (format, *dispositif)* are films screened during the festivals? In-depth knowledge about the particularities and unique history of the event(s) under scrutiny will prevent one from raising less appropriate research questions. For example, when studying a small, local film festival, it would be irrelevant to make the impact of the festival on the national film industry one's central concern. An example of a well-focused question for a festival about human trafficking, on the other hand, would be how it deals with the pitfall of

"poverty porn" (see Faguet 2009; Ross 2011) in its programming practices?[11]

3   **Determine their position in the festival world and cultural field.**
Despite our emphasis thus far on the differences between film festivals, and the necessity to determine what identifies and characterizes a specific event, it is equally crucial to realize that film festivals are never stand-alone events. They are part of the film festival world as well as the larger cultural field. This film festival world is in constant flux, with new festivals being initiated while others discontinue their activities. While the concept of the international film festival circuit has been rightfully criticized for its inaccurate connation of an orchestrated network of festival events (see the discussions in Chapters 2 and 3 by Julian Stringer and Skadi Loist), the rationale that film festivals gain significance in relation to each other still holds. This is not to say that each festival has a relation to every other festival, nor that relations are fixed; rather it points to the constant positioning (competitive, antagonistic, or complementary) of festival organizations in an ever-changing institutional and cultural landscape. Inquiry into festivals' positioning will reveal hierarchies and other power relations that work upon festivals' potential impact. It is important to understand, in addition, that impact can occur on different levels: that international or local; large, small, or medium-sized; and general or specialized events all speak to different stakeholders and thus have divergent discursive weight (see Chapter 9 by Diane Burgess and Brendan Kredell).

4   **Draw on points 1–3 to formulate a topical research question.**
With knowledge about festival history and the current debates in festival studies, as well as your case studies and their position in the festival world, one is ready to formulate a topical research question. The topicality of the question can reside in its contribution to existing research and discussions, or be motivated by developments and transformations in professional practice. Many of the most interesting questions tend to pertain to areas in which the selected cases have most discursive weight; this may be questions about community and representation in the case of identity-based film festivals, or the innovative use of audience participation of certain online film festivals. A good example of a non-case-study based question would be the role of the city of Melbourne in the promotion of film festival culture in Australia (see Chapter 9 by Diane Burgess and Brendan Kredell for other examples of research questions).

Because many film festivals are complex events, research questions need to be specific about which aspects will be included in the context of your project. Are you interested in a festival's impact on culture? Then you may want to focus on its programming, analyze curatorial strategies, or study the history of prizes. If your interest lies instead with festivals' relation to the industry, you could turn to the study of film festival markets or funds (see Chapter 12 by Tamara L. Falicov), interview film-makers or producers that frequent festivals, or examine festivals as revenue stream. On the institutional level, festivals can be studied as cultural organizations, mapping how they function and what is subject to change—for example, as a result of trends in cultural policy. One can also explore festivals as events, and consider the ways in which the festival set-up informs reception. In Chapter 4 Janet Harbord discusses festivals' peculiar relation to space and time, with the latter being her focus. This avenue offers rich possibilities for projects on festivals' relation to their host city, regional positioning, or tensions between national (political) interests and cultural specificity, on the one hand, and cosmopolitan aspirations and the demands of a globalized world on the other.

5   **Choose a theoretical framework and method(s) that will best help you answer your questions *and* are feasible.**
Research in film festival studies tends to be topic-driven. Given the complexity of the film festival world—with octopus arms into the realms of culture, economics, and politics—and the many differences between individual festivals, it really is one's research question that determines what theories to draw upon and which methods to deploy (see Chapter 9 by Diane Burgess and Brendan Kredell). There is a young tradition in film festival studies that builds on notions like the public sphere (see Chapter 5 by Cindy Hing-Yuk Wong), uses Pierre Bourdieu's cultural sociology (see Chapter 6 by Marijke de Valck), and addresses issues of globalization, but there is yet a wealth of further theoretical frames waiting to be brought to bear on film festivals. In terms of methodology a lot of festival studies include fieldwork and interviews (see Chapter 7 by Toby Lee). Critical analysis of the variety of texts that is churned out with each festival edition is equally common. A particular challenge for the researcher of film festivals is the availability of and access to sources. Ger Zielinski points out in Chapter 8 how a lack of resources hinders many festivals in keeping an archive, with the loss of precious material as a result. Fieldwork and interviews in their turn may be obstructed by festival staff who may not be willing to let one look behind the scenes, or who are simply too busy to collaborate. Each festival research project needs to take these practicalities into account and consider the feasibility of its set-up carefully before proceeding.

Celebrating film festivals

The name chosen for the Pluk de Nacht Open Air Film Festival is a savvy play on words. It takes the Latin aphorism *carpe diem*—usually translated as "seize the day" ("pluk de dag" in Dutch) and uttered as incitement to enjoy the moment—and turns this into "seize the night" to mark the unique selling proposition of the festival's concept: open-air film screenings after sunset. *Carpe diem* is a wonderful phrase to use in the context of film festivals. It encompasses what may be our main attraction to these events: their complete embrace of the present moment. Festivals take place in the here and now. They invite people to engage with cinema in ways that are uniquely tied in with the space and time of the festival event. Therefore, the festival experience, we suggest, should never be simply theorized; it beckons to be lived. For all the necessary distinctions and valuable frames we may apply, it is our celebration of film festivals—going there, participating, experiencing, performing—that brings us closer to an understanding of the question what film festivals are. Not because we would bring home neat definitions, but because it is only after having breathed the festival atmosphere and become one with its rhythms that we can begin to grasp our love for them.

Film festivals have multiplied ever since their inception in the European Interbellum. Many have wondered if their growth will ever come to a halt, or reach the point where a paring back is inevitable.[12] So far, this hasn't happened. Part of the answer to the conundrum of film festivals' persistent proliferation simply seems to be that people care. We believe they matter, and thus continue to flock to them. Why do they matter? The wonderful films that are screened, often exclusively, at festivals constitute a key reason; the festival environment provides a sound second; and the possibility of sharing the experience with others a good third. Film festivals are, in short, about three "F"s: films, festivals, and friends. They offer a unique combination of corporeal, visceral, and mental stimulation, engaging multiple senses, offering intellectual stimuli, and allowing social connection.[13] Thanks to this particular mix of ingredients festivals have established themselves as the nodes where cinephilia, the love for cinema, is kept alive.

Film festivals have become an essential part of global film culture. By studying them, we learn not only about festivals, but about film, film history, industry, and much more. Festivals are the sites and occasions where discursive patterns emerge that teach us about film culture, aesthetics, politics, activism, cosmopolitanism, and its counter-movements. It is in the condensed time of the festival event, the bustling spaces of ritualized environments, and the printed words of festival discourse that a myriad of interests are played out. Like cinema itself, festivals act as a metaphorical window onto the world. Festivals possess a unique potential to set agendas and to intervene in the public sphere. They can influence our aesthetic tastes, our political beliefs, and our outlook upon life. Put simply, film festivals may change our perception of the world.

Not many people know the second part of the sentence in which the Roman poet Horace wrote his famous phrase *carpe diem* in 23 BCE: "*Carpe diem, quam minimum credula postero*," which can be translated as "Seize the day, put very little trust in tomorrow." The meaning of this text is decisively *not* to ignore the future, but rather to take action today—in the present—to create a better future. For Horace, in other words, *carpe diem* did not signify the glorification of a hedonistic approach to life, but a call to action. Likewise, film festivals are not simply about self-indulgent pleasures. Beyond the fun and frivolity, the showing off and smooching, there is a serious undertone. Celebrating film festivals means celebrating film as art, film as a political tool, and film's invaluable role in society. By studying film festivals you will participate in such celebration.

Notes

1 The four friends that founded the Pluk de Nacht Open Air Film Festival are Jurriaan Esmeijer, Caspar Sonnen, Henne Verhoef, and Emilio Troncoso Larrain.
2 Pluk de Nacht: www.plukdenacht.nl/en/about-the-festival/ (August 26, 2015).
3 International major film festivals are typically what Mark Peranson (2008) has called "business festivals," events for which industry professionals constitute the most important stakeholder. In order to attract representatives from the industry these festivals do more than simply screen films; they facilitate the business that takes place at festivals. The organization of markets, funds, and training initiatives has taken a flight in the new millennium (see De Valck 2014).
4 The Film Festival Research Network (FFRN) is an informal network of academics and professionals working for or interested in film festivals. Its main aim is to facilitate knowledge exchange and to further research and critical thinking on film festivals. The network was founded in 2008 by Marijke de Valck and Skadi Loist, who continue to manage the website and coordinate the activities. Apart from the website, which includes the regularly updated annotated bibliography of film festival studies, and additional resources such as festival listings and syllabi, the network offers a mailing list (with *c.*550 subscribers in 2015), provides assistance in the organization of annual conference meetings in Europe (NECS) and North America (SCMS), and acts as a liaison for collaboration with other organizations and initiatives.
   On the topic of identity-based film festivals consult section 9.1. of the annotated bibliography at www.filmfestivalresearch.org.
5 BiFan Website, "History: Summary—19th (2015)," http://history.bifan.kr/eng/summary/19th_summary.htm, accessed November 13, 2015.
6 Since the establishment of the Network of Asian Fantastic Film in 2008, moreover, the festival positions and promotes itself as a regional hub for genre film production in Asia.
7 See section 9.2.d of the annotated bibliography on www.filmfestivalresearch.org.
8 San Francisco Silent Film Festival website, "Mission & History," www.silentfilm.org/about/mission-history, accessed August 20, 2015.
9 The concept of *dispositif* in film theory goes back to its use by Michel Foucault, and subsequent interpretations by theorists like Giorgio Agamben, Jean-Louis Baudry, and Vilém Flusser. Depending on which theoretical origin is preferred, film scholars use the term to point to the apparatus of cinema, film's medium specificity or the cultural traditions that determine films' (bodily and social) reception.
10 An interesting trend that may be linked to the omnipresence of smartphones is "vertical cinema," films conceived to be projected on a flipped, vertical screen.
11 "Poverty porn" may be understood as the exploitation of images of the poor or underprivileged by playing on the emotional response of Western audiences, often with the additional aim of raising donations.
12 See for example the interview with Robert Redford on *IndieWire* (Kohn 2013) or Pierre-Henri Deleau, former head of Cannes' Director's Fortnight in *Daily Variety* (cited in Turan 2002: 8).

13 For more reading and a groundbreaking approach to film festivals that combines embodied sensations and intellectual analysis see the book *Curating Africa in the Age of Film Festivals* by Lindiwe Dovey.

References

De Valck, M. (2012) "Finding Audiences for Films: Programming in Historical Perspective," in J. Ruoff (ed.) *Coming Soon to a Festival Near You: Programming Film Festivals*, St Andrews: St Andrews Film Books, pp. 25–40.

De Valck, M. (2014) "Supporting Art Cinema at a Time of Commercialization: Principles and Practices, the Case of the International Film Festival Rotterdam," *Poetics*, 42, pp. 40–59.

Dovey, L. (2015) *Curating Africa in the Age of Film Festivals*, New York: Palgrave Macmillan.

Faguet, M. (2009) "Pornomiseria: Or How Not to Make a Documentary Film," *Afterall: A Journal of Art, Context and Enquiry*, 21, pp. 5–15.

Fossati, G. (2011) *From Grain to Pixel: The Live of Archival Film in Transition*, Amsterdam: Amsterdam University Press.

Kohn, E. (2013) "Sundance 2013: Robert Redford Says There Are Too Many Film Festivals," *IndieWire*, January 17, www.indiewire.com/article/sundance-2012-robert-redford-says-there-are-too-many-film-festivals (August 27, 2015).

Loist, S. (2012) "A Complicated Queerness: LGBT Film Festivals and Queer Programming Strategies," in J. Ruoff (ed.) *Coming Soon to a Festival Near You: Programming Film Festivals*, St Andrews: St Andrews Film Books, pp. 157–172.

Peranson, M. (2008) "First You Get the Power, Then You Get the Money: Two Models of Film Festivals," *Cineaste*, 3(3), pp. 37–43.

Ross, M. (2011) "The Film Festival as Producer: Latin American films and Rotterdam's Hubert Bals Fund," *Screen*, 52(2), pp. 261–267.

Turan, K. (2002) *Sundance to Sarajevo: Film Festivals and the World They Made*, Berkeley, CA: University of California Press.

Part I

History

Introduction

Brendan Kredell

Appropriately, this book begins with the history of film festivals—both as events and as objects of study. At a time when festivals number into the thousands, seemingly filling every imaginable niche and day on the calendar, it is easy to take for granted that the modern film festival was always so. Of course, it was not. In the decades since what we now regard as the first film festival, held in Venice in 1932, festivals have grown exponentially in both scope and scale, and they now command a place of central importance in global film culture. How exactly we got from there to here remains a complicated question; as we shall see, what exactly we mean by "here" is all the more vexed.

In this part, our authors approach the history of film festivals from a variety of vantage points, yielding different insights into the development of festivals over time, and the impact of that history on the contemporary festival ecosystem. In the first chapter, Dorota Ostrowska considers the history of the Festival de Cannes, which despite not being the world's oldest (a title it cedes to Venice), remains its most iconic. Ostrowska argues that by closely scrutinizing the history of Cannes, we can identify distinct patterns in the films that have been selected there, leading her to conclude that the Festival de Cannes has played an outsized role in the development of the aesthetics of the contemporary festival film.

Julian Stringer focuses his attention on the history of film festivals in East Asia. He argues that only by considering spatial relations can we properly understand both the regional history of film festivals and also the way that East Asia is situated with larger global flows of power. Resisting essentialist discourses that would seek to clearly define "Asian festivals" and mark them as other to the dominant festivals of the West, Stringer instead focuses our attention on tensions within the history of film festivals in Asia. What is more, he contends, the existing model of global festival regulation has been organized in such a way as to reinscribe the hegemony of European film festivals; his chapter closes with a call for more sustained research into the relationship between global festival regulator FIAPF and the newer, non-European festivals of the world.

In her chapter, Skadi Loist takes the long view, considering the organizational logics that we have applied to the study of film festival history themselves. In particular, she is interested in the notion of a circuit, and its many connotations; at a minimum, as she explains, festivals represents circuits of films, money, and people, and the "wiring" of those circuits varies tremendously. As Loist traces out in her chapter, these circuits are overlaid upon and integrated into existing structures of the media industries and of society more generally; as broader structural change in turn affects the workings of festival circuits, we witness one of the ways in which cinema culture is directly impacted by social forces.

Of course, it goes without saying that this part is necessarily incomplete in its overview of film festival history. A critical historiography of film festivals is still very much a work-in-progress; Marijke de Valck (2007) offers a three-part periodization of festival history that has been influential in this regard. Operationalizing the notions of flow and circuit described in Loist's chapter here, Cindy Hing-Yuk Wong's account (2011) of the historical evolution of festivals is especially valuable insofar as it highlights the interconnectedness of large and small festivals within a global exchange of cinema.

As Stringer suggests, there remains an implicit Eurocentrism to film festival history, and thus recent histories of festivals in Africa (Dovey 2015), Asia (Iordanova and Cheung 2011; Chan 2011), and Latin America (Barrow and Falicov 2013) have helped decenter our understanding of film festival studies, opening new avenues for inquiry in the process. Equally welcome in this regard are histories that focus our attention on festivals beyond the so-called "Big Three" of Cannes, Venice, and Berlin; this would include recent histories on Leipzig (Kötzing 2004; Moine 2014), Edinburgh (Stanfield 2008; Lloyd 2011), and Busan (Ahn 2011), among others.

And yet, despite these and many other examples of festival histories too numerous to cite here, the overwhelming conclusion one must reach after considering the state of historical research into film festivals is that much research remains to be done—that for every question answered, several more present themselves anew. As Francesco Di Chiara and Valentina Re (2011) argue, the stakes are high not only for the burgeoning field of film festival studies, but for our broader understanding of cinema history. In a real sense, festivals are to cinema what journalism is to history: a "first rough draft," in Philip Graham's famous phrase, a real-time effort to make some sense of the cinemas of the world. Here, I would go one step further: not only do festivals serve as cinema history's first rough draft, but they are the sites where its forgotten treasures are given new life, and the public squares in which its hidden audiences gather. By studying the history of film festivals, we gain insight into how cinema history comes to be.

References

Ahn, S. (2011) *The Pusan International Film Festival, South Korean Cinema and Globalization*, Hong Kong: Hong Kong University Press.

Barrow, S. and T. Falicov (eds.) (2013) "Latin American Cinemas Today," special issue of *Transnational Cinemas*, 4(2).

Chan, F. (2011) "The International Film Festival and the Making of a National Cinema," *Screen*, 52(2), pp. 253–260.

De Valck, M. (2007) *Film Festivals: From European Geopolitics to Global Cinephilia*, Amsterdam: Amsterdam University Press.

Di Chiara, F. and V. Re (2011) "Film Festival/Film History: The Impact of Film Festivals on Cinema Historiography. *Il cinema ritrovato* and Beyond," *Cinémas: Revue d'études cinématographiques | Cinémas: Journal of Film Studies*, 21(2/3), pp. 131–151.

Dovey, L. (2015) *Curating Africa in the Age of Film Festivals: Film Festivals, Time, Resistance*, New York: Palgrave Macmillan.

Iordanova, D. and R. Cheung (eds.) (2011) *Film Festivals and East Asia*, St Andrews: St Andrews Film Studies.

Kötzing, A. (2004) *Die Internationale Leipziger Dokumentar- und Kurzfilmwoche in den 1970er Jahren*, Leipzig: Leipziger Universitätsverlag.

Lloyd, M. (2011) *How the Movie Brats Took Over Edinburgh: The Impact of Cinéphilia on the Edinburgh International Film Festival, 1968–1980*, St Andrews: St Andrews Film Studies.

Moine, C. (2014) *Cinéma et guerre froide: Histoire du festival de films documentaires de Leipzig (1955–1990)*, Paris: Publications Sorbonne.

Stanfield, P. (2008) "Notes Toward a History of the Edinburgh International Film Festival, 1969–77," *Film International*, 6(4), pp. 62–71.

Wong, C. H.-Y. (2011) *Film Festivals: Culture, People, and Power on the Global Screen*, New Brunswick, NJ: Rutgers University Press.

1 Making film history at the Cannes film festival

Dorota Ostrowska

Introduction

Among A-list film festivals the Festival de Cannes has been unchallenged as the key event in the film festival calendar since its inception in 1946. Cannes' role in shaping canons of arthouse cinema contributed to the festival's enduring importance. This chapter explores the history of the Cannes film festival in relation to arthouse cinema across four periods when particular types of films were recognized as innovative for a combination of aesthetic, critical, industrial, or political reasons. The chapter starts with the exploration of the idea of "humanist film" which was linked with the pacifist goals embraced by Cannes in its early days and a result of specific programming policies of the festival; it then moves on to explore "critics' film" associated with the increasingly important role of critics and producers at the festival in the early 1960s; it proceeds to explain the emergence of the "director's" or "auteur film" throughout the late 1960s and 1970s; and finally, the chapter focuses on the idea of "Cannes film" which is the result of recent changes in production practices whereby film festivals both are a meeting place for the industry, and also act as creative film producers themselves through the festivals' film development initiatives and funds. This chapter will chisel out the enduring characteristics of these historic Cannes film categories, which are compounded in today's category of a festival film.

Humanist films

The idea to create an international film festival in Cannes emerged in France in 1937–1939 as a direct response to the political change in Italy, home of the first film festival, *La Mostra di Venezia* (Venice Film Festival). In the late 1930s, in line with Mussolini's government, *La Mostra* was becoming more politically radicalized toward Fascism with countries such as the United States, the United Kingdom, and France no longer willing to attend the Italian event (Mazdon 2007: 16). This was in stark contrast to the early days of the Venice Film Festival, whose first two editions in 1932 and 1934 were organized in association with the International Educational Cinematographic Institute,[1] which itself had been established in 1928 by the League of Nations in response to the carnage of World War I and in the wake of various pacifist movements of the nineteenth century. This Institute was housed in Rome at the expense of the Fascist government.

The first Cannes film festival was planned for September 2, 1939 but the German invasion of Poland on September 1 brutally interrupted the festival after the screening of the opening film *The Hunchback of Notre Dame* (1939, dir. William Dieterle) (Jungen 2014). When the festival finally took place for the first time in 1946 it was driven by the vision of a cosmopolitan event underpinned by the ideal of humanist, populist, and pacifist cinema. The earliest regulations of the Cannes film festival stated clearly that "the aim of the festival is to encourage the development of the cinematic art in all its forms and to establish a spirit of collaboration among film producing countries" (Festival regulations 1946). The actual process of film submission and film selection supported the festival's "spirit of collaboration" which determined the character of the festival more than aesthetic concerns. The films were selected and submitted by the national boards or national producers' associations. The festival organizers were not able to see the films until just a few weeks or sometimes even days before the festival. These viewings were focused on confirming that the technical quality of the copy was adequate rather than to pass any aesthetic judgments. Often the copies were coming very late, which precluded the festival organizers from engaging in any meaningful curatorial activity.

The festival regulations focused on encouraging the participation from the main film-producing countries such as the United States and the United Kingdom to boost the importance of Cannes from the industry's point of view, and on maximizing the number of countries that were invited to participate. The level of film production in every country determined the number each could submit, and only countries with which France had diplomatic relationships could be invited. This was a particularly sensitive issue in the immediate postwar period, which took a few years to resolve in relation to the former Axis powers of Germany and Japan. Overall, the festival organizers together with the French foreign office were focused on assuring that no participant felt offended or sidetracked. The direct result was that quite regularly films were forced to be withdrawn from the festival in response to the protests from different countries, and the air of political scandal usually accompanied the Cannes festival editions. The producers, who were members of the national producers' associations in different Western countries, mattered for the way in which the festival was programmed. These associations, such as the British Film Producers' Associations (BFPA), were responsible for selecting which films were submitted for competition at the Cannes film festival and for bearing some of the costs associated with the submission. For socialist countries, where the state took over the role of the producer, the selection and submission was done by the specially set-up national boards and committees. Commercial interests and Cold War politics were the flavor of the month in the early years of the Cannes film festival.

The idea of cinema as a vehicle for universal peace can be traced back to the nineteenth-century belief in the power of the new means of transportation such as railways and new media of communications, in particular the telegraph, to bring peace and progress (Mattelart 1999). Cinema as a medium of communication was inscribed into this utopian vision, which gained particular strength in the period of silent cinema. The experience of World War I as well as the transition to sound brought into sharp focus the concerns about cinema's power to be a vehicle for peace in the era of extreme ideologies and growing nationalisms, which the advent of sound was exacerbating. Marcel Lapierre's 1932 book, written in the early days of the talkies in France, *Le cinéma et la paix*, attacked the question of sound cinema as a vehicle for peace head on. Lapierre argued that cinema "can become an excellent vehicle for peace" but he did not really spell out what kind of films could achieve this goal (1932: 92).[2] The fact that he discussed peace films by surveying war films made since the beginning of cinema in the major film-producing countries gave an interesting twist to his arguments.

It was in the immediate aftermath of World War II and in the charged atmosphere of the impending political debacle between the two Cold War camps that first breakthroughs in the cinematic art took place with new films from Italy, Poland, and the Soviet Union winning the main festival awards. They were: Roberto Rossellini, *Roma Città Aperta/Rome Open City* (Grand Prix, Cannes 1946), Vittorio de Sica, *Miracolo a Milano/Miracle in Milan* (Grand Prix ex-aequo, Cannes 1951), Vittorio de Sica, *Umberto D.* (1952), Andrzej Wajda, *Kanał/Canal* (Special Jury Prize ex-aequo, Cannes 1957), Mikhail Kalatozov, *Letiat zhuravli/Cranes Are Flying* (Palme d'Or, Cannes 1958), Girgori Chukhrai, *Ballada o soldate/Ballad of a Soldier* (Cannes 1960). These films helped redirect the pacifist efforts of the festival organizers from purely political and diplomatic ends toward aesthetic and formal ones.

The celebration of new film movements unveiled at the Cannes film festival in the 1940s and 1950s could thus be seen as an outcome of the fusion of different ideas spanning peace efforts following both World Wars. Unsurprisingly, Italian neo-realism, the Polish School, and Soviet cinema made in the period of the post-Stalinist Thaw had some important characteristics in common. They were all films belonging broadly to the genre of war films and shared a strong antiwar message which Lapierre might have envisioned. They also corresponded to the characteristics of educational film promoted on the pages of the *International Review of Educational Cinematography* in that they were embracing the aesthetic of documentary filmmaking. While positioning themselves as reconstructions of the events of World War II, they were also vehicles of peace education inscribed in the climate of the postwar peace efforts, which were threatened by the rising tensions associated with the Cold War. Importantly, they were not American but were made by either left-leaning Italian film-makers or directors from the socialist states and the Soviet Union.

Their critical reception emphasized their "humanity" as well as universalism of the message they conveyed, and the realist portrayal of human lives in extreme situations. The idea of humanism proved to be very potent in the period when Europe was polarized toward the opposing ideologies of the Cold War. Humanism was smoothing over these differences while it glanced over the divisions imposed by nationality, race, class, gender, or ideology. It was rooted in "the myth of essential and universal Man: essential, because humanity—human-ness—is the inseparable and central essence, the defining quality, of human beings; universal, because the essential humanity is shared by all human beings, of whatever time and place" (Davies 1997: 24). Humanist films were embracing "a truly human point of view," a perspective of an individual living in the world along with the fellow human beings (ibid.: 21). Such views chimed with the political objectives of Cannes and the festival's utopian and universalizing ideal.

The film critics writing about "humanist films" at Cannes were also noting the films' documentary and realist roots. André Bazin reviews of Italian neo-realism (2004), Ado Kyrou's writing on the Polish School (1957), and Georges Sadoul's work on post-Stalinist Soviet filmmaking (1958) each valued the style of the films, heralding them as breaking new aesthetic ground and making interesting stylistic interventions. In that period critical emphasis was placed not on the director but on the fact that these were groups of films produced under a particular national umbrella. The accent on the place of provenance of the films rather than their origins in terms of authorship was due to the programming strategies, which dominated at the Cannes film festival in that period. Retrospectively, these films came to be viewed as representative of both aesthetic film movements and oeuvres of auteurs. However, this process did not take place until the category of the auteur film was firmly established throughout the 1960s.

The festival's focus on cultivating the spirit of collaboration resulted in the emergence of the category of humanist films, which were defined by film critics attending the festival. The focus on politics dominating the accounts from the festival makes it impossible to see the humanist films in purely stylistic terms. Given the Cold War tensions, which ran high at the festival, the category of humanist film is as much political as it is a critical and aesthetic one. It was the critics' decision to establish their own independently curated sidebar of the festival in the early 1960s—inspired by the presence of the film market (Marché du Film) running parallel to the main festival—which helped redefine the festival's objectives more clearly toward aesthetics and style, this time with the focus on non-European films.

Critics' films

Since the early 1960s press reports from Cannes were emphasizing the fact that the festival's main competition was very disappointing and the awards the result of political compromise. At the same time they remarked with great enthusiasm that there were a lot of interesting films to be seen in the market in Cannes (Marché du Film) set up in 1959 by the Syndicat Français des

Producteurs de Films/French Union of Film Producers (Benghozi and Nénert 1995). Any film producer could book their film in for the market, and many of them did. By 1964 there were about 300 films screened in the small cinemas dotted along Cannes' main street, rue d'Antibes, where the Cannes film market was located (Zamot 1964). Screened as the same time as the actual festival program, the market films gave an impression of a parallel film festival happening away from the pomp of the Palais des Festival, the craze surrounding the stars, and the hustle and bustle of the Croisette. Not bound by any diplomatic or political constraints, the commercially driven market of film in Cannes was doing something which the main festival did not; namely, it offered a strong sense that there was a lot of new cinema made in the world which deserved attention and exposure. In the words of the critics it was the market rather than the main competition that made the trip to Cannes worthwhile for those interested in an overview of the global film production (Ibid).

And there were many intriguing developments in cinema across the world since the breakthrough of the French Nouvelle Vague at the turn of the 1950s and 1960s. "New cinemas" were mushrooming everywhere, invented by young filmmakers who were creating highly politicized and nonconformist portraits of their generation. They were critical of the dominant social and economic structures, and freely mixed documentary and fictional cinema to generate films that were formally experimental and challenged the established narrative norms. The films were fictionalized documents of their times created by the youth which was coming of age. They were also unlike the humanist films not only in their distanced relationship to the themes of the World War II but also in their sheer cultural diversity and the interest in difference—which was made evident through formal experiments and critical engagement with the problems of the here and now. These problems were pressing with extremes of wealth and poverty in some parts of the world, and the accelerated economic growth in the others leaving vast groups in society marginalized and struggling to find their place. A new kind of cinema, which was as much fiction as an anthropological or sociological essay, was needed to give account and engage with the everyday reality. While World War II was still present as a theme, there were other wars and colonial conflicts gaining momentum and demanding representation which the new cinemas provided.

French critics attending Cannes were the first ones to capitalize on these new creative trends, which were sending shockwaves through cinema worldwide and through the Cannes film market. In 1962 the critics set up an independent screening section, *La Semaine de la Critique* (Critics' Week) under the auspices of *L'Association Française de la Critique* (French Critics' Association) and ran it at the time of the main festival. The selection committee was made up mostly of French critics and some foreign ones who lived in France, and was headed by Georges Sadoul, an influential communist film critic writing for the left-wing publication *Les Lettres françaises*. The section's aim was to show films of first- or second-time filmmakers, which had not yet been screened at any major international film festival. The films were usually low-budget, sometime censored in their country of origin, and aesthetically drawing their inspiration from North American Direct Cinema and French *cinéma vérité* whose works were also screened as part of the Critics' Week (*Football*, dir. Richard Leacock; *Seul ou avec d'autres/Alone or with Others*, dir. Denys Arcand; *Showman*, dir. Albert and David Maysles). Many of the films shown in the first editions of the Critics' Week came to be recognized as those which launched the New Iranian Cinema (*Nights of the Hunchback/Shabe ghuzi*, 1965, dir. Farokh Ghafari), Czechoslovak New Wave (*Something Different/Onecim jinem*, 1963, dir. Vera Chytilova; *Diamonds of the Night/Demanty Noci*, 1964, dir. Jan Nemec; *The Sun in a Net/Slnko v sieti*, 1962, dir. Stefan Uher), New German Cinema (*Die Parallelstrasse/The Parallel Street*, 1962, dir. Ferdinand Khittl) and New American Cinema (*Goldstein*, 1964, dir. Philip Kaufman; *Andy*, 1965, dir. Richard C. Sarafian).

In spite of their importance at the time of their screening in Cannes many of these films are forgotten and hardly seen nowadays which is indicative of the dynamics of film festivals. Festivals offer exposure to aesthetically and politically important films, which find it difficult nonetheless to survive outside the film festival circuit. That said, some of the films have become classics: *Adieu Philippine* (1962, dir. Jacques Rozier), *Before the Revolution/Prima della Rivoluzione* (1964, dir. Bernardo Bertolucci), *Walkover* (1965, dir. Jerzy Skolimowski). The directors' participation with their early films in the Critics' Week helped them launch their careers as auteurs. The impact of the films shown as part of the Critics' Week should be thus most productively understood as a rupture or intervention into the fabric of the main festival which then resonated in the canons of film history. The critics' films were a signal as to where new and interesting cinema was originating from. This is different from canon-building, which can only happen retrospectively after the emotions of the festival subside and the stock of the films lauded at the festivals can be assessed according to different criteria such as national cinema or authorship.

The Critics' Week committee was soliciting about eight films each year that made it to the final selection directly from the producing countries rather than relying on the selection of the national film boards or national producers' associations as was the case with the main competition. There was a greater flexibility regarding film formats, which could have been both 16mm and 35mm, making the Critics' Week more open to experimental films than the Cannes main film selection. The Critics' Week wanted to be a sidebar (a section of the festival) where the discovery of young talent could happen, but it took some time to work out the parameters of the relationship between the main festival and the Critics' Week. The result was an agreement whereby the Critics' Week was a selection of films screened at the time of the Cannes film festival and programmed independently by critics. It was agreed that the screenings of the main competition and the Critics' Week would be arranged in such a way as to avoid clashes. The Critics' Week was to focus on the debut and second features to present "a panorama of new world cinema of high quality." There was no specific prize which was attached to the Critics' Week, only a "diploma" of participation, and the main festival did not cover the costs of the Critics' Week (Sadoul 1965: 3).

What the Critics' Week shared with the competitive section of the Festival was the desire to include films from as many countries as possible and in this way to present a panorama of the emerging film talent globally. It differed in its selection method: the Critics' Week made numerous approaches often directly to directors, national film institutes or producers to solicit films. Moreover, the emphasis had firmly shifted from the rhetoric of international peace and collaboration, humanism, and brotherhood through cinema to cinema itself, where the films came to be considered as the pulse of the national cultures lived and felt by the audiences and captured and expressed by the emergent film talent. It is important to note that while the critics controlled the film selection, they were also the only audience for the films as screenings were off limits to anyone who was not a film critic, which indicated the importance of the market dynamics in regard to this sidebar. Although the Critics' Week began to transform the festival itself by making it more sensitive to the aesthetic, social, and political aspects of the films screened there, it also underlined the festival as an event meant for film industry professionals rather than for the general public.

Because the Critics' Week successfully focused on first-time talent which could be developed and showcased in the future at Cannes and other international film festivals, it worked as a kind of bridge between the main festival and the film market. In this way it closed an important gap in the operation of the main festival, which was aware of the film market but had no practical way of engaging with it mostly because of the strict diplomacy-driven rules underpinning the main selection. By collaborating with the market and international film critics, the Critics' Week managed to change the main festival. However, that did not mean that it transformed the festival's core aspect—the dependence of the film selection on choices of the national boards. It was the events surrounding the establishment of *La Quinzaine des Réalisateurs* (Directors' Fortnight) which changed the festival in the most profound ways by putting emphasis on the figure of a film director, and also that of a film festival curator.

Auteur films

By the early 1970s, as a result of the May 1968 events in Paris, the decline of the American studios, and the success of the new festival's initiatives such as the Critics' Week, the role of FIAPF[3] and its members diminished on the film festival circuit. In the wake of students' anti-establishment and anti-government strikes, May 1968 brought with it a wave of protests in Paris against the decision to dismiss Henri Langlois (Harvey 1978). Langlois was a founder and a long-standing head of the *Cinémathèque française*, a key figure in the French film world and a formative presence for the French New Wave filmmakers (Roud 1983). The protest originating in Paris continued in

Cannes on the opening night of the festival. A group of filmmakers including Jean-Luc Godard, François Truffaut, and Roman Polanski pressured the director of the festival, Robert Favre le Bret, to suspend it in view of the protests taking place in Paris to which Favre le Bret reluctantly agreed. The interruption of the festival in such a way meant that the festival selection and programming practices, established at the end of World War II, were challenged in an unprecedented way. This would transform the festival into a much more politically independent organization in terms of its programming choices.

Instrumental to this change was the emergence of film directors, who were organized in France into the newly founded *La Société des Réalisateurs de Films* (SFR) (Directors' Association). The Association was created in May 1968 in order "to defend the artistic, moral, professional and economic freedom to create and to participate in the development of new cinematic structures" (Thévenin 2008: 50). One of the reflections of these complex changes on the film festival circuit was the new sidebar at Cannes independently programmed by the directors themselves, called *La Quinzaine des Réalisateurs* (The Directors' Fortnight) (ibid.). For the first time the figure of the auteur was acknowledged as the key and independent agent in the creative process of filmmaking and film festival exhibition. Films of specific directors were deemed "auteur films" and sought out for screening at the festival. The increasing importance of directors in the context of the festival also meant a much more personal and direct relationship between individual artists and festival programmers with the filter of the national boards and producers' associations being removed or its role significantly limited.

At the beginning, the Directors' Fortnight was called *Cinéma en Liberté* (Cinema Set Free), which reflected the goals of the directors linked to it. They envisioned a section of the Cannes film festival as a kind of "counter-festival" which would be "organized and controlled by French filmmakers, directed toward the cinema of discovery, toward new cinemas, the Third-World productions and the underground of all kinds" (Thévenin 2008: 72). One of the key differences between the Critics' Week and the Directors' Fortnight was a much more militant attitude that the new section's organizers took toward the main festival. Unlike the ones running the Critics' Week, those behind the Directors' Fortnight were not seeking peaceful cohabitation with the main section but rather wanted to challenge it. A very large number of films were included in the Directors' Fortnight (nearly 70 films in its first year in 1969 as opposed to eight for the Critics' Week), which reflected the inclusive character of the new section and the support that the initiative of the French directors elicited in the filmmaking community worldwide. This community was starved for an international platform to showcase their films, which the Directors' Fortnight finally provided. The important point was the insistence on the fact that the films do not belong to critics, producers, or national film boards but to the directors who make them. Despite its militant attitude and much more inclusive programming strategies it is safe to say that

the Directors' Fortnight could not have existed without the earlier trailblaz-
ing efforts of the Critics' Week, which was the first section to present a true
alternative to the main festival. While the Critics' Week was focusing on
debuts and second films, the Directors' Fortnight was emphasizing the agency
of the auteur in relation to the films it championed.

Many of the radical transformations to the festival culture introduced by
the Critics' Week and the Directors' Fortnight were a result of the enduring
impact of the French New Wave, which was in many ways a critical development for the whole history of the Cannes film festival. The French New
Wave was a complex and multifaceted phenomenon whose many differences
were played out and negotiated in the context of the Cannes film festival.
The New Wave mattered for the valorization of criticism and its link to production, as many of the New Wave filmmakers were originally critics. It was
also important for the way it recognized and valued the first-time directors;
the French New Wave directors were just that (Ostrowska 2008). It was the
link between the New Wave and the Cannes film festival that triggered the
emergence of the Directors' Association, as it was the action of the directors
linked to the French New Wave that resulted in the suspension of the festival
in May 1968 and the reform of its curatorial practices in the following years
(Thévenin 2008). In many ways the trajectory of the Cannes film festival
during the 1960s and 1970s, from the establishment of the Critics' Week to
that of the Directors' Fortnight, paralleled the transition of the New Wave
filmmakers from film critics to film auteurs.

For the first three years the Directors' Fortnight was programmed by a
group of filmmakers, but in time the process became more institutionalized
and streamlined. At the same time the criteria for the selection continued to
be driven solely by aesthetic concerns. The idea was

> to show in Cannes films without any diplomatic or political pressure, dis-
> regarding the box office or fashions, in a way which was free in any pos-
> sible way, ignoring budgets and means of production, formats and length,
> and opinions of the jury
>
> (Thévenin 2008: 80)

It was Pierre-Henri Deleau who ran the section for some 30 years and who
became famous for reserving the right of the final selection, what he called
"the final cut," to himself. The strength of his position as a curator was something quite new and unparalleled in Cannes until Gilles Jacob took over the
position of the director of the Cannes film festival in 1978, leaving his own
stamp on it, and opening the doors for a more subjective and personalized
format of festival programming.

The main programming innovation introduced by the Directors' Fortnight
in comparison to the Critics' Week and the main festival was that the films
for the Directors' Fortnight were solicited directly from the filmmakers themselves, whereby a director or his/her assistant were sending a 35 mm copy of

a finished film to the festival and on some occasions a representative of the selection committee would even visit the set during the shoot. This meant that the distance between the sidebar and the artists was reduced, removing any intermediaries including a selection committee, producers, or even critics. In this way the films in the sidebar were believed to truly mirror the political and social mood in different corners of the world: "the winds of freedoms in the Western countries in 1973 and the situation of the countries suffering under dictatorships and totalitarianisms in South America, Asia and Eastern Europe were reflected in the new [film] aesthetic" (Thévenin 2008: 92–93). This enlargement or widening also occurred in relation to the audiences, which were free to attend the screenings of the sidebar without an accreditation. This practice was in stark contrast to the Critics' Week and the main competition, which were closed off to the general public.

The artistic freedom of the festival and the films screened there was tightly linked to the questions of censorship firmly in place in France. Due to the main festival selection committee's reliance on the government's cultural politics and its diplomatic efforts, the Cannes film festival was deeply implicated in the practices of censorship (Latil 2005; Thévenin 2008). Olivier Thévenin argues that the filmmakers wanted to change the festival by lifting the constraints that censorship imposed on festival practices. The independence and freedom with which the Directors' Fortnight was run started a series of changes within the practices of the main festival, whose selection was becoming more independent. The main festival came to reflect some important characteristics of the Directors' Fortnight (and the Critics' Week earlier on): the focus on new talent, first-time films, productions from all over the world, and the growing role of the festival director as a curator. Drawing on the example of the Directors' Fortnight, Gilles Jacob transformed the main competition, set up a new sidebar, *Un Certain Regard* (1978), and also a cross-festival award, the *Caméra d'Or* (1978), which all ended up being marked by his curatorial choices (Benghozi and Nénert 1995: 69). These changes to the festival were intensified in the early 1990s and culminated in the emergence of a new category of films, the "Cannes film," which paved the way for a "festival" film.

Cannes films

Until the early 1970s two ideological conceptions of filmmaking coexisted at the Cannes film festival, inscribed into the dynamics of the Cold War, and associated with either Western or socialist cinema. Western films, including the American ones, were seen as almost exclusively driven by commercial concerns, while Eastern European and Soviet films, unburdened by money issues, not only offered a different vision of the world and human relations, but also engaged in aesthetic experimentation, which was missing from Western filmmaking. The film festival screenings in Cannes presented quite a few counterexamples to this highly polarized and caricatured vision of the state of cinema in the world. However, what remained unchallenged was the fact that films made in the socialist East were not subject to the same pressures of the marketplace as those produced in the West. This is why the Cannes film festival became a platform where new ways of financing and supporting films through other channels than private funds were tested (Ostrowska 2014). Drawing on the example of socialist film industries, state subsidies were seen as an obvious way to support the making of more daring and experimental films in Europe. It took some time before the festival itself was in a position to propose a way to develop new projects (Benghazi and Nénert 1995: 65).

The development of the Cannes market played a key role in the process of the emergence of what I propose to call "Cannes film." The 1980 decision to integrate the Marché du Film and the festival was a sign of the recognition of the significance and value of these face-to-face meetings and conversations among industry professionals, and the efficiency with which they could take place at the time of the festival (ibid.: 72). Jérôme Paillard became the General Director of the Cannes Film Market in 1995 and made it grow during the period when the American independent cinema was re-launched with the help of companies such as Miramax. This development coincided with an increase of market share for independent films produced in different corners of the world. For the first time in history there was money available, which producers were willing to put into independent and arthouse cinema, the type of films that various festival sidebars had championed since the early 1960s. The Cannes film festival finally embraced its new role—that of a matchmaker between talent and money through a series of networking initiatives at the development stage of film production—which in turn led to the growth of the aforementioned new category of films.

The idea that arthouse films have to be funded in some special way, which is not determined exclusively by commercial concerns, had been gaining currency on the international film festival circuit concurrently with the emancipation of auteur cinema from national cinemas. In respect to these "uprooted" auteur films Lúcia Nagib talked about "the itinerant trajectory of the auteurist trait, which in the international context, has acquired the quality of a national contribution to a transnational language" (Nagib 2006: 102). Thus this new kind of arthouse films championed by Cannes belongs to the emerging transnational cinema fostered by the film festival networking opportunities and funds[4]. It is possible to be a renowned filmmaker on the film festival circuit with little support from one's own country of origin. This has been historically the case with African filmmakers who reside in France and show their films at film festivals, Latin American filmmakers (Ross 2011; Falicov 2010) and more recently with the directors of the Romanian New Wave (Wong 2011). The result of these processes are films which cater to the political and aesthetic tastes of those who enable their production in the first place—film festivals such as Cannes.

Formally these films—no matter whether they come from Western or non-Western countries—are indebted to the modernist and realist aesthetics of the European arthouse. However, they do not form a uniform group in formal terms; such uniformity would have defied the whole ethos of discovery and innovation to which international film festivals are strongly committed. Rather, the festivals promote and support talent, i.e., individual filmmakers who show potential to blossom into auteurs, the artists whose films are an expression of a unique filmmaking style and vision. In the context of the festivals these overlapping authorial visions form a patchwork of styles and formal experiments, which express appreciation and passion for cinema and commitment to testing, expanding, and exploring the boundaries of the medium.

In the context of other international film festivals the role of Cannes in relation to contemporary arthouse films is unique in that Cannes does not have a specific development or production fund to support projects and filmmakers that they value. Rather, the symbolic power of Cannes in regard to new projects lies in the commercial power of the market, which is its part. The festival itself does not fund films but it gives access and helps filmmakers navigate the biggest film industry trade convention in the world—the Marché du Film in Cannes. This soft power applied at the development stage of new films translates into projects, which later on often flourish on the A-list film festival circuit (Ostrowska 2010). The result is a film, which could be high on aesthetic value, with a stamp of Cannes approval on it from the start, but with little box-office appeal. The reason Cannes films deserve to be put in a separate category is because this festival functions as the key reference point for other international film festivals and the film industry worldwide. How and why Cannes has managed to establish and maintain its position as a festival of such great importance is a complex question, which cannot be fully explored here. It is enough to say that most of the arthouse films that become successful on the film festival circuit and gain critical acclaim did benefit from the relationship with the Cannes film festival either at the development stage or when they were screened in one of the Cannes sidebars.

Films that pass through Cannes in the development stage morph into what came to be known as "festival films" when they are completed (Elsaesser 2005; Wong 2011; de Valck 2012). Jonathan Rosenbaum described them as "destined to be seen by professionals, specialists, or cultists but not the general public because some of these professionals decided it won't or can't be sufficiently profitable to warrant distribution" (Wong 2011: 66). The role that Cannes plays in relation to these films is nearest to that of a creative producer because of the special care and attention they take in helping the films come to existence. Cannes' films that develop into festival films are contemporary examples of arthouse and auteur films often drawing on a formally and thematically challenging vocabulary, which this kind of cinema developed historically (Neale 1981; Bordwell 2004).

The appearance of festival films which are the result of the networking activities of the international film festivals such as Cannes as well as of an internationalizing tendency, which has been part and parcel of the film festival culture from its inception, bring the history of the international film festival circuit full circle. Cannes and other major international film festivals are about advancing the cinematic art and international collaboration, not so much among the film-producing nations nowadays but rather among the film industry professionals who come from many different corners of the world to attend the international film festivals. This is what Marijke de Valck calls the "self-referencing" stage in the film festival history, when the utopian vision, which has underpinned the very idea of the international film festivals from their inception, has been realized in a very particular way (De Valck 2012).

Conclusion

The four types of films discussed in this chapter were important for Cannes' ability to reinvent itself on the one hand, and for the process of reshaping the arthouse film culture on the other. With these new categories of film emerging in the context of Cannes, the festival has successfully managed to preserve its role as a trendsetter and a reference point for producers, critics, directors, and festival programmers worldwide. At the same time, with new stakeholders coming to prominence at different periods in the festival history, such as critics or directors, the festival has found the way to respond and address changes and transformations taking place in the wider arthouse cinema culture while reshaping and redefining them further in the course of the film festival event.

Once a type of film emerged at a particular junction of the Cannes history; it became integrated into the fabric of arthouse film culture and directly affected the ways in which future films screened at the festival were evaluated. In this way there were elements of humanist films in critics', auteur, and Cannes films, while auteur films are the main framework through which the festival films are understood nowadays as well as the category that has been used retrospectively to frame humanist and critics' films. While it is clear that the categories of films that emerged in the context of Cannes, such as critics', directors', and Cannes films, are enduring ones, humanist film appears to be more historical designation. The war film genre associated with humanist films has undergone changes and transformations since the time of Italian neo-realism and the Polish School. What remains of it is the militant and contestatory element associated with humanist films, which underpins any drive toward formal innovation and desire for political relevance in arthouse cinema.

To conclude, the success of the Cannes film festival is built around its ability to respond to the changes taking place in film industry worldwide by restructuring the festival's architecture to accommodate new trends, new films, and new directors. At the same time it is the festival sidebars (the Critics' Week, the Directors' Fortnight and more recently *Un Certain Regard* and *Caméra d'Or*) that by remaining highly selective, ultimately reinforce the festival's position as a trendsetter in the world of the arthouse cinema.

Notes

1 During its existence the Institute published a monthly magazine called *International Review of Educational Cinematography* exploring ideas regarding the educational value of cinema. The Institute and the journal provided a unique international canvas woven out of the idealistic vision about the progress of cinematic art, international collaboration and anti-Americanism on which the ideal of cinema as a universal art form was based (Druick 2008: 77).
2 All translations are mine unless indicated otherwise.
3 Various national producers' associations, including the French Union of Film Producers and the British Film Producers' Association, were in turn grouped in the International Federation of Film Producers' Associations (FIAPF). The FIAPF's main objective was to remove obstacles to free film trade worldwide. The international film festival circuit was the main arena where this goal was to be advanced. The organization is probably best known for overseeing the expansion of the film festival circuit by granting the status of an A-list festival to those which they believed to be worthy in commercial and political terms (Moine 2011, 2013). This meant the festivals which could offer the greatest commercial advantage to the producers.
4 International Film Festival in Rotterdam and the Berlinale have also played an important part in this process thanks to their funds: the Hubert Bals Fund and the World Cinema Fund, respectively. For detailed account how these funds operate, see Chapter 12 in this book by Tamara L. Falicov.

References

Bazin, A. (2004) *What is Cinema?* revised edition, vol. 1 and 2, trans. H. Gray, Berkeley, CA: University of California Press.

Benghozi, P. and C. Nénert (1995) "Création de Valeur Artistique ou Économique: Festival International du Film de Cannes au Marché du Film," *Recherche et Applications en Marketing*, 10(4), pp. 65–76.

Bordwell, D. (2004) "The Art Cinema as a Mode of Film Practice," in L. Braudy and M. Cohen (eds.) *Film Theory and Criticism. Introductory Readings*, 6th edition, Oxford: Oxford University Press, pp. 774–782.

Davies, T. (1997) *Humanism*, London: Routledge.

De Valck, M. (2012) "Finding Audiences for Films: Programming in Historical Perspective," in J. Ruoff (ed.) *Coming Soon to a Festival Near You: Programming Film Festivals*, St Andrews: St Andrews Film Books, pp. 25–40.

Druick, Z. (2008) "'Reaching the Multimillions': Liberal Internationalism and the Establishment of Documentary Film," in L. Grievson and H. Wasson (eds.) *Inventing Film Studies*, Durham, NC: Duke University Press, pp. 66–92.

Elsaesser, T. (2005) "Film Festival Networks: The New Topographies of Cinema in Europe," in *European Cinema: Face to Face With Hollywood*, Amsterdam: Amsterdam University Press, pp. 82–107.

Falicov, T. (2010) "Migrating From South to North: The Role of Film Festivals in Funding and Shaping Global South Film and Video," in G. Elmer, C. H. Davis, J. Marchessault, and J. McCullough (eds.) *Locating Migrating Media*, Lanham, MD: Lexington Books, pp. 3–21.

"Festival International du Film de Cannes Règlement 1946," Bibliothèque du Film (BiFi), Paris, FIFA 33 B5.

Harvey, S. (1978) *May '68 and Film Culture*, London: BFI Publishing.

Jungen, C. (2014) *Hollywood in Cannes: The History of a Love-Hate Relationship*, Amsterdam: Amsterdam University Press.

Kyrou, A. (1957) "Le visage féminine de la révolution," *Positif*, 21.

Lapierre, M. (1932) *Le cinéma et la paix*, Paris: Cahiers bleu.

Latil, L. (2005) *Le festival de Cannes sur la scène international*, Paris: Nouveau monde.

Mattelart, A. (1999) *Histoire de l'utopie planétaire: De la cité prophétique à la société globale*, Paris: La Découverte.

Mazdon, L. (2007) "Transnational 'French' Cinema: The Cannes Film Festival," *Modern and Contemporary France*, 15(1), pp. 9–20.

Moine, C. (2011) "La FIAPF, une Fédération de Producteurs au cœur des relations internationales après 1945," in L. Creton, Y. Dehée, S. Layerle and C. Moine (eds.) *Les producteurs: Enjeux créatifs, enjeux financiers*, Paris: Nouveau monde éditions, pp. 249–266.

Moine, C. (2013) "La Fédération international des associations de producteurs de films: un acteur controversé de la promotion du cinéma après 1945," *Le Mouvement Social*, 243, pp. 91–103.

Nagib, L. (2006) "Going Global: The Brazilian Scripted Film," in S. Harvey (ed.) *Trading Culture: Global Traffic and Local Cultures in Film and Television*, Eastleigh: John Libbey, pp. 95–103.

Neale, S. (1981) "Art Cinema as Institution," *Screen*, 22(1), pp. 11–39.

Ostrowska, D. (2008) *Reading the French New Wave: Critics, Writers and Art Cinema in France*, London: Wallflower.

Ostrowska, D. (2010) "International Film Festivals as Producers of World Cinema," *Cinéma & Cie: International Film Studies Journal*, 10(14/15), pp. 145–150.

Ostrowska, D. (2014) "Polish Films at the Venice and Cannes Film Festivals: The 1940s, 1950s and 1960s," in E. Mazierska and M. Goddard (eds.) *Polish Cinema in a Transnational Context*, Rochester, NY: University of Rochester Press, pp. 77–94.

Ross, M. (2011) "The Film Festival as Producer: Latin American Films and Rotterdam's Hubert Bals Fund," *Screen* 52(2), pp. 261–267.

Roud, R. (1983) *A Passion for Films: Henri Langlois & the Cinémathèque Française*, London: Secker & Warburg.

Sadoul, G. (1958) "Quand passent les cigognes," *Les Lettres françaises*, May 8.

Sadoul, G. (1965) "La Quatrième Semaine Internationale de la Critique Française," pp. 3–4 in XVIIIe Festival International du Film Cannes 1965. SIC IV. Semaine Internationale de la Critique Présentée par l'Association Française de la Critique du Cinéma, p. 3, BiFi, FIFA 891 B143.

Thévenin, O. (2008) *La S.R.F et la Quinzaine des Réalisateurs. 1968–2008; une construction d'identités collectives*, Montreuil: Aux lieux d'être.

Wong, C. H.-Y. (2011) *Film Festivals. Culture, People, and Power on the Global Screen*, New Brunswick, NJ: Rutgers University Press.

Zamot, R. (1964) [untitled], *L'Express* (Neuchâtel), May 23 [no page number], BiFi FIFP 16–22 B2 (1964), FIF Presse 21 Festival 1964.

Further reading

Jungen, C. (2014) *Hollywood in Cannes*, Amsterdam: Amsterdam University Press. (The book examines the dynamics of Cannes film festival's relationship to Hollywood.)

Latil, L. (2005) *Le festival de Cannes sur la scène international*, Paris: Nouveau monde. (The book focuses on the ways in which Cannes film festival was shaped by the Cold War politics.)

Ostrowska, D. (2014) "Three Decades of Polish Film at the Venice and Cannes Film Festivals: the 1940s, 1950s and 1960s," in E. Mazierska and M. Goddard (eds.) *Beyond the Border: Polish Cinema in a Transnational Context*, Rochester, NY: Rochester University Press, pp. 77–94. (The chapter focuses on the presence and critical reception of Polish films at Cannes and Venice film festivals in the Cold War period.)

Schwartz, V. (2007) "The Cannes Film Festival and the Marketing of Cosmopolitanism," in *It's So French! Hollywood, Paris, and the Making of Cosmopolitan Film Culture*, Chicago, IL: Chicago University Press, pp. 56–99. (The chapter explores the ways in which Cannes film festival was a vehicle for reinventing French cinema as cosmopolitan.)

Thévenin, O. (2008) *La S.R.F et la Quinzaine des Réalisateurs. 1968–2008; une construction d'identités collectives*, Montreuil: Aux lieux d'être. (The book presents history of the emergence of one of the most important sidebars of Cannes film festival: *La Quinzaine des Réalisateurs*/Directors' Fortnight.)

2 Film festivals in Asia

Notes on history, geography, and power from a distance

Julian Stringer

The history of film festivals is inseparable from the geography of film festivals. When critics and historians seek to understand how and why festivals were first established, as well as how and why the number of all manner of events has proliferated so dramatically in recent years, it is necessary that they also consider where festivals have (or have not) been set up and where they have (or have not) flourished. The spatial dimension of analysis complements the temporal dimension. Each constitutes the other's shadow.

Despite the fact that geographical analysis potentially provides one of the key approaches to film festival studies, this method remains to date relatively underdeveloped.[1] However, there are indications that this situation may be in the process of changing as new scholarly endeavors are brought to maturity. For example, the important *Film Festival Yearbook* series published by St Andrews Film Studies has already devoted volumes to East Asia (Iordanova and Cheung 2011) and to the Middle East (Iordanova and Van de Peer 2014), while the first volume in Palgrave Macmillan's equally important Framing Film Festivals book series is given over to Africa (Dovey 2015). It is to be hoped that similar future publications will chart this terrain in ever-greater depth and detail while also extending the focus to other regions of the world.

What does a geographical approach contribute to the scholarly understanding of film festivals? The entwining of an examination of space (geography) with time (history) is significant for a number of reasons. First, apprehending the spatial characteristics of any festival provides a potent means of grasping its relevance to social practices: in other words, because space is always socially produced as well as continuously situated, each and every individual event is embedded in historically specific social relationships.[2] Second, developing this methodology allows researchers to identify geographically meaningful patterns among festival locations on all continents across time.[3] Third, and inescapably related to this endeavor, it also illuminates the extent to which groupings of festivals constitute a global circuit or network of interrelated phenomena (Stringer 2001; Iordanova and Rhyne 2009). Finally, pursuing geographically-oriented research opens up the question of similarities and differences among diverse events, especially as these relate to the comparative workings of power—a vital issue which inevitably arises once any historical or contemporary aspect of festivals is subject to the slightest degree of analytical scrutiny.[4]

These last two points—that festivals constitute a network of interlinked junctures and that power relations unavoidably flow between and underpin its constituent parts—are especially worth pursuing in the context of the present chapter. Some scholars have questioned whether a film festival circuit really exists, asking if it is helpful to conceptualize such a sprawling collection of seemingly random and disparate events in relation to one another (Iordanova and Rhyne 2009). Yet as I argue below, there is at the very minimum at least one perfectly good reason for claiming that a circuit does indeed exist, and, moreover, that its underlying power structure may be revealed by historical examination of its spatial characteristics. The fact I am referring to is a key datum that has nevertheless been frequently and upsettingly overlooked by the scholarly literature.

In order to establish the terms of the analysis that follows, two further assertions are worth highlighting at this point. One, it is necessary to underline the core observation that the film festival is originally a European phenomenon; it is a creature of the Europe region that then went global. This is one of the key arguments made by Marijke de Valck in her pioneering monograph *Film Festivals: From European Geopolitics to Global Cinephilia*. In De Valck's words:

> Film festivals started as a European phenomenon. The first festival was organised on New Year's Day 1898 in Monaco. Other festivals followed in Torino, Milan, and Palermo (Italy), Hamburg (Germany) and Prague (Czechoslovakia). The first prize-winning festival was an Italian movie contest in 1907, organised by the Lumiere brothers [...]. *La Mostra Internazionale d'Arte Cinematographico* [Venice] was the first film festival to be organised on a regular basis [...]. The immediate post-Second World War period offered Europe its first festival boom. Film festivals were a purely European phenomenon during this period and more and more countries decide to follow the example of Venice and Cannes, and found their own festivals. Events were organised in Locarno (1946), Karlovy Vary (1946), Edinburgh (1946), Brussels (1947), Berlin (1951), and Oberhausen (1954), among other places. Like the first festival in Venice, these festivals were all established for a combination of economic, political, and cultural reasons.
>
> (2007: 47, 49)

Two, a further and complementary position is that in more recent years it is the Asia region that has emerged as especially important to the continual advancement of the film festival.[5] In terms of both festivals and associated film industries, Asia constitutes the new vanguard; more exactly, as Dina Iordanova (2011: 1) puts it, "[t]he most exciting developments in world cinema over the past two decades are linked to East Asian countries such as

China, Japan and South Korea." According to this reading, the significance of well-established European events like those staged annually in Venice, Cannes, and Berlin has shifted relative to the growth of newer festivals hosted each year in Hong Kong, Shanghai, Busan, and other East Asian locations.[6]

This chapter unravels an ongoing and paradoxical geopolitical arrangement concerning the rise of major international film festivals (as well as smaller events of all tiers of scale) in East Asia and other parts of the region. It does so by advancing a dual engagement with the issues of space and time identified above. On the one hand, the account offered below presents a brief overview of the historical importance and growing contemporary significance of the abundance of festivals now operative in this particular part of the world. On the other hand, it identifies continuities in Europe's arguably secure position as the long-term locus of global festival power.

Film festivals in Asia

The history—or more properly, the histories—of film festivals in Asia has—or rather have—yet to be written. While a few specialist accounts are available and more work is currently being prepared, there has to date been little sustained examination of this important area of activity.[7] However, when more detailed studies do start to appear, and in greater number, they will doubtless help to drive home a fundamental point—namely, that there is no one or singular "Asia." Rather, there are multiple versions of Asia, and hence, various ways of comprehending and narrating the establishment and growth across decades of a large number of different kinds of festivals in this area.[8] By the same token, future studies will need to grapple, too, with the full complexity of the crisscrossing historical and geographical trajectories that characterize and define the range of occurrences under discussion.

English-language academic research has focused in the main on three stages in the historical development of multiple kinds of festivals in Asia. First, from the mid-1950s a pan-Asian event, the Southeast Asian Film Festival—the oldest continuous film festival in Asia—fulfilled the important function of introducing Asian audiences and filmmakers to other Asian movies while building fresh business connections among industry leaders in several countries (Yau 2003; Lee 2012, 2014; Baskett 2014).[9] Second, the decades from the 1970s to the 1990s witnessed the establishment of a series of flagship events in distinct parts of East Asia, including Hong Kong, Tokyo, and Busan.[10] Third, recent years have brought the beginnings of a reconfiguration of festivals along the Southeast Asia axis, for example with the setting up of the Singapore International Film Festival and the Bangkok International Film Festival, alongside continued growth and vibrancy in East Asia.[11] Of particular significance in the latter regard are prolonged activities in the People's Republic of China, especially the unceasing attempt by government authorities to push the recently established Beijing International Film Festival, a resource-rich "late adopter" (Strandgaard Pedersen and Mazza 2011) founded in 2011, as a prestige event of global standing.

The dominant narrative that emerges from the various but still relatively few published accounts of festivals in Asia currently available is of regional cooperation coexisting with competiveness inside a cauldron of geopolitical pressures. In these terms, early initiatives such as the Cold War-era Southeast Asian Film Festival, while notably reluctant to draw distinctions between the constituent parts of the region, nevertheless served only an ad hoc union of nations comprising a small number of "friendly" clients allied to the United States. By contrast, the rise at the end of the twentieth century of major East Asian events like Hong Kong, Tokyo, and Busan was stimulated by (among other complex factors) ambitious city branding priorities on the part of ostensibly autonomous local governments (Stringer 2001; Ooi and Strandgaard Pedersen 2010). Moreover, a further shift in the dynamic relations among Asia's myriad festivals is being driven at the present time both by enhanced prospects for ASEAN (Association of Southeast Asian Nations) members such as Thailand and Malaysia and the powerful global force of China's spectacular economic growth.

The nascent literature on Asia generated by film festival studies encompasses numerous dimensions of these interlinked phenomena. For example, scholarly accounts demonstrate the role of city economies and infrastructures (Vogel 2012), port city settings (Lee and Stringer 2012a), and inter-city rivalries (Ahn 2012). (Just as the Hong Kong International Film Festival provided a model for the Busan International Film Festival, the Beijing International Film Festival appears keen to outstrip the achievements and profile of the Shanghai International Film Festival.) Then, too, other commentaries pay attention to the discrete networks, or counter-networks, that have grown up for particular forms of cinema, including documentary (Nornes 2009), animation (Kinoshita 2012), and gay, lesbian, and queer filmmaking (Kim 2007). Researchers have also discussed connections with other forms of identity politics (Kim 2005 [1998]), meditated on the representation of various Asian cinemas on festival screens (Zhang 2002; Stringer 2005, 2011 [2002]; Wu 2007; Gerow 2013) and tracked the fortunes of individual companies at domestic and overseas events (Sun 2015).

It is also necessary to be aware of the variety of events that make up the totality of film festivals in Asia. Aside from the numerous major international showcases already mentioned, these include mid-size celebrations of non-corporate cinema (Seoul Independent Film Festival), long-established platforms for short films (Image Forum Festival, based in Tokyo), television festivals (Shanghai TV Festival), women's film festivals (the Women Make Waves Film Festival, based in Taipei), and so on.[12] All of these, as well as an abundance of other kinds of audiovisual jamborees not listed here, will surely have their parts to play in future assessments of activities in the vast swathes of the Earth that comprise "Asia" broadly defined.

In navigating the numerous outputs that constitute this emerging body of research, it is helpful to ponder a subtle distinction in critical terminology. Some writers talk about "Asian film festivals"—a phrase that seemingly emphasizes the cultural commonality, or "Asian-ness," of the specific events in question. Against this, though, may be posited use of the simple pragmatic term "film festivals in Asia." (This is obviously the wording adopted in the present chapter.)[13] What are the benefits of this latter mode of expression? To begin with, it emphasizes the centrality of geography to any relevant inquiry. In addition, by refusing to ascribe a collective pan-continental identity to the region's varied events, the notion of "film festivals in Asia" avoids smoothing over the (often highly significant) dissimilarities between them. Indeed, it reiterates instead the fundamental point that there is no one or singular regional unit; by contrast, "Asia" is a highly contingent term whose shifting meanings are subject to the divergent historical and cultural relations that various societies have to this imaginary entity. Use of this particular form of words similarly paves the way for other forms of spatial mapping, for example considerations of the local, the trans-local, the trans-regional and the trans-urban, joined with intellectual approaches to "media capital" (Curtin 2007), or the core location criteria underpinning the growth of specific production, distribution and exhibition centers. In short, the analytical descriptor "film festivals in Asia" carries several advantages. It assists in the battle against essentialist thinking while facilitating research methods that more fully account for the region's historically complex, multilayered, and ever-shifting festival dynamics.

The term "film festivals in Asia" carries one further benefit as the basis for an historical and geographical analysis of regional events of all tiers of scale. Unlike the phrase "Asian film festivals," which suggests a harmonious bloc of cognate happenings, it potentially introduces into these relationships suggestive notes of disjuncture and difference (Appadurai 1990). To put it another way, it more readily suggests the existence of power dynamics among the complex crisscrossing trajectories that characterize and define the range of the continent's festivals. Events in diverse locations in Asia are linked to one another by coexisting and asymmetrical relationships of cooperation and competition, via shifting variables such as relative size and status as well as the ability (or inability) to attract and retain valuable resources like investment and sponsorship. For all of these reasons regional circuits of interrelated phenomena can be said to exist in Asia even if their ad hoc natures makes them difficult to perceive let alone identify.

Nevertheless, and regardless of which critical terminology is ultimately used, it is important to also grasp a more tangible way in which power dynamics shape and penetrate the film festival phenomenon in Asia (and elsewhere). This entails a very different form of spatial mapping. Let us therefore now turn to this highly suggestive yet frequently overlooked aspect of the international film festival circuit.

Power from a distance

While the summary outlined above shows that numerous methods exist for investigating conditions of force and influence among film festivals in Asia, the remainder of this chapter spotlights a more hidden side of the topic. This perspective only comes into view when issues of history and geography are placed in a fresh geopolitical context. Once revealed, though, it drives home the argument that a global circuit or network of interrelated events does indeed exist.

Groupings of festivals in Asia—and, by extension, in all other parts of the world—constitute linked phenomena because the continent's events dwell in the orbit of an organizing core. For instance, some secure sizeable competitive advantage by trumpeting their "official" status. Others, such as "unofficial" public exhibitions in China (Nakajima 2006), build identities as subterranean alternatives to these formally sanctioned showcases. What and where is this focused center? And who gets to bless some festivals while sidelining others?

The International Federation of Film Producers Associations, or Fédération Internationale des Associations de Producteurs de Films (FIAPF), was founded in France in 1933 as, among other functions, the regulatory body for film festivals worldwide. This is a key role it has retained ever since. The organization's purpose is explained in the mission statement available on its website (FIAPF 2015):

> FIAPF's members are 35 producer organizations from 30 countries on five continents, FIAPF is the only organization of film and television producers with a global reach. FIAPF's mandate is to represent the economic, legal and regulatory interests which film and TV production industries in five continents have in common. [...] FIAPF is also a regulator of international film festivals, including some of the world's most significant ones. FIAPF International Film Festivals Regulations are a trust contract between the film business and the festivals who depend on their cooperation for their prestige and economic impact.[14]

> FIAPF's role as a regulator of international film festivals is to facilitate the job of the producers, sales agents and distributors in the management of their relationships with the festivals [...]. Accredited festivals are expected to implement quality and reliability standards that meet industry expectations [...]. FIAPF's role is also to support some festivals' efforts in achieving higher standards over time, despite economic or programming challenges which often stem from a combination of unfavourable geopolitical location, budgets, and a difficult place in the annual festivals' calendar. This is particularly relevant in the context of the unequal levels of resources and opportunities between film festivals in the Southern and Northern hemispheres.[15]

As Dina Iordanova (2009: 27) perceptively notes, FIAPF constitutes the "only clearly articulated attempt to 'network' festivals officially according to certain criteria."[16] These principles encompass, most pertinently, the organization's notorious global accreditation system, whereby all manner of events are divvied up into four separate categories: Competitive Feature Film Festivals (also known as the "A-list"), Competitive Specialized Feature Film Festivals (also known as the "B-list"), Non-Competitive Feature Film Festivals, and Documentary and Short Film Festivals. Events that fail to secure, or do not care to pursue, accreditation status are obliged to function without FIAPF's assistance. While for some festivals not being involved with FIAPF is certainly an option—as the cases of the Hong Kong International Film Festival and the Sundance Film Festival, to cite just two, readily attest—such an arrangement also carries potential downsides. For the weight of FIAPF's international gravitas and clout is such that any event that does not participate (for whatever reason) in its accreditation process runs the risk of being perceived as a maverick outsider. More specifically, it will be shut out from accessing "the flow of quality cinema" that ostensibly marks the "special position within the assigned regions" (Iordanova 2009: 28) enjoyed by those festivals that do work closely with the organization.

Festivals in Asia in a position to play the FIAPF game can expect to benefit in numerous ways. They are cushioned by the sanction of official status and granted formal visibility on the global festival map. This in turn can result in enhanced branding and other commercial opportunities. In particular, monetary and symbolic values attach like limpets to FIAPF's "A" and "B" lists, and these may form influential pull factors in the scramble among rival events to secure precious (and ever more mobile) transnational investments. The prestige that accompanies ratification by FIAPF depends, in part, upon adherence to the organization's assorted rules: these stipulate, for example, just how many premieres and other kinds of films must be shown at such-and-such a category of event. By these and other means, FIAPF-friendly festivals are in a position to cherry-pick (albeit competitively between themselves) the most sought-after new titles of world cinema while non-accredited events have to make do as best they can.

Against this, capitulation to FIAPF inevitably leads to an individual festival relinquishing a measure of control over its own destiny. Power is deferred elsewhere. Moreover, while the effects of FIAPF's accreditation system have spread far and wide, critics note its ongoing idiosyncrasies. For instance, the decree that at any point in time only one festival from a given nation can be included in the "A-list" spurs events to vie with each other for this coveted status.[17] The logic of distinguishing between events in the "A-list" and "B-list" categories has also been questioned. Such a seemingly arbitrary way of cordoning off comparable festivals has

> raised eyebrows because it places smaller and less established events such as Shanghai in the same league as Cannes and Venice, among the 12 festivals in the first category. The second category, or "competitive specialised" section, endorses 26 film festivals, including the Pusan

International Film Festival, which is widely regarded as Asia's most influential film festival and more prestigious than Shanghai.

(Shackleton 2007)

In line with virtually all of FIAPF's actions, the exact justification for such a precise ordering of particular events is seldom given public airing.[18]

In short, FIAPF ranks individual events on the international film festival circuit, distributes rare resources, controls prestige, and consolidates the sense of an interlinked global festival network. For all of these reasons it must be deemed a significant force in the organization of film festivals in Asia. Like some outsize butterfly-effect, FIAPF's daily exertions generate magnified repercussions on the other side of the world. It touches events of all tiers of scale—even those that want nothing to do with it can scarcely avoid the sweep of its structuring influence. Yet despite this, critics and historians appear to know next to nothing about how the organization itself actually functions. Based on the available evidence, it seems to be a self-appointed cabal staffed by shadowy figures charged with mysterious portfolios. There is no reason to suppose that this state of affairs is likely to alter anytime soon.

It is in these terms that power from a distance operates upon film festivals in Asia (and elsewhere). FIAPF's singular capabilities extend both across space (from its geographical roots outside the continent) and time (from the secure international profile it has managed to maintain for an impressive eight decades). If the film festival is indeed a European phenomenon, a creature of the region that then went global, it is not just because the first events were founded in Europe. It is also because the economies and cultural politics of festivals in all parts of the world have always had to contend with the simple fact of FIAPF's existence. Moreover, while the dominant narrative that emerges from published accounts of festivals in Asia is of regional competition coexisting with competitiveness, one of the hands that stokes the cauldron of geopolitical pressures within which all of this takes place belongs to FIAPF. The organization represents the most visible power structure in the festival world. Attending to its influence can thus only enhance comprehension of the complex relationship between global and local power dynamics in festival histories and geographies.

The festivals and associated film industries of China, Japan, and South Korea may today be in the vanguard of world cinema. Prospects may be looking up for events located in ASEAN countries as well as other hitherto less active parts of the continent. But the unchanging paradox is that for all manner of festivals in Asia important business continues to germinate thousands of miles away, behind closed doors, from inside a certain address: the International Federation of Film Producers Associations, 9, rue de l'Échelle, 75001 Paris, France.

Conclusion

This chapter has sought to offer a brief narrative of the historical importance and growing contemporary significance of film festivals in Asia. At the same time, it has pointed to a habitually neglected trait of the globalized festival circuit—namely, the power and influence wielded on it and through it by a spectral organization of uncertain characteristics.

The preceding case study's relevance to the historical understanding of film festivals more generally is twofold. On the one hand, many events in Asia embody distinct identities and unique stories. Their innovations, in conjunction with the continent's continuing economic strength and China's high ambitions for its media industries, are likely to drive the festival circuit for years to come. On the other hand, the fact that festivals in Asia have to deal with FIAPF's regime of global power is indicative of experiences shared the world over by untold numbers of (otherwise very dissimilar) kinds of events. FIAPF may be based outside a particular region, but it will typically play a strong hand on activities in that region all the same.

At the same time, it is important to observe that scholarship on this topic would benefit from increased knowledge and understanding. Nuances of thought deserve to be developed. For example, for how much should FIAPF's long-standing pedigree and pivotal role in the global organization of festivals count when set against the growing consequence of the other interrelations—cultural, economic, geographical, historical, and political—that also impact upon circuits, or counter-circuits, of festivals in Asia? FIAPF is symptomatic of how power relationships constrain festivals and exercise a systemic authority on otherwise disparate events. Yet in today's digital and increasingly interconnected world, new forces and synergies may well rise to challenge FIAPF's authority.

In addition, heady questions can be asked about how FIAPF's status as regulator of international festivals relates to its core business as an organization of film and television producers. To be sure, when it comes to the former area of activity the fundamental Eurocentrism of the FIAPF enterprise is self-evident: of the 15 accredited A-list festivals, nine are based in Europe. But FIAPF simultaneously appears to be exerting a declining influence on the world's associated movie industries. Consider in this respect the fact that while half of FIAPF's member nations are European, half are not. Furthermore, that among the countries listed in 2013 by UNESCO as the most productive filmmaking nations are several (including South Korea, the United Kingdom, Italy, and France) that do not belong to the international trade group that ostensibly promotes their industries.[19] Such figures provide tantalizing glimpses into the true complexities of the trade and traffic in cinema internationally, but they remain glimpses all the same. A substantial geographical analysis of the history of film festivals in Asia, and in the entirety of the world for that matter, cannot be told until a more precise cartography of FIAPF's connections to specific industries, as well as its presence in particular countries and continents, is mapped much more fully than it has been to date.

In conclusion, culturally- and historically-specific geographical analysis of spatial dynamics will always reveal something of interest and importance about the international film festival circuit. More than that, it will always reveal a power relationship. Unravelling the true diversity and impact of these conditions of force and influence among film festivals in Asia is a daunting but exciting challenge for the future. To undertake it will require the combined talents and efforts of a dedicated cadre of researchers toiling away on multiple fronts. This task will hopefully be achieved once a sufficient cohort of scholars is able and willing to undertake the endeavor.

Acknowledgments

Thank you to Marijke de Valck, Brendan Kredell, and Skadi Loist for generous feedback on an earlier draft of this chapter.

Notes

1 For examples of existing studies, see Stringer (2001), Harbord (2002: 59–75), Falicov (2010), Ooi and Strandgaard Pedersen (2010), Bissell (2012), Lee and Stringer (2012a), and Gutiérrez and Wagenberg (2013). At the time of writing, no researcher has attempted to produce a substantial geographical analysis of the history of film festivals: in these terms, the field has yet to be mapped. On the other hand, many accounts of the establishment and growth of individual events do exist and these often provide useful information on the reasons why a new initiative was established in this or that particular destination. Indicative examples of such work include Smith (1999) and Corliss and Darke (2007).

2 Besides geography and history, a third especially important aspect of film festival culture is the role of human agency, or people, organized into business practices. As well as providing one of the few attempts to produce a historical chronology of festivals, De Valck (2007), along with Elsaesser (2005), proposes a valuable model of actor-network-theory. Word constraints prevent a people-centered and business-oriented perspective from being pursued here. However, recent forays in this direction may be found in Rhyne (2009), Loist (2011), Fischer (2013) and Stringer (forthcoming).

3 Film festival studies may benefit greatly from extended consideration of the "spatial turn" in geography, history, and other academic disciplines (see, *inter alia*, Lefebvre 1991 [1974]; Soja 1989; Davis 1992 [1990]). Although not directly concerned with festivals, two recent collections (Rhodes and Gorfinkel 2011; Hallam and Roberts 2013) provide stimulating analyses of various aspects of location and the moving image.

4 This is to say that the film festival is inherently political. Scratch the surface of any of its geographical or historical dimensions and you will always find a power relationship.

5 Due to lack of space, I put to one side here consideration of the definition of the concepts of "Asia" and "Asian cinema." For relevant discussions of these topics, see, among other sources, Berry et al. (2009) and Eleftheriotis and Needham (2006); see also note 8 (below). The Udine Far East Film Festival, held annually in Udine, Italy, is one of the most important annual showcases of what it terms "popular Asian cinema." Its programming philosophy and rationale is analyzed by Lee and Stringer (2012b).

6 The Venice Film Festival was founded in 1932, the Cannes film festival in 1946, and the Berlin International Film Festival in 1951; the Hong Kong International Film Festival was founded in 1977, the Shanghai International Film Festival in 1993, and the Pusan International Film Festival in 1996. The latter changed its name to the Busan International Film Festival in 2011.

7 Bibliographies of key readings have been assembled by Fischer (2011) and by Marijke de Valck and Skadi Loist's Film Festival Research Network (2015). A new collection of writings on the burgeoning number of Chinese film festivals, edited by Chris Berry and Luke Robinson, is forthcoming.

8 This truism also applies of course to other regions of the world such as Europe and the Middle East. For an indication of the inevitable brevity and tentativeness—given word constraints—of the treatment offered in this chapter, consult the definition of "Asia" offered by the *Collins English Dictionary*:

> *n* the largest of the continents, bordering on the Arctic Ocean, the Pacific Ocean, the India Ocean, and the Mediterranean and Red Seas in the west. It includes the large peninsulas of Asia Minor, India, Arabia, and Indochina and the island groups of Japan, Indonesia, the Philippines, and Sri Lanka; contains the mountain ranges of the Hindu Kush, Himalayas, Pamirs, Tian, Shan, Urals, and Caucasus, the great plateaus of India, Iran, and Tibet, vast plains and deserts, and the valleys of many large rivers, including the Mekong, Irrawaddy, Indus, Ganges, Tigris, and Euphrates.

For references to scholarly work on festivals based in the continent of Asia but outside the vital centers of East Asia, consult Fischer (2011) and the Film Festival Research Network (2015).

9 As Yau explains (2003: 279, 290), this event was established in 1954 under the title of the Southeast Asian Film Festival; it was then renamed the Asian Film Festival in 1957 and subsequently as the Asia-Pacific Film Festival. Forty-seven editions were held between 1954 and 2002.

10 The Tokyo International Film Festival was established in 1985. On the Hong Kong event, see Wong (2011); on Busan, see Ahn (2012).

11 On the Singapore International Film Festival, established in 1987, see Chan and Chua (2011); on the Bangkok International Film Festival, established in 2003, see Kong (2009).

12 The dates of the founding of these respective events are Seoul Independent Film Festival (1975), Image Forum Festival (1986), Shanghai TV Festival (1986), the Women Make Waves Film Festival (1993).

13 The discussion that follows is adapted from Lee and Stringer's (2013) analysis of "film noir in Asia."

14 Cf. Welcome note of the FIAPF website, www.fiapf.org/default.asp (accessed August 28, 2015).

15 Cf. "International Film Festivals" page on the FIAPF website, www.fiapf.org/intfilmfestivals.asp (accessed August 28, 2015).

16 See also Ma (2012).

17 This situation goes some way to explaining the nature of the Beijing International Film Festival's current relationship with the Shanghai International Film Festival. As the latter is classified under the Competitive Feature Film rubric, nominally putting it on equal terms with Berlin, Cannes and Venice, the former gives every impression of striving to usurp its position.

18 For a sense of the intensely political nature of all of this—as well as some indication of the correspondingly high stakes involved—consider one of the rare public statements, uttered in 2007, by then-FIAPF president Andres Vicente Gomez (who was succeeded in the role in 2009 by Luis Alberto Scalella), in defense of the organization's decision to include Shanghai in its first category (quoted by Shackleton 2007):

Considering on one hand that piracy in China is still a very critical concern for the film industry, and on the other hand, the current access market restriction for foreign movies, FIAPF strongly believes in the role of the Shanghai International Film Festival. This event is one of the rare legitimate windows to offer and to promote a large selection of foreign movies to a numerous local audience with optimum screening conditions.

19 See www.uis.unesco.org.

References

Ahn, S. (2012) *The Pusan International Film Festival, South Korean Cinema and Globalization*, Hong Kong: Hong Kong University Press.

Appadurai, A. (1990) "Disjuncture and Difference in the Global Cultural Economy," *Public Culture*, 2(2), pp. 1–24.

Baskett, M. (2014) "Japan's Film Festival Diplomacy in Cold War Asia," *The Velvet Light Trap*, 73, pp. 4–18.

Berry, C., N. Liscutin, and J. D. Mackintosh (eds.) (2009) *Cultural Studies and Cultural Industries in Northeast Asia: What a Difference a Region Makes*, Hong Kong: Hong Kong University Press.

Bissell, W. C. (2012) "When the Film Festival Comes to (Down)Town: Transnational Circuits, Tourism, and the Urban Economy of Images," in M. Peterson and G. W. McDonogh (eds.) *Global Downtowns*, Philadelphia, PA: University of Pennsylvania Press, pp. 160–185.

Chan, F. and D. Chua (2011) "Programming Southeast Asia at the Singapore International Film Festival," in D. Iordanova and R. Cheung (eds.) *Film Festival Yearbook 3: Film Festivals and East Asia*, St Andrews: St Andrews Film Studies, pp. 125–141.

Corliss, K. and C. Darke (2007) *Cannes: Inside the World's Premier Film Festival*, London: Faber and Faber.

Curtin, M. (2007) *Playing to the World's Biggest Audience: The Globalization of Chinese Film and TV*, Berkeley, CA: University of California Press.

Davis, M. (1992 [1990]) *City of Quartz: Excavating the Future in Los Angeles*, London: Vintage.

De Valck, M. (2007) *Film Festivals: From European Geopolitics to Global Cinephilia*, Amsterdam: Amsterdam University Press.

Dovey, L. (2015) *Curating Africa in the Age of Film Festivals*, New York: Palgrave Macmillan.

Eleftheriotis, D. and G. Needham (eds.) (2006) *Asian Cinemas: A Reader and Guide*, Edinburgh: Edinburgh University Press.

Elsaesser, T. (2005) "Film Festival Networks: The New Topographies of Cinema in Europe," in *European Cinema: Face to Face With Hollywood*, Amsterdam: Amsterdam University Press, pp. 82–107.

Falicov, T. L. (2010) "Migrating from South to North: The Role of Film Festivals in Funding and Shaping Global South Film and Video," in G. Elmer, C. H. Davis, J. Marchessault, and J. McCullough (eds.) *Locating Migrating Media*, Lanham, MD: Lexington Books, pp. 3–21.

FIAPF (Fédération Internationale des Associations de Producteurs de Films, or International Federation of Film Producers Associations) (2015). Online. www.fiapf.org.

Film Festival Research Network (2015) "Film Festival Research Bibliography: Asia." Online. www.filmfestivalresearch.org.

Fischer, A. (2011) "Bibliography: Film Festivals and East Asia," in D. Iordanova and R. Cheung (eds.) *Film Festival Yearbook 3: Film Festivals and East Asia*, St Andrews: St Andrews Film Studies, pp. 267–275.

Fischer, A. (2013) *Sustainable Projections: Concepts in Film Festival Management*, St Andrews: St Andrews Film Studies.

Gerow, A. (2013) "Retrospective Irony: Film Festivals and Japanese Cinema History," in A. Marlow-Mann (ed.) *Film Festival Yearbook 5: Archival Film Festivals*, St Andrews: St Andrews Film Studies, pp. 189–199.

Gutiérrez, C. A. and M. Wagenberg (2013) "Meeting Points: A Survey of Film Festivals in Latin America," *Transnational Cinemas*, 4(2), pp. 295–305.

Hallam, J. and L. Roberts (eds.) (2013) *Locating the Moving Image: New Approaches to Film and Place*, Bloomington, IN: Indiana University Press.

Harbord, J. (2002) *Film Cultures*, London: Sage.

Iordanova, D. (2009) "The Film Festival Circuit," in D. Iordanova and R. Rhyne (eds.) *Film Festival Yearbook 1: The Festival Circuit*, St Andrews: St Andrews Film Studies, pp. 23–39.

Iordanova, D. (2011) "East Asia and Film Festivals: Transnational Clusters for Creativity and Commerce," in D. Iordanova and R. Cheung (eds.) *Film Festival Yearbook 3: Film Festivals and East Asia*, St Andrews: St Andrews Film Studies, pp. 1–33.

Iordanova, D. and R. Cheung (eds.) (2011) *Film Festival Yearbook 3: Film Festivals and East Asia*, St Andrews: St Andrews Film Studies.

Iordanova, D. and R. Rhyne (eds.) (2009) *Film Festival Yearbook 1: The Festival Circuit*, St Andrews: St Andrews Film Studies.

Iordanova, D. and S. Van de Peer (eds.) (2014) *Film Festival Yearbook 6: Film Festivals and the Middle East*, St Andrews: St Andrews Film Studies.

Kim, J. (2007) "Queer Cultural Movements and Local Counterpublics of Sexuality: A Case of Seoul Queer Films and Videos Festival," *Inter-Asia Cultural Studies*, 8(4), pp. 617–633.

Kim, S. (2005 [1998]) "'Cine-Mania' or Cinephilia: Film Festivals and the Identity Question," in C.-Y. Shin and J. Stringer (eds.) *New Korean Cinema*, Edinburgh: Edinburgh University Press, pp. 79–91.

Kinoshita, S. (2012) "The Spirit of the Hiroshima International Animation Festival, 1985–2010," in J. Ruoff (ed.) *Coming Soon to a Festival Near You: Programming Film Festivals*, St Andrews: St Andrews Film Studies, pp. 201–213.

Kong, R. (2009) "The Sad Case of the Bangkok Film Festival," in R. Porton (ed.) *Dekalog 3: On Film Festivals*, London: Wallflower, pp. 122–130.

Lee, N. J. Y. and J. Stringer (2012a) "Ports of Entry: Mapping Chinese Cinema's Multiple Trajectories at International Film Festivals," in Y. Zhang (ed.) *A Companion to Chinese Cinema*, Oxford: Wiley-Blackwell, pp. 239–261.

Lee, N. J. Y. and J. Stringer (2012b) "Counter-Programming and the Udine Far East Film Festival," *Screen*, 53(3), pp. 301–309.

Lee, N. J. Y. and J. Stringer (2013) "Film Noir in Asia: Historicizing South Korean Crime Thrillers," in A. Spicer and H. Hanson (eds.) *A Companion to Film Noir*, Oxford: Wiley-Blackwell, pp. 480–495.

Lee, S. (2012) "It's Oscar Time in Asia! The Rise and Demise of the Asia-Pacific Film Festival, 1954–1972," in J. Ruoff (ed.) *Coming Soon to a Festival Near You: Programming Film Festivals*, St Andrews: St Andrews Film Studies, pp. 173–187.

Lee, S. (2014) "The Emergence of the Asian Film Festival: Cold War Asia and Japan's Reentrance to the Regional Film Industry in the 1950s," in D. Miyao (ed.)

The Oxford Handbook of Japanese Cinema, Oxford: Oxford University Press, pp. 226–244.

Lefebvre, H. (1991 [1974]) *The Production of Space*, trans. D. Nicholson-Smith, Oxford: Blackwell.

Loist, S. (2011) "Precarious Cultural Work: About the Organisation of (Queer) Film Festivals," *Screen*, 52(2), pp. 268–273.

Ma, R. (2012) "Celebrating the International, Disremembering Shanghai: The Curious Case of the Shanghai International Film Festival," *Culture Unbound*, 4, pp. 147–168.

Nakajima, S. (2006) "Film Clubs in Beijing: The Cultural Consumption of Chinese Independent Films," in P. G. Pickowicz and Y. Zhang (eds.) *From Underground to Independent: Alternative Film Cultures in Contemporary China*, Oxford: Rowman & Littlefield, pp. 161–187.

Nornes, A. M. (2009) "Bulldozers, Bibles, and Very Sharp Knives: The Chinese Independent Documentary Scene," *Film Quarterly*, 63(1), pp. 50–55.

Ooi, C.-S. and J. Strandgaard Pedersen (2010) "City Branding and Film Festivals: Re-evaluating Stakeholder's Relations," *Place Branding and Public Diplomacy*, 6(4), pp. 316–332.

Rhodes, J. D. and E. Gorfinkel (eds.) (2011) *Taking Place: Location and the Moving Image*, Minneapolis, MN: University of Minnesota Press.

Rhyne, R. (2009) "Film Festival Circuits and Stakeholders," in D. Iordanova and R. Rhyne (eds.) *Film Festival Yearbook 1: The Festival Circuit*, St Andrews: St Andrews Film Studies, pp. 9–22.

Shackleton, L. (2007) "FIAPF Defends Film Festival Accreditation System," *Screen Daily*, July 9. Online. www.screendaily.com/fiapf-defends-film-festival-accreditation-system/4033493.article.

Smith, L. (1999) *Party in a Box: The Story of the Sundance Film Festival*, Salt Lake City; UT: Gibbs Smith.

Soja, E. (1989) *Postmodern Geographies: The Reassertion of Space in Critical Social Theory*, London: Verso.

Strandgaard Pedersen, J. and C. Mazza (2011) "International Film Festivals: For the Benefit of Whom?" *Culture Unbound*, 3, pp. 139–165.

Stringer, J. (2001) "Global Cities and the International Film Festival Economy," in M. Shiel and T. Fitzmaurice (eds.) *Cinema and the City: Film and Urban Societies in a Global Context*, Oxford: Blackwell, pp. 134–144.

Stringer, J. (2005) "Putting Korean Cinema in Its Place: Genre Classifications and the Contexts of Reception," in C.-Y. Shin and J. Stringer (eds.) *New Korean Cinema*, Edinburgh: Edinburgh University Press, pp. 95–105.

Stringer, J. (2011 [2002]) "Japan 1951–1970: National Cinema as Cultural Currency," in D. Iordanova and R. Cheung (eds.) *Film Festival Yearbook 3: Film Festivals and East Asia*, St Andrews: St Andrews Film Studies, pp. 62–80.

Stringer, J. (forthcoming) *Regarding Film Festivals*, New York: Palgrave Macmillan.

Sun, Y. (2015) "Shaping Hong Kong Cinema's New Icon: Milkyway Image at International Film Festivals," *Transnational Cinemas*, 6(1), pp. 67–83.

Vogel, A. (2012) "Film Festivals in Asian Cities," in P. W. Daniels, K. C. Ho, and T. A. Hutton (eds.) *New Economic Spaces in Asian Cities: From Industrial Restructuring to the Cultural Turn*, Abingdon and New York: Routledge, pp. 67–86.

Wong, C. H.-Y. (2011) *Film Festivals: Culture, People, and Power on the Global Screen*, New Brunswick, NJ: Rutgers University Press.

Wu, C.-C. (2007) "Festivals, Criticism and International Reputation of Taiwan New Cinema," in D. W. Davis and R.-S. R. Chen (eds.) *Cinema Taiwan: Politics, Popularity, and State of the Arts*, Abingdon and New York: Routledge, pp. 75–91.

Yau, K. S.-T. (2003) "Shaws' Japanese Collaboration and Competition as Seen Through the Asian Film Festival Evolution," in A.-L. Wong (ed.) *The Shaw Screen: A Preliminary Study*, Hong Kong: Hong Kong Film Archive, pp. 279–294.

Zhang, Y. (2002) *Screening China: Critical Interventions, Cinematic Reconfigurations, and the Transnational Imaginary in Contemporary Chinese Cinema*, Ann Arbor, MI: University of Michigan Press.

Further reading

Many of the key works on film festivals in Asia are listed in the References. As already indicated, more complete bibliographies have been compiled by Fischer (2011) and by the Film Festival Research Network (2015). Students wishing to keep up to date with relevant developments on the festival circuit are recommended to consult the excellent website *Film Business Asia* (www. filmbiz.asia). To date no history of FIAPF has been published. Indeed, its internal workings remain a complete mystery.

3 The film festival circuit

Networks, hierarchies, and circulation

Skadi Loist

When speaking with filmmakers, producers, film funders, and journalists, the term "film festival circuit" is widely used. Yet, the concept seems to be lacking a clear definition; when looking at its usage, an array of meanings can be discerned. On the one hand, the film festival circuit is an all-encompassing idea, covering the entire landscape of a few thousand-odd festivals. On another level, when talking about "the circuit" practitioners and journalists have a select number of top-tier festivals in mind. To complicate matters further, when speaking about a specific film or project the term circuit becomes relational, referring to the trajectory of a specific product through a global network of festivals. Evidently, "circuit" is a volatile and contingent term.

This chapter shifts the focus from single festivals and their individual aims and strategies to the creation of a circuit with its spatial and temporal dimensions, which play out in the hierarchies between festivals, sub-circuits, and calendars. The first section of this chapter focuses on the theoretical conceptions that try to account for the complex dimensions of a festival ecosystem that comprises various stakeholders. The remainder of the chapter positions these dynamics within the historical development of the global film festival phenomenon as it is embedded in larger shifts in culture, society, politics, and media industries. While looking at the growth and diversification of the festival model, it also considers the establishment, proliferation, and consolidation of the film festival circuit.

Conceptions of the festival world

The metaphor of a film festival "circuit" has been used by film critics and film professionals since the late 1950s and the image of the international film festival circuit "implies a kind of free circulation, an open system of film prints moving effortlessly around the earth. They alight at one node or another for projection and enjoyment, before returning to their circuitous path home" (Nornes 2014: 258). Festival industry databases, such as the submission platform Withoutabox, currently list more than 6,000 festivals in operation globally as part of the vast festival landscape.[1] Obviously, not all of those events operate in the same way or are equally connected; instead the festival phenomenon is marked by great diversity, differentiation, and hierarchical stratification, and what constitutes the circuit for a specific professional or film is highly relational.[2]

Since one can only visit a limited number of festivals in a year, the personal composition of the circuit depends on specific interests of the attendee, which may vary depending upon her professional interests (as a filmmaker, critic, or distributor, for example). Active film professionals usually refer to the festival circuit as encompassing the 10–15 festivals that they attend or actively follow in one calendar year when scouting for films and talent.[3] They will pick their festivals depending on their position within the larger network and their value to the interests of distributors and filmmakers.

Both interpretations of the circuit metaphor—whether it denotes films or people circulating through festivals—are linked to the business side of this world. The top-tier events are often marked by the presence of a film market: in some cases, such as the European Film Market (EFM), held in conjunction with the Berlinale, or the Marché du Film of the Festival de Cannes, these are officially sanctioned by the festival. Other top-tier events host "quasi-markets," such as the ones at the Toronto International Film Festival (TIFF) and Sundance Film Festival; the American Film Market is an example of a market with influence on the festival calendar which exists without an accompanying festival. Other international film festivals of the second tier occupy a position between this seasonal cycle of top-level industry events. By focusing on particular cinemas, they complement the broader festivals and offer the potential for personalized, individual circuits. These festivals can serve, for instance, as a source festival for national/regional cinemas, or as leading events in parallel or sub-circuits, e.g., for documentary or LGBT/Q films.

In the academic world, scholars have tended to be critical about the use of the term circuit, because it does not extend to include the broad landscape of film festivals: more than 6,000 festivals in operation globally, each of which are increasingly networked and interconnected, marked both by competition and collaboration over films, talent, sponsors, and audiences. In the wake of sociological theorizations of systems, networks, and flows,[4] this connected festival world has been conceptualized as a film festival "network" by Thomas Elsaesser (2005) and Marijke de Valck (2007). De Valck discusses the value of Bruno Latour's actor-network-theory and how it can favorably be applied to the film festival circuit. She stresses the potential to capture the complexity of the festival system by utilizing his "notion of a network as a relation to living and non-living actors" (De Valck 2007: 101). In this conception, film professionals, films, and accreditation systems equally have agency within the network. However, she also points to the concept's limitations, as scales and hierarchies cannot be mapped by this approach.

Elsaesser and De Valck point to the European roots of the festival network and discuss it in relation to Hollywood. They stress that the festival network cannot easily be put up as a singular "other" of Hollywood, not least because

Hollywood is also an important actor within the network necessary for the attention economy that is part of the value-addition machine connected to the red carpets. Nevertheless they focus largely on the European centers and the global impact of the Hollywood industry. From this initial focus, film festival studies has moved forward to increasingly pay attention also to events and circulation patterns outside the European and North American "centers." Focusing on film festivals in Asia, Julian Stringer (2001) and Abé Mark Nornes (2014) have both discussed the geographic disparities on the festival network.[5] While there are several other A-list festivals beyond the "big three" European ones (Cannes, Berlin, Venice), those seem not to hold the same status on the international circuit. Nornes attributes this to old engrained (post-)colonial structures as well as language barriers, which are borne out of a long-standing Eurocentric "first Europe, then elsewhere"—or respectively a "first Hollywood, then elsewhere"—stance, that have hindered free flow and exchange, and resulted in the ignorance of European and North American film cultures and their festivals, discounting the significance of non-Western film cultures (Nornes 2014: 246).

Extending the "circuit" metaphor, Nornes then suggests that Western Eurocentrism and ignorance has created a blockage in the circuit of free flow, which resulted in a discharge of energy in a short circuit (ibid.). Despite its negative connotations, this "short" has had a positive, energetic effect—just as with an electrical short, sparks went flying. Here, he refers to the establishment of the energetic Yamagata International Documentary Film Festival in 1989. While it was largely ignored by the international circuit, it became a highly influential event, promoting a vibrant, dedicated documentary film scene and influencing the creation of several documentary film festivals throughout Asia (ibid.: 251).

Beyond the professional circuit (or Nornes' "short circuit"), several other "parallel circuits" that function along specific geographic or thematic logics have been studied in the *Film Festival Yearbook* series.[6] Pushing further from where the series leaves off and following critiques of disparity both on the circuit and in scholarly attention, Papagena Robbins and Viviane Saglier assert that a "focus on a network woven around diversity, tensions, ruptures, and inequalities suggests an underlying new conception of networks beyond the coherence that was once given in the beginning years of film festival studies" (Robbins and Saglier 2015: 4). Instead of following the "circuit" metaphor further, they offer a few other terms in the hopes of providing new avenues for the study of the vast, complex festival world. For one, they point to the notion of an "archipelago"—used by Joshua Neves (2012) and Michel Frodon (2014) to refer to regional networks of festivals developing along the margins of globalization in Southeast Asia and the Arab world, respectively— and suggest that this term "allows thinking of rupture and continuity simultaneously" (Robbins and Saglier 2015: 4). In a further step they propose taking a different look at festival networks by mobilizing Gilles Deleuze and Félix Guattari's concept of the "ever-expanding and decentralized rhizome rather than the self-reflexive and enclosed modern system theory that Elsaesser and De Valck" used and demand "that we revise assumptions of a world organization based on strict centers and peripheries" (ibid.).

As these conceptual struggles suggest, in recent years the changing dynamics of the festival world have opened up yet another interpretation of "the circuit." This refers not only to the exhibition of films, but also to their distribution, leading to an increased emphasis on the classic sense of circuit and its business ramifications. Here circulation—not only of film, but increasingly of personnel such as consultants, programmers, critics, and buyers—on the "festival treadmill" (Iordanova 2009: 33) gains significance. This leads in another step to a third interpretation of the circuit: the circulation of money, for instance in the form of distribution revenue or film production funds flowing through the increasing number of markets and production workshops on the festival circuit.

Along with other non-traditional distribution routes, such as diasporic circuits, online distribution, and shadow economies,[7] festivals have become an important networked global distribution route for "alternative cinema."[8] The massive growth of the festival world has increased the strength of network effects and the significance of the "long-tail effect" for this alternative distribution network (Iordanova 2010). A host of smaller networks now exist to serve specific audiences or "minor genres"; these networks operate differently than the general narrative feature film norm and create their own niche markets and industries, building parallel circuits while also being interconnected with the general network. Depending on themes and form, after a top-tier festival premiere, a film will further trickle down second- and third-tier events and simultaneously move along the multiplicity of rhizomatic channels of parallel thematic circuits for documentary, human rights, animation, women's, or LGBT/Q film festivals.

The significance of the interconnectedness of the circuit is not only recognized by scholars of festival studies and world cinema but also by distributors. Increasingly these routes do not only constitute exhibition platforms, but actually contribute (modestly) as a revenue stream for films, as sales agents and distributors increasingly ask for screening fees, akin to the film rental fees for an eclectic scattered limited release. The Film Collaborative, an independent film representative and consultancy nonprofit, suggests that depending on the film's characteristics (such as premiere status and niche), income between the four-digit to the higher end of the five-digit range can be generated on the festival run alone (The Film Collaborative 2013). Beyond the increasing professionalization and proliferation of the festival network, festivals increasingly are becoming also production platforms, or "industry nodes" (Iordanova 2015).

Historical background

The complex structures of the film festival circuit are the result of several decades-old developments, leading from the European establishment of the film festival model in the 1930s to a contemporary vast global network with several parallel, sub-, and short circuits in the system. The model and function of film festivals has changed over time, along with film culture and cultural policies at large. Festivals' ability to constantly adapt and renew has helped the film festival model to survive, self-sustain, and thrive to this day (De Valck 2007: 35–36).

Marijke de Valck proposes three main phases in the development of the European film festival landscape, which she relates to major shifts in the circuit and industry:

> The first phase runs from the establishment of the first reoccurring film festival in Venice in 1932 until 1968, when upheavals began to disrupt the festivals in Cannes and Venice, or, more precisely, the early 1970s, when these upheavals were followed by a reorganization of the initial festival format (which comprised film festivals as showcases of national cinemas). The second phase is characterized by independently organized festivals that operate both as protectors of the cinematic art and as facilitators of the film industries. This phase ends in the course of the 1980s when the global spread of film festivals and the creation of the international film festival circuit ushers in a third period, during which the festival phenomenon is sweepingly professionalized and institutionalized.
>
> (2007: 19–20)

While De Valck situates the creation of a circuit in the last phase, the historical development of the festival phenomenon from its inception is a foundational background for understanding the network structure of festivals. These three phases serve as reference points in the following historical survey of the festival circuit development.

From the film festival model to a rising network

The film festival model of an annual event was only established when film as a medium had already existed for nearly four decades. Between the first film presentations in Berlin and Paris in 1895 and the establishment of the stable film festival model in the early 1930s, film had transitioned from being a new medium with an air of mass spectacle measured against legitimate art forms like theater and opera to a regarded art form of its own. During this time several one-off events, including film contests, conferences, industry fairs, and avant-garde shows took place throughout Europe that served as important precursors to the festival model (Hagener 2014). Several early film festivals were founded as side bars of larger art expositions, in part as an effort to gain legitimacy for film as an art form. The Venice Film Festival started in 1932 under the umbrella of the Venice Biennale and the Edinburgh Film Festival as part of the Edinburgh International Festival in 1947 (Wong 2011: 44). By the 1950s the status of film had considerably changed, and the Berlinale was specifically founded outside the *Festspielwochen* in 1951 to stress the American sentiment of film as mass culture, not elite art (ibid.: 42).

De Valck dates the first phase of the film festival development from the successful establishment of the Venice Film Festival in Venice in 1932. The model put forward by the Venice Biennale resolved the crisis of European film production, distribution, and exhibition. What had formerly been disadvantages—language barriers, which came to the fore with sound film, and the onset of nationalistic sentiments, which had also contributed to the failure of the cosmopolitan avant-garde movement—were turned into advantages by offering national cultural pride an international platform. In this phase, the festival invited nations to submit their own best films, and the model of national selection and competitions, a sort of "Olympics of film," was born (De Valck 2007: 24, 53). This was later adopted by other festivals, and prevailed through the late 1960s. Yet the move by festival organizers to co-opt nationalist sentiment would have lasting consequences. The political connection of the Venice Film Festival to Mussolini and his Fascist regime eventually led democratic countries to boycott it and organize a counter-festival in Cannes.[9] Also directly entangled with geopolitics and culture, the Berlinale became a major player in the emerging Cold War climate.

Aside from these politically motivated festivals, other events were established by cinephile groups. Two such examples are the festivals founded in Locarno (1946) and Edinburgh (1947). The Locarno festival was initially envisioned as event for Italian cinema and an Italian public. Edinburgh was founded in the context of an international festival city not as state initiative but by a cinephilic association, the Edinburgh Film Guild (Moine 2013).

Although the "big three" film festivals—Cannes, Venice, and Berlin—are quintessential examples of the European film festival phenomenon, the festival model was not long confined to Europe. It quickly went global after World War II. Along with European additions in Karlovy Vary, Czechoslovakia (1946), Locarno, Switzerland (1946), Bilbao, Spain (1946), Edinburgh, UK (1947), San Sebastian, Spain (1953), and London, UK (1956), major festivals were also founded in Melbourne, Australia (1951), India (1952; moving from Mumbai via Delhi to Goa), Mar del Plata, Argentina (1954), Sydney, Australia (1954), the Asia-Pacific region (1954, with rotating locations), San Francisco, USA (1957), and Moscow, Russia (1959). Thus, the building of regional networks goes as far back as the 1950s. Although the Asia-Pacific Film Festival had no great impact on the international circuit, it shows early efforts to connect film industries in Asia regionally (Nornes 2014: 249).

This early globalized proliferation of the film festival model already shows tendencies of a network. The International Federation of Film Producers Associations (FIAPF), which held the monopoly on the regulation of film festivals in the early decades of the festival circuit, in a move to protect the prestige of the festivals in Venice and Cannes, denied Berlin's application for the A-list status in 1950 (Jacobsen 2000: 18). The Berlinale, thus, was not allowed to hold juried international competitions. FIAPF was concerned about the proliferation of the festival circuit and feared for the diminishing interest in—and, thus, vanishing impact of—the premiere festivals. The right to international premieres meant that a certain amount of fresh high-quality product had to be available. As soon as FIAPF started to regulate the festivals and create the "A-list" festivals, the idea of a circuit became visible. The festivals had to be regulated spatially and temporally—in terms of calendar and geopolitics. Thus, it fostered and protected the status of Venice and Cannes. With the move to protect the flow of product to premiere showcases, a hierarchy was introduced to the network. This decision was only overruled in the late 1950s, when Berlin and Karlovy Vary were awarded the A-list status in 1956, San Sebastian in 1957, and Locarno in 1958 (Moine 2013).

The A-list and other "specialized" categories were not spread evenly. A clear preference for Western European and North American festivals can be discerned. Cold War politics played a significant role when the already established Czech film festival in Karlovy Vary had to share A-list status with a new event in the Russian capital, Moscow; it was forced to go biannual in 1959 as the FIAPF decided to only grant one festival in the Eastern bloc such privilege (Moine 2013). These decisions point to the early influence of producers and the industry on the film festival world, an influence that continues to be strong. Today, as Mark Peranson (2008) shows, the industry exercises its control over festivals not through FIAPF but the even more powerful figure of the sales agent.[10]

However, not all of the festivals founded in the 1950s and 1960s were conceived as international platforms for national cultural exhibition and competition striving for A-level status. A number of festivals with smaller reach were founded with a focus on local film or specific genres and techniques. Along with the hierarchies introduced by the FIAPF accreditation system, this marks the beginning of the differentiation of the film festival network into different tiers and sub-circuits of specialized festivals.

Specialized sub-circuits with festivals operating as national cinema showcases for "minor film genres"—for instance short film, documentary, or animation—first grew slowly in the 1960s and then proliferated substantially from the 1980s onward. Standing outside the mainstream commercial film production and exhibition system, these "minor film genres" developed separate financing, production, and exhibition routes (Vallejo 2016). Starting as professional showcases and market fairs, some of these film festivals grew to become "field-configuring events" (Rüling 2011). They soon built their own collaborative networks, production workshops, and distribution routes, as is visible in the parallel festival circuits devoted to short film, documentary, and animation.[11]

The festival model spread across the whole globe rapidly. By the 1960s, all continents and regions featured major regional and international film festivals. Australia was among the first to establish major festivals in Melbourne (1951) and Sydney (1954), growing out of a cinephile community as well as cultural political interests hoping to boost local film production through international competition (Hope and Dickerson 2011; Stevens 2013). In the late 1960s, festivals also appeared in Africa, with the first editions of the *Journées Cinématographique de Carthage* in Tunisia and *Festival panafricain du cinéma et de la télévision de Ouagadougou* (FESPACO) in Burkina Faso in 1969 (Turan 2002: 65–80; Ruoff 2008). A number of festivals in Asia followed, for instance the Golden Horse Film Festival in Taipei (1962), the Hong Kong International Film Festival (1977), and the Fajr International Film Festival in Tehran (1982). The oldest festival in Latin America goes back to 1954 with the Mar del Plata Film Festival (Argentina), followed by international festivals in São Paulo, Brazil, and Havana, Cuba (1976) (Gutiérrez and Wagenberg 2013).

Diversification, parallel circuits, and niche markets

From the 1960s onward, new forms of festivals appear in reaction to social needs as well as to insufficiencies of established festivals and their traditional formats. In the decades after the initial establishment of the film festival model, smaller festivals with a variety of agendas emerge. They start to make use of the festival format to present national cinemas on an international stage (Tehran or Cuba); they champion Third (World) Cinema to counter a West European bias (Pesaro, Rotterdam); they counter the premiere hierarchies of the competitive A-list festivals by surveying the best cinema from other festivals (London, Vienna); and they provide a platform for new voices in independent filmmaking (Sundance).

Not only the addition of smaller festivals changed the nature of the film festival circuit: the large A-list festivals also changed their model considerably in this period. The disruption of the 1968 Cannes film festival edition heralded the end of the era of national programming and signaled the beginning rise of the festival programmer. Various A-list festivals coped with the demands of critics and young filmmakers—think of the *Nouvelle Vague* or the New German Cinema in the wake of the Oberhausen Manifesto—in a very similar way. The Cannes film festival broadened as institution to include under its heading the *Semaine de la Critique* and the *Quinzaine des Réalisateurs*, founded in 1962 and 1969 respectively, as parallel selections along the official main competition. The Berlinale similarly expanded and integrated the *Forum des Jungen Films*—which had started as a counter-festival in 1968 organized by the *Freunde der Deutschen Kinemathek* around Erika and Ulrich Gregor—in 1970 into its fold as an independently curated section. A decade later in 1980, the festival created the *Infoschau* (later renamed Panorama) section to cover the middle ground between the main competition, which featured big productions from arthouse or commercial cinema, and the Forum, which was leaning toward the avant-garde art film spectrum. These two histories show exemplarily how the big general festivals changed their formats by expansion to reconcile the diverging demands from cinephiles, critics, filmmakers, and industry.

Another response was the establishment of general showcases in the form of "festivals of festivals," which sidestepped the fierce competition that comes with demands of premiere status. London had started this model in 1956 and in 1976 a similar festival was started in Toronto (Wong 2011: 48).

Along with the spatial spread and hierarchies, the temporal order of the circuit and the position on the yearly calendar has a big impact on the selection and further marketing. The yearly film cycle is structured around festivals and markets, awards such as the Oscars, and prominent dates for theatrical releases. Since Berlin moved from its original June date to February in 1978 in order to avoid being sandwiched between Cannes in May and Venice in September, the big three are spread out quite evenly on the calendar. This helps retain their dominant position within the yearly premiere cycle. However, as the circuit has gotten more crowded and influence of festivals and industry players has shifted over the decades, the competition about premieres and calendar positions has gotten fiercer.[12]

On a second-tier level, festivals such as Sundance and Rotterdam, which were established in the late 1970s without accreditation, sought to secure their position as significant events outside the reach of FIAPF by placing emphasis on independent film and art film (De Valck 2014). The United States Film Festival was created in 1978 in Salt Lake City, Utah. In 1980 it relocated to the ski-resort town Park City, Utah. When the festival was taken over by Robert Redford's Sundance Institute in 1985 and changed its name to Sundance Film Festival, it started to collaborate with Hollywood industry executives, eventually becoming the most influential independent film hub for the US (Wong 2011: 49). Thus, like other major North American festivals (Telluride, SXSW) its position and rank now depends more on clout with industry than FIAPF.

Thus far, the second phase in festival history can in sum be characterized by the differentiation of the festival landscape and a shift toward political and cinephile programming. The generally politicized era of the 1960s and various new social movements provide the cultural context that served as a breeding ground for the establishment of a variety of identity-based festivals in the 1970s: women's film festivals, indigenous, gay and lesbian, and Black/African American film festivals.[13] Each struggle or movement used arts and culture as activist tools, where film screenings in community settings were part of general awareness-raising endeavors. All of these festivals were first established as safe spaces and gathering spots for identity issues, to constitute and consolidate communities with specific causes. While they continue to be community spaces, they have oftentimes also gradually grown to become alternative distribution networks and brokers for specific themes, representations, and filmmakers.

The trend of significant differentiation on the circuit continues with a vast number of specialized festivals appearing in the following decades. Various "diasporic" or "ethnic" film festivals, catering to what Benedict Anderson (1991) has called "imagined communities," appear in an increasingly globalized world (Iordanova and Cheung 2010). A broad spectrum of activist festivals focus on a number of newly discussed social causes, such as disabilities, human rights, and ecology. Human rights film festivals have been especially organized to create a professional network of festivals, which also serves as an alternative distribution system (One World 2009).

Proliferation, eventization, and networked professionalism

Since the 1980s onward, festivals have become a prominent form of event culture that has spread all over Europe and moved on globally. Generally, the 1980s and 1990s were a time of massive proliferation of the festival model, for which several related terms such as "eventization," "festivalomania," "festivalization," and "festival epidemic" popped up in the festival literature. By the 2000s, scholars and festival professionals started to discuss the saturation of the circuit and its potential negative effects.

Whereas the first phase was majorly influenced by national diplomatic strategies, and the second by new politics and social movements, this third era has been most impacted by a complex shift of several interlocking cultural and economic agendas. One major trend that has had significant impact on arts and culture was the rise of neoliberalism, which pushed the welfare state to start using the business logic of privatization. Culture, which used to be a field that was supported with public funds, because it was deemed important for the formation of a coherent national identity, has increasingly turned into a value-generating creative industry. This ideological shift in the funding landscape directly impacted festivals by introducing a neoliberal corporate business logic into cultural institutions (Rhyne 2009).

Such economic shifts have become visible all over the world since the 1990s. The breakdown of socialist structures in economy and culture had a direct impact on the festival landscape when long-established festivals such as Karlovy Vary were challenged by newcomers such as the Prague Film Festival in a "showdown of festivals," with clashing entrepreneurship and post-communist management of culture (Iordanova 2006). In the wake of the handover of Hong Kong from the UK to China in 1997, the Hong Kong International Film Festival has seen many structural changes including the incorporation of the festival (Cheung 2009). After the financial crisis of 2008 hit the markets and the cultural sector lost further funding opportunities, the drive to neoliberal corporate models has seen a further push (Vallejo 2016). The dismantling in 2011 of the Film Council in the UK has had a profound impact on film and festival culture there.

It is not only changing economic systems that have influenced and tested long-established festivals. New dynamics in the global city constellation have brought about new players with powerful funders backing them, so that newly founded festivals are challenging the established circuit. The global nature and broadness of the phenomenon is visible in the diversity of newcomers, which range from the Busan International Film Festival and Market—which has risen to become a major player in the Asian market—to the star-backed Tribeca Film Festival—which set out to boost development in downtown New York after the trauma and destruction of 9/11—to newly founded festivals in European capitals such as Zurich, Rome, and Copenhagen—which challenge their long-standing, established national counterparts in Locarno, Venice, and Gothenburg (Strandgaard Pedersen and Mazza 2011). The proliferation, especially of well-funded new festivals, contributes to the sweeping professionalization and potential homogenization of the circuit that De Valck mentions (2007: 20).

Globalization itself also goes hand in hand with a rising trend of regionalization. The global city paradigm ensures competition on both national and international levels. While for a long time the nation-state had been the defining element in cultural identity, transnational transactions among regional or global cities have largely supplanted the old model. Today, global cities compete for funds and economic gains, for tourism, and for what Richard Florida (2003) has termed the "creative class," and thus become the driving force for cultural development. As public funders are increasingly interested in tourism profits and elevating the public cultural image of a city, festivals are funded with the logic of creative industries, with an eye on jobs for creative workers and their positive impact on the city image. These shifting interests are directly observable in changes to funding models, which have moved both money and focus from arts and culture to business development funds.

Festivals have always interacted with the film industry, giving them a platform to meet, network, and showcase work. But from the 1980s onward, festivals underwent a major shift. They moved from being passive platforms and facilitators for the film industry to becoming intermediaries and increasingly active players in all aspects of the film industry themselves (Rüling 2011).[14] The move of festivals to become active players also reflects the changing hierarchies and power dynamics. With the shifts in the film industry in the digital era, increasing film production, the proliferation of the festival circuit, and the shrinking availability of screens for theatrical release, festivals jockey for a position on the circuit but also for a position within the ever-shifting and expanding film exploitation chain. As the competition for major premieres makes it increasingly difficult to tell whether the sales agent or the programmer has the upper hand in the programming choices (Peranson 2008), festivals strive to become independent of certain industry mechanisms by becoming active agents themselves. Thus, since the mid-2000s festivals have moved increasingly into various segments of training and funding of all stages of film production and distribution, adding markets, talent campuses, and script writing labs, while also facilitating co-production markets, and distributing film funds.[15]

Conclusion

The above-mentioned trend of festivals becoming increasingly involved with the film industry or acting as a quasi-industry in their own right brings us full circle to the beginning of the chapter. The term "film festival circuit" is foremost an industry term, which is versatile, contingent, and relational. In an attempt to bring light into the increasing complexity of the festival world, film festival studies have criticized the hierarchical view in which "circuit" is often used synonymous with the elite A-list.

In order to understand the intricate interconnections of the festival world with its hierarchical tiers and parallel/sub-circuits, it is helpful to consider long-term historical developments. As the above historical narrative shows, the development of the film festival circuit has been marked by complex shifts in film culture writ large. The festival model of a showcase for national film art of the 1930s has moved toward an ever-broader spectrum of festivals and programming strategies. In response to shifting cultural demands new festival models have appeared while the top-tier events have continually evolved. In addition, larger-scale economic shifts, such as the spread of a neoliberal market logic after the end of the Cold War and the rise of the global city paradigm have encouraged an eventization and further proliferation of the circuit. As festivals have proliferated to more than 6,000 events today, the network has become increasingly differentiated. This has gone hand in hand with business interests of the commercial film industries as well as thriving world cinema circulation through the circuit. In view of those broader tendencies, which tend to get lost in the current hype and glitz of the media buzz, film festival studies turn to the broader analytic concepts trying to capture the festival phenomenon at large. Instead of the industrial "circuit," new terms and concepts—such as network, archipelago, rhizome, disruptive short circuits, or periphery—are brought to bear on the festival ecosystem and the analytical scope broadened to include the wide range of events from seemingly marginal geographies and topics.

Notes

1 Various industry platforms connected to and working with the festival circuit give very different numbers and are usually careful to state that their respective listings are representative but not comprehensive. Industry-driven platforms, such as Filmfestivals.com, Withoutabox.com, or Filmfestivallife.com—which are essentially portals for film professionals, filmmakers, and programmers—or the Festivals Directory of the British Council, aim to provide comprehensive lists, listing between 1,300 and 6,000 entries. Since film festivals are acknowledged as international platforms to promote national cinemas, a number of national film agencies list their own festival directories. However, these institutions provide highly selective listings—usually limited to a number of international festivals which could be categorized as festivals with international impact (A-list and second-tier festivals), or top-tier festivals of specialized circuits, such as short film, documentary, animation, or children's film festivals. Thus these lists cover seldom more than 200 festivals.
2 From the point of view of a specific film, the circuit can for instance refer to the network of 260 active LGBT/Q film festivals that represent the potential festival run and thus alternative exhibition route for an LGBT/Q-themed documentary or independent film (Loist 2013, 2014a).

3 See for instance Neil Young's account of his festival travels as a film critic and festival programmer (Steinhart 2015).

4 Major theorists referred to here are Niklas Luhmann, Bruno Latour, and Manuel Castells. See also Harbord (2002) and Elsaesser (2005).

5 See also Chapter 2 in this book by Julian Stringer.

6 The series has set out to chart a wide range of festivals, geographically (East Asia and Middle East) as well as thematically (activism, diaspora, archive) to address issues beyond the specifics of the select A-list festivals (Iordanova and Cheung 2010, 2011; Iordanova and Rhyne 2009; Iordanova and Torchin 2012; Marlow-Mann 2013; Iordanova and Van de Peer 2014).

7 These new forms of distribution have come into the focus of recent film industry studies (Lobato 2012; Iordanova 2010, 2015; Verhoeven 2011).

8 Within the ongoing discussions on how to conceptually frame globalization and film culture, these "alternative" cinemas have been conceptualized either as "peripheral cinema," "world cinema," or "global art cinema" (see Iordanova 2010; Nichols 1994; Galt and Schoonover 2010).

9 On the historical development of the Cannes film festival, see Chapter 1 of this book by Dorota Ostrowska.

10 There is no comprehensive study available discussing the concrete impact of the FIAPF on the development of the film festival circuit, yet. Only selective periods or issues have been studied (Moine 2011, 2013). The organization itself provides very little information in its web presence, with many regulations and materials only accessible to members.

11 In 1954, the oldest international short film festival was established in Oberhausen, Germany. Renowned short film festivals followed in Bilbao, Spain (1959), Tampere, Finland (1969), and Clermont-Ferrand, France (1979). The Edinburgh Film Festival originally started out in 1947 with a documentary focus and the support of John Grierson and Paul Rotha, but opened to fiction in 1950. Dedicated documentary film festivals followed in Leipzig, Germany, Belgrade, Serbia (1959), in Krakow, Poland (1961) and Nyon, Switzerland (1969) (Vallejo 2014, 2016). In 1960, the first animation film festival was held in Annecy, Switzerland, with festivals following in Mamaia, Romania (1966–1970), Cambridge/Cardiff, UK (1968), Zagreb, Croatia (1972), and Ottawa, Canada (1976) (Rüling 2011).

12 For instance, it would be very interesting to try and untangle the complex relations between influential actors at play when Venice Film Festival, Montreal World Film Festival, Telluride Film Festival, and Toronto International Film Festival (TIFF) routinely fight over premieres during the crowded fall season. While the former two are nominally A-list festivals and TIFF is officially accredited as "Non-Competitive Feature Film Festival," the hierarchies are not at all clear as the constant grumbling between TIFF and Venice—especially over premieres of North American films often going to TIFF—attest. Here, clout with industry and an eye on the market seems to trump FIAPF protectionism.

13 For a more detailed historical account of the development of identity-based and social concern film festivals, see Loist (2014b: 82–103).

14 This shift has also been accompanied by an ever-growing army of festival professionals traveling the circuit, which appear to have formed a separate layer of film industry professionals in the 2000s. Among those new intermediaries are consultants, often former programmers who offer advice on how to enter or navigate the circuit with your film; sales agents and special festivals handlers of sales companies; lawyers; festival film representatives; and newly emerged business-to-business platforms like Cinando, FestivalScope or Eventival which serve the smooth interaction between festivals, programmers, buyers, and talent in the connected festival network.

15 For a detailed account of the production activities of film festivals, see Chapter 12 in this book, by Tamara L. Falicov.

References

Anderson, B. (1991 [1983]) *Imagined Communities: Reflections on the Origin and Spread of Nationalism*, revised and extended ed., London: Verso.

Cheung, R. (2009) "Corporatising a Film Festival: Hong Kong," in D. Iordanova and R. Rhyne (eds.) *Film Festival Yearbook 1: The Festival Circuit*, St Andrews: St Andrews Film Studies, pp. 99–115.

De Valck, M. (2007) *Film Festivals: From European Geopolitics to Global Cinephilia*, Amsterdam: Amsterdam University Press.

De Valck, M. (2014) "Supporting Art Cinema at a Time of Commercialization: Principles and Practices, the Case of the International Film Festival Rotterdam," *Poetics*, 42, pp. 40–59.

Elsaesser, T. (2005) "Film Festival Networks: The New Topographies of Cinema in Europe," in *European Cinema: Face to Face With Hollywood*, Amsterdam: Amsterdam University Press, pp. 82–107.

Florida, R. (2003) "Cities and the Creative Class," *City & Community*, 2(1), pp. 3–19.

Frodon, J.-M. (2014) "The Film Festival Archipelago in the Arab World," in D. Iordanova and S. Van de Peer (eds.) *Film Festival Yearbook 6: Film Festivals and the Middle East*, St Andrews: St Andrews Film Studies, pp. 15–26.

Galt, R. and K. Schoonover (eds.) (2010) *Global Art Cinema: New Theories and Histories*, New York: Oxford University Press.

Gutiérrez, C. A. and M. Wagenberg (2013) "Meeting Points: A Survey of Film Festivals in Latin America," *Transnational Cinemas*, 4(2), pp. 295–305.

Hagener, M. (2014) "Institutions of Film Culture: Festivals and Archives as Network Nodes," in M. Hagener (ed.) *The Emergence of Film Culture: Knowledge Production, Institution Building, and the Fate of the Avant-garde in Europe, 1919–1945*, New York: Berghahn, pp. 283–305.

Harbord, J. (2002) *Film Cultures*, London: Sage.

Hope, C. and A. Dickerson (2011) " 'Give It a Go You Apes:' Relations Between the Sydney and Melbourne Film Festivals, and the Early Australian Film Industry (1954–1970)," *Screening the Past*, 30, http://screeningthepast.com/?p=256 (September 1, 2015).

Iordanova, D. (2006) "Showdown of the Festivals: Clashing Entrepreneurships and Post-Communist Management of Culture," *Film International*, 4(5), pp. 25–37.

Iordanova, D. (2009) "The Film Festival Circuit," in D. Iordanova and R. Rhyne (eds.) *Film Festival Yearbook 1: The Festival Circuit*, St Andrews: St Andrews Film Studies, pp. 23–39.

Iordanova, D. (2010) "Rise of the Fringe: Global Cinema's Long Tail," in D. Iordanova, D. Martin-Jones, and B. Vidal (eds.) *Cinema at the Periphery: Industries, Narratives, Iconography*, Detroit, MI: Wayne State University Press, pp. 23–45.

Iordanova, D. (2015) "The Film Festival as an Industry Node," *Media Industries*, 1(3), pp. 7–11.

Iordanova, D. and R. Cheung (eds.) (2010) *Film Festival Yearbook 2: Film Festivals and Imagined Communities*, St Andrews: St Andrews Film Studies.

Iordanova, D. and R. Cheung (eds.) (2011) *Film Festival Yearbook 3: Film Festivals and East Asia*, St Andrews: St Andrews Film Studies.

Iordanova, D. and R. Rhyne (eds.) (2009) *Film Festival Yearbook 1: The Festival Circuit*, St Andrews: St Andrews Film Studies.

Iordanova, D. and L. Torchin (eds.) (2012) *Film Festival Yearbook 4: Film Festivals and Activism*, St Andrews: St Andrews Film Studies.

Iordanova, D. and S. Van de Peer (eds.) (2014) *Film Festival Yearbook 6: Film Festivals and the Middle East*, St Andrews: St Andrews Film Studies.

Jacobsen, W. (2000) *50 Years Berlinale: Internationale Filmfestspiele Berlin*, Berlin: Nicolai.

Lobato, R. (2012) *Shadow Economies of Cinema: Mapping Informal Film Distribution*, London: Palgrave Macmillan/BFI.

Loist, S. (2013) "The Queer Film Festival Phenomenon in a Global Historical Perspective (the 1970s–2000s)," in A. Fléchet, P. Gœtschel, P. Hidiroglou, S. Jacotot, C. Moine, and J. Verlaine (eds.) *Une histoire des festivals: XXe–XXIe siècle*, Paris: Publications de la Sorbonne, pp. 109–121.

Loist, S. (2014a) "Rêves transversaux: La circulation des films *queer* dans le réseau des festivals," trans. B. Rollet, *Diogène: Revue internationale des sciences humaines*, 245, pp. 80–103.

Loist, S. (2014b) "Queer Film Culture: Performative Aspects of LGBT/Q Film Festivals," PhD thesis, Hamburg: Universität Hamburg.

Marlow-Mann, A. (ed.) (2013) *Film Festival Yearbook 5: Archival Film Festivals*, St Andrews: St Andrews Film Studies.

Moine, C. (2011) "La FIAPF, une Fédération de Producteurs au cœur des relations internationales après 1945," in L. Creton, Y. Dehée, S. Layerle, and C. Moine (eds.) *Les producteurs: Enjeux créatifs, enjeux financiers*, Paris: Nouveau monde, pp. 249–266.

Moine, C. (2013) "La Fédération internationale des associations de producteurs de films: un acteur controversé de la promotion du cinéma après 1945," *Le mouvement social*, 243, pp. 91–103.

Neves, J. (2012) "Media Archipelagos: Inter-Asian Film Festivals," *Discourse*, 34(2/3), pp. 230–239.

Nichols, B. (1994) "Discovering Form, Inferring Meaning: New Cinemas and the Film Festival Circuit," *Film Quarterly*, 47(3), pp. 16–30.

Nornes, A. M. (2014) "Yamagata–Asia–Europe: The International Film Festival Short Circuit," in D. Miyao (ed.) *The Oxford Handbook of Japanese Cinema*, Oxford and New York: Oxford University Press, pp. 245–262.

One World International Human Rights Documentary Film Festival (2009) *Setting Up a Human Rights Film Festival: A Handbook for Festival Organizers Including Case Studies of Prominent Human Rights Events*, Prague: People in Need.

Peranson, M. (2008) "First You Get the Power, Then You Get the Money: Two Models of Film Festivals," *Cineaste*, 33(3), pp. 37–43.

Rhyne, R. (2009) "Film Festival Circuits and Stakeholders," in D. Iordanova and R. Rhyne (eds.) *Film Festival Yearbook 1: The Festival Circuit*, St Andrews: St Andrews Film Studies, pp. 9–39.

Robbins, P. and V. Saglier (2015) "Introduction. Other Networks: Expanding Film Festival Perspectives," *Synoptique*, 3(2), pp. 1–8.

Rüling, C.-C. (2011) "Event Institutionalization and Maintenance: The Annecy Animation Festival 1960–2010," in B. Moeran, and J. Strandgaard Pedersen (eds.) *Negotiating Values in the Creative Industries: Fairs, Festivals and Competitive Events*, Cambridge: Cambridge University Press, pp. 197–223.

Ruoff, J. (2008) "Ten Nights in Tunisia. Le Journées Cinématographiques de Carthage," *Film International*, 6(4), pp. 43–51.

Steinhart, D. (2015) "Dispatches from the Dark: A Conversation with Neil Young at the 2015 International Film Festival Rotterdam," *NECSUS: European Journal of Media Studies*, 4(1): www.necsus-ejms.org/dispatches-from-the-dark-a-conversation-with-neil-young-at-the-2015-international-film-festival-rotterdam/ (October 27, 2015).

Stevens, K. (2013) "See It at a Festival Near You: The Film Festival as Exhibition Practice in Melbourne, 1952–2012," PhD thesis, Melbourne: Monash University.

Strandgaard Pedersen, J. and C. Mazza (2011) "International Film Festivals. For the Benefit of Whom?" *Culture Unbound: Journal of Current Cultural Research*, 3, pp. 139–165.

Stringer, J. (2001) "Global Cities and International Film Festival Economy," in M. Shiel and T. Fitzmaurice (eds.) *Cinema and the City: Film and Urban Societies in a Global Context*, Oxford: Blackwell, pp. 134–144.

The Film Collaborative (2013) "December 2013, #1. The Film Collaborative's Festival Real Revenue Numbers and Comments regarding Transparency Trends," December 2, www.thefilmcollaborative.org/_eblasts/collaborative_eblast_124.html (September 1, 2015).

Turan, K. (2002) *Sundance to Sarajevo: Film Festivals and the World They Made*, Berkeley, CA: University of California Press.

Vallejo, A. (2014) "Industry Sections: Documentary Film Festivals Between Production and Distribution," *Iluminace: časopis pro teorii, historii a estetiku filmu | Journal for Film Theory, History, and Aesthetics*, 26(1), pp. 65–82.

Vallejo, A. (2016) "The Rise of Documentary Festivals: A Historical Approach," in A. Vallejo (ed.) *Documentary Film Festivals: History, Politics, Industry*, New York: Columbia University Press, in press.

Verhoeven, D. (2011) "Film Distribution in the Diaspora: Temporality, Community and National Cinema," in R. Maltby, D. Biltereyst, and P. Meers (eds.) *Explorations in New Cinema History: Approaches and Case Studies*, Malden, MA: Wiley-Blackwell, pp. 243–260.

Wong, C. H.-Y. (2011) *Film Festivals: Culture, People, and Power on the Global Screen*, New Brunswick, NJ: Rutgers University Press.

Further reading

Elsaesser, T. (2005) "Film Festival Networks: The New Topographies of Cinema in Europe," in *European Cinema: Face to Face With Hollywood*, Amsterdam: Amsterdam University Press, pp. 82–107. (Seminal chapter on the conception of the festival network and its position vis-à-vis European cinema.)

Iordanova, D. and R. Rhyne (eds.) (2009) *Film Festival Yearbook 1: The Festival Circuit*, St Andrews: St Andrews Film Studies. (The first volume of the series includes several different approaches to discuss the circuit topic.)

Nichols, B. (1994) "Discovering Form, Inferring Meaning: New Cinemas and the Film Festival Circuit," *Film Quarterly*, 47(3), pp. 16–30, and Nichols, B. (1994) "Global Image Consumption in the Age of Late Capitalism," *East-West Film Journal*, 8(1), pp. 68–85; reprinted in D. Iordanova (2013) *The Film Festivals Reader*, St Andrews: St Andrews Film Studies, pp. 29–44. (These two companion articles are the first dedicated academic discussions on film reception and circulation on the festival circuit.)

Vallejo, A. (ed.) (2016) *Documentary Film Festivals: History, Politics, Industry*, New York: Columbia University Press. (In this volume on the sub-circuit of documentary film festivals several chapters cover issues of the circuit from different stakeholder perspectives.)

White, P. (2015) *Women's Cinema, World Cinema: Projecting Contemporary Feminisms*, Durham, NC: Duke University Press. (Account of the circulation of cinema made by women, which considers the festival circuit as one influential avenue.)

Part II
Theory

Introduction

Marijke de Valck

Film festivals do not suffer from a lack of attention. People that visit festivals talk about festival matters at length, in casual conversation as well as more serious discussions. There is also a long tradition in journalistic writing; the press has covered festivals since their inception, and has continued to report on them since. However, it is only quite recently that film festivals have become the object of academic interest. The study of film festivals sets itself apart from media coverage, public debate, and everyday talk, with its grander ambitions to explain film festivals as a phenomenon. Theory offers explanations that transcend the single observation, experience, or example.

It is important to keep in mind that theories are sets of ideas, not facts that have been proven. To theorize means to suggest ideas about what is possibly true or real. It is a rational and contemplative way of generalized, abstract thinking that can be used to explain facts or events. Since the field of film festival studies is relatively young, it has drawn upon theories from established disciplines in the humanities and social sciences to develop approaches for thinking about film festivals. As stated in the Introduction, however, there is yet a wealth of theories to be explored.

The chapters in this section present three theoretical frameworks for the study of film festivals. Janet Harbord takes on festivals' special relation to time, applying the notion of contingency, which has also been used to theorize early cinema, to frame and explain festivals' attraction in contemporary society. Her approach is rooted in film studies and media archaeology. Cindy Hing-Yuk Wong engages with several theories of the public sphere to investigate the diversity among film festivals, directing specific attention to the constitution of festival publics and the way some festivals speak to what has been theorized as counterpublics. Marijke de Valck turns to the work of cultural sociologist Pierre Bourdieu and explores how working with three of his key concepts—field, capital, and habitus—can improve our understanding of the value and function of film festivals in society.

While the three topics tackled in this section—festivals' temporal dimensions, their ability to influence political action, and to add value—have spurred substantial conceptual thinking, there are plenty of other theoretical traditions that inform the existing body of scholarly writing on film festivals.

For instance, many scholars have been interested in the specific spatial dimensions of the film festival world, and turned to globalization theories (Stringer 2001), network and system theory (Elsaesser 2005; De Valck 2007), or have drawn upon studies of tourism and urban development (Derrett 2004; Kredell 2012). Subsequently, there is a substantial amount of research that exposes the unequal power relations within the globalized festival circuit, and that raises important theoretical questions about the ways in which film festivals bring the local, regional, and global together, often mixing a commitment to cultural specificity with cosmopolitan aspirations (Diawara 1994; Nichols 1994; Dovey 2015). There is also a growing concern with the business side of film festivals that is visible in the use of stakeholder theory (Rhyne 2009), organizational studies perspectives (Moeran and Strangaards Pederson 2010), and notions like precarious labor (Loist 2011). But even this extended overview of existing theoretical frames is just a tip of the iceberg. Depending on one's interest and particular research question, one may turn to different theoretical traditions to try and explain a specific aspect or dynamics of the fascinating world that film festivals make.

References

Derrett, R. (2004) "Festivals, Events and the Destination," in I. Yeoman, M. Robertson, J. Ali-Knight, S. Drummond, and U. McMahon-Beattie (eds.) *Festival and Events Management: An International Arts and Culture Perspective*, Amsterdam: Elsevier Butterworth-Heinemann, pp. 32–51.

De Valck, M. (2007) *Film Festivals: From European Geopolitics to Global Cinephilia*, Amsterdam: Amsterdam University Press.

Diawara, M. (1994) "On Tracking World Cinema: African Cinema at Film Festivals," *Public Culture*, 6(2), pp. 385–396.

Dovey, L. (2015) *Curating Africa in the Age of Film Festivals: Film Festivals, Time, Resistance*, London and New York: Palgrave Macmillan.

Elsaesser, T. (2005) "Film Festival Networks: The New Topographies of Cinema in Europe,"in *European Cinema: Face to Face With Hollywood*, Amsterdam: Amsterdam University Press, pp. 82–107.

Kredell, B. (2012) "T.O. Live With Film: The Toronto International Film Festival and Municipal Cultural Policy in Contemporary Toronto," *Canadian Journal of Film Studies | Revue Canadienne d'Études Cinématographiques*, 21(1), pp. 21–37.

Loist, S. (2011) "Precarious Cultural Work: About the Organization of (Queer) Film Festivals," *Screen*, 52(2), pp. 268–273.

Moeran, B. and J. Strandgaard Pedersen (eds.) *(2010) Negotiating Values in the Creative Industries: Fairs, Festivals and Competitive Events*, Cambridge: Cambridge University Press.

Nichols, B. (1994) "Global Image Consumption in the Age of Late Capitalism," *East-West Film Journal*, 8(1), pp. 68–85.

Rhyne, R. (2009) "Film Festival Circuits and Stakeholders," in D. Iordanova and R. Rhyne (eds.) *Film Festival Yearbook 1: The Festival Circuit*, St Andrews: St Andrews Film Studies, pp. 9–39.

Stringer, J. (2001) "Global Cities and International Film Festival Economy," in M. Shiel and T. Fitzmaurice (eds.) *Cinema and the City: Film and Urban Societies in a Global Context*, Oxford: Blackwell, pp. 134–144.

4 Contingency, time, and event

An archaeological approach to the film festival

Janet Harbord

The argument proposed here is that an analysis of time as it is manifested by the film festival illuminates both the particularity of the festival's structure and the continuation of its appeal. Equally, through the study of a film festival as a model or figural form we are able to comprehend our contemporary experience of time as it has mutated from a regulated clock-time of the early twentieth century to a more amorphic modality at the beginning of the twenty-first century. In summary, at cinema's inception over a century ago the populace encountered a new temporal regime that forced them to inhabit life as a series of units designated by schedules and conforming to standardized timetables. Cinema famously played it both ways, colluding with the uniformity of an increasingly mass culture in its roll-out of repetitive exhibition programs, but it also broke with the demanding nature of working life in the provision of a new spectacular culture of distraction. If factory life meant clocking in, cinema culture equaled release from duty. If we travel forward 100 years, the patterns of life and the experience of time have radically changed in a climate of deregulation and deinstitutionalization. Both work and leisure (including film viewing) in the process of relocating to the home have become mixed up and overlapping. The collective nature of film viewing is all but lost as film is dispersed across technological forms, locations, and times. In short, the dominant concept of time at the beginning of this century is one of distributed nonalignment. The film festival, however, operates a temporality that runs counter to the deregulated environment in which it exists.

To a certain extent this argument runs counter to the paradigmatic features of the film festival as they have been established in a growing body of scholarship that identifies its effectiveness and appeal through spatial terms (De Valck 2007; De Valck and Loist 2009). It is useful to enumerate the most prominent of these at the beginning. First, film festivals provide for film cultures that would otherwise remain marginalized by a dominant, high-budget cinema. These "alternative" films may be minority language, or they may focus on identitarian politics, or they may locate themselves within a minority aesthetic such as cult cinemas. Second, collectively festivals operate routes of distribution where each autonomous site also belongs to a series of nodes that secure the circulation of films across national territories. More specifically, film festivals serve as circulators of non-English-speaking films that carry high commercial risk to exhibitors. A third function of film festivals is to secure a role for film as a public culture to be debated in a semi-structured environment involving specialists and nonspecialists. Finally, film festivals are events tied to place, part of the calendar of local rituals that perform and enact the specific nature and appeal of a location for both inhabitants and visitors. They may be understood through the discourse of tourism, reproducing a form of nationalism as culture at a local level. Within a spatial framework, the function and appeal of film festivals is inseparable from the context of globalization, understood here as the shorthand term for the domination of commerce and political relations by multinationals, most visibly manifest in transborder flows of culture and people, and the production of what Marc Augé memorably named "non-place" (Augé 1995). Within an era of globalization, the film festival operates as a bulwark against its deterritorializing effects; the model of enclosure that defines the film festival may be said to create an enclave to protect against the deracinating effects of global capitalism, retaining and marking the distinctive identity of each festival location and its cultural offering.

Yet while this broad sweep of geopolitical context illuminates the significance of film festivals as a spatial phenomenon, the temporal features of these events have something further to contribute to our understanding. Film festivals are intense temporal happenings that are on the one hand unique events, and on the other, cyclical rituals repeated annually or on occasion biannually. They inhabit the intersection where, borrowing from Claude Lévi-Strauss (1962), the synchronic (events taking place simultaneously) crosses the diachronic (events taking place chronologically). At this intersection a conversion of structure and event takes place. As annual events, film festivals are productive of a sense of cyclical calendar time sustained through rites that transform events into structures. Conversely, as structures that contain happenings that are singular and unrepeatable, such as those created by contingencies of weather, accident, or explosive commentary, film festivals are open to the transformation of structure into events. If the former tends to absorb all events into a historical continuity, lodged under the festival name as a standard bearer across time, then the latter crumbles the structure into individual fragments as events. The festival is able to move between or hold together these two opposing modalities through its power of conversion: diachrony (the festival as an historical occurrence) mutates into synchrony (the axis of events that occur at one moment in time). This movement is the focus of this chapter.

How does the conversion of structure into event take place? In simple terms, there is a movement from continuous time into the instant through the live event that in some way misfires. The instant is an experience of time generated by contingencies that may be described as accidents or controversies, but their purpose is to demonstrate an unrecorded live temporality. In so doing, these instants resonate with an earlier moment in cinema: the time of the "actuality" film, which crafts for the instant a dimension that is separate from the past and the future. For live-time to register as such in the early genre of actualities, something has to get away, to escape control: the unforeseen obstruction of an object's path, the misfiring of an intention, and the automatism of systems that have a non-human life of their own all function to undermine the planned order of the day and demonstrate to us that time is running uncontrollable and "live." What I want to propose here is that this characteristic of early actuality film has become a century later a critical component in the model of the film festival. Festivals have captured and become efficient choreographers of the scandalous mishap that places us (and itself) in the moment of the now, managing both to facilitate and to contain directors making scandalous comments, actors who smoke in prohibited areas, and scaffolding that is prone to collapse. These contingencies never threaten to dissolve the structure of the festival; on the contrary, they serve to support its temporal particularity at the intersection of diachrony and synchrony.

In addressing the relationship between these historically distant practices, one of which is a genre and the other a type of event, the approach adopted in this chapter is an archaeological one following in the tradition of the media-focused scholarship of Siegfried Zielinski, Jussi Parikka, and Erkki Huhtamo, and the film-focused engagements of Mary Ann Doane, Thomas Elsaesser, and Tom Gunning. The definition of media archaeology proffered by Jussi Parikka is a critical process that "looks for conceptual cuts through which to open up new agendas of research and analysis,"[1] working against a chronological account of media's development by privileging relationships across time, identifying connections that are in fact "out of time" in a teleological sense (Parikka 2010: xiv). Siegfried Zielinski, writing about his archaeological intention in *Deep Time of the Media*, articulates his goal as the uncovering of dynamic moments in the history of media that "abound and revel in heterogeneity," a heterogeneity previously overlooked in the narration of media as a causal line of development (Zielinski 2002: 11). In archaeological practice, contemporary forms of media are seen to resonate most potently with objects and practices overlooked in the dominant historical account. In bringing these two moments into relation, the contemporary is relativized and "render[ed] more decisive" (ibid.: 10).[2] What I am proposing here is that the moment of cinema actualities, most prevalent in cinema between 1900 and 1907, illuminates a critical component of contemporary film culture: the making legible of time and making a particular moment matter. In both early cinema and in the contemporary film festival, the abstract intangible substance of temporality is made visible through the same process, which is the foregrounding of contingency through the structural accommodation of risk.

What, we may ask, is at stake in each of these moments in the making legible of time? The dialectic of risk and its containment first staged in early cinema actualities is identified by Mary Ann Doane as the emergence of cinematic time in its full complexity. According to Doane, the cinema served a purpose in its manufacture of time as a release of pressure from the newly instituted clock-time of factory work, railroad timetables, and other forms of standardization, presenting in actualities the disruption of a relentless linear temporality (Doane 2002: 17). The film festival, in its manifestation of a structure punctuated by contingency, addresses the anxieties of an inverse state: the potential free fall of deregulated time. In the terms of Italian political philosopher Maurizio Lazzarato, labor practices at the end of the twentieth century are characteristically forms of immaterial labor requiring the worker to invest (time and emotional qualities) into the making of a commodity, be that an object, a service, or data. Investments of this nature deliver responsibility to the worker who is at liberty to organize her own time and labor. The rhythms of work dictate other areas of life and indeed, as Lazzarato argues, "in this kind of working existence it becomes increasingly difficult to distinguish leisure time from work time," continuing "in a sense, life becomes inseparable from work" (Lazzarato 1996: 137).

The process that Lazzarato describes is dependent on deregulated time, which is manifest variously in the labor practices of contemporary film culture. (One example would be the simultaneous release of film across a range of platforms, which has not only enabled film to be viewed at any time, but has facilitated the online reviewing of films, formerly an activity of paid labor, as a leisure activity.) It is also the case that the economic model of the film festival is dependent on a degree of "affective" labor, which may typically come in the form of volunteers or interns, or interviewers of cast and crew, who receive public recognition and professional association with the festival rather than economic remuneration.[3] Yet despite these affinities with the climate of deregulation, I will argue, the structure of the film festival is productive of a form of time that opposes the broader deregulation of socio-temporal boundaries in its emphatic deployment of real-time within its structure. The festival model has built into its form a managed contingency whose function it is to produce a moment of real-time, a time that cannot be harnessed for productive labor, nor for the ethos of a deregulated time of deferral and displacement, but can only be an affective and emphatic "now." The festival, like early cinema actualities, retains the risk of a live event unfolding in real-time, in the singular instant of the here and now. It creates a moment that seems paradoxically to suspend the moment, to produce what George Kubler describes as "the instant between the ticks of a watch" (Kubler 1962: 15). In what follows, the moment of actuality in early cinema is explored through Doane's account of an emerging temporality of both modernism and cinema, the features of which are subsequently located in the practices of the contemporary film festival.

Actuality: being there (and not)

In Mary Ann Doane's account of cinema at the turn of the twentieth century, the emergence of what she names cinematic time is embedded in the dynamic forces of modernity. Far from an abstract concept, "[t]ime was indeed *felt*—as a weight, as a source of anxiety, and as an acutely pressing problem of representation" (Doane 2002: 4). She continues, writing that "[m]odernity was perceived as a temporal demand," a demand for a consensual measure of time operating across space, necessitated by railroad timetables and telegraphy, and a demand for bodies to be regulated by a centralized timescale in industrial labor practices (the factory). The measure of time is ideologically part of a rationalization of behavior, a measure of energy expended in a given period that can be calculated as an economic outcome (wages). Pocket watches were the accessory of the late nineteenth century, the body adorned with its own regulatory device that connected the individual to the clock-time of capitalist production. Watches, for Doane, are not simply an accessory but a visualization of time as a series of units, amenable to calculation and standardization: "Time becomes uniform, homogenous, irreversible, and divisible into verifiable units" (Doane 2002: 6).

In one sense, cinema complies with the demand to fashion time into discrete units that run at predictable (albeit diverse) lengths. Film visualizes time, it measures and makes manifest the time of viewing compared to other open-ended activities such as reading or looking at a painting. It appears to mirror the measured units of work time with measured units of leisure time, all delivered by a film strip that runs forward through the projector in mimesis of Taylor's factory production belt. But in another sense cinema in its earliest and most popular manifestation performs a resistance to the rationalization of experience as knowable, linear, and recordable in its fascination with contingency. The picturesque turns dramatic in many early films as a result of contingencies in the elements, such as in Louis Lumière's *Boat Leaving the Harbor* (*Barque sortant du port*, 1895). In this film, three men row out from a harbor toward the open sea while a group of women and children watch from the pier (or rather parade themselves to the camera as they feign watching the boat). The boat makes good progress but is then caught by a sea swell and turned sideways, set off course and possibly endangered at the moment at which the film reel ends. Dai Vaughn writes that the distinguishing feature of the film is the response of the men to the elements: "the men must apply their efforts to controlling it; and, by responding to the challenge of the spontaneous moment, they become integrated into its spontaneity" (Vaughn 1990: 65). Clearly the film sequence is not staged in any way, and what marks early cinema is this encounter with the unpredictable and what we might think of as *untimely* events that expose the notion of rational control and total management as fallacy.

The period of early film, before its heterogeneous elements have sedimented into a particular narrative form was, according to Tom Gunning, characterized by anomalies (1990: 86). Among these anomalies was the actuality film, a one-reel movie that reveled in the witnessing of an act or event. In what was to become a genre, the recorded time of the film as a fixed sequence of actions butts up against the live-time of the event. The actuality film is a demonstration of the unruly nature of the world and the reliable nature of film. Up until 1907 or thereabouts (the date being the subject of ongoing debate), the actuality film was the dominant cinematic form, and "for a brief time the cinema seemed to be preoccupied with the minute examination of the realm of the contingent, persistently displaying the camera's aptitude for recording" (Doane 2002: 141). Doane provides the example of Thomas Edison's *Electrocuting an Elephant* (1903), the short and desperately sad film in which an elephant, Topsy, is to be killed (her punishment for having taken the lives of three men). The film records the preparation of the event with the elephant being walked toward the site of electrocution. Several figures move from right to left in front of the camera, followed by a jump cut to the scene where the elephant's feet are being attached to the equipment. There is then a moment of stasis and the sideways collapse of this huge animal's body, smoke rising from her feet. At this point another shadowy figure moves in front of the camera into the foreground of the picture.

The paradox that is contained in this sequence is the demand for opposing assurances, a request granted by cinema. The film fulfills the requirement to record or literally document a scenario that is preplanned and cannot be repeated or experienced at a later date—"death would seem to mark the insistence and intractability of the real in representation," writes Doane (2002: 145)—and yet cinema allows the scene to be witnessed elsewhere at a later date as a recording. Simultaneously, the film attests to the liveness of the event by the way in which it elides real time in a jump cut, a cut that remains undisguised. The cut eliminates dead time in preparation for the time of death, as it were. The shadowy figures in the foreground also play out an accidental foray into the frame, and in so doing, demonstrate that the filming of a live event is open to disruption, or at least visual noise. The film frames the event literally, and yet the frame is disrupted. The singular moment of the elephant's death becomes a thing recorded and yet also eluding the record, the camera acting as witness but yet unable to attribute meaning to what it records.

In its earliest manifestation, cinema attested to the limits of the control of time and events, upending or even complementing rationalization with the specter of chance. Contingency exploded onto the cinematic screen to reveal happenings, curiosities involving accidents and hazards, thus making contingency *legible*. "Contingency, detail, visual 'noise' are part of what the camera, the photograph, whether still or moving, brings with it," writes Vicky Lebeau in her consideration of cinema's relation to *infans* (being without speech) in its earliest days. She continues,

> in fact, as far as the emergence of film as a medium for telling stories is concerned, the problem was how to turn that excess of the visual to the purposes of narrative (of knowing where to look, as it were)
>
> (Lebeau 2008: 25)

Cinema later turns that excess into a feature of comic films where the capers of slapstick gesture became the *accidental performed*. Lisa Trahair describes slapstick as "a continuum of action that spans from physical violence, to elemental decomposition, to mechanical repetition, to stylization" as the contingent became embedded within the narrative tradition of film precisely as style (Trahair 2007: 48). With this generic development of the contingent as comedy, a genre came to facilitate for the audience an infectious bodily response to the polarities of urban chaos and automated life; the toppled, beaten, falling body of Buster Keaton or of Charlie Chaplin ignited laughter in the audiences of early cinema precisely because they were seated safely outside of the spectacle, for they were looking in on the scene that was always already over.

Cinema became adept at turning the excesses and anomalies of early film to the purposes of narrative through multiple practices involving the manufacture of a visual syntax, production techniques, economic motivation, and the standardization of viewing practices. But this moment of early cinema remains a significant instance for its illumination of a paradox at the heart of modern life: the demand for routine, a working rhythm of daily life where leisure was distinguished from labor time, and conversely, the desire for singular experience, differentiation and contingency. In the actuality film and its near kin (as it mutated into documentary and newsreel films), cinema provided both, deploying the appeal and threat of contingency contained within the temporal parameters of the cinema program: film viewing as an anticipation of the unexpected and hazardous, but safe within the knowledge that the event has already happened (and is therefore contained) in a time prior to screening. In Doane's reading, cinema afforded a type of safety valve for the pressures of modern temporality, a release from the demands of an increasingly rationalized experience of time always already measured, calculated, and given value in advance, appearing to harness the unknowable aspects of the modern world. The requirement of a safety valve or a defense against the ravaging effects of rationalism and commodified time is identified not only by Doane, but by cultural critics of the early twentieth century. In Siegfried Kracauer's (1963) reading of cinema, it was of course the abstract rhythm of film images that delivered the spectator to a state of pleasurable distraction, and in Walter Benjamin's (1955) account, boredom, or the freedom to think in nonrational modes, written up in Leo Carney's (1998) account as ennui and drift.

Contingency reworked: from the accidental to the controversial

The dual times and demands of cinema characterizing the modern era migrate from the film text to the event itself in the contemporary. The model of the film festival develops over a course of a century to harness different energies and anxieties concerning time and the rhythms of everyday life. More specifically in the current era, the film festival ameliorates the effects of deregulated time by making time matter in two seemingly opposing ways. On the one hand, the time of the film program is a structured temporality; the running time of films is stated on the program and the schedule for the whole event set out in advance, providing a temporal rhythm that deregulation has eliminated from other areas of everyday life. Yet on the other hand, the festival harnesses the time of contingency through live events that bookend screenings, introducing into the offering the singularity of an experience that cannot be reproduced at a later date or location.

The contemporary manifestation of contingency is not the incidental intrusion or accident but more often than not a seemingly casual statement that registers as a controversy. The boundary between contingency and controversy, chance and intention, is, however, not a distinct one. The live events of the festival fall somewhere upon a spectrum that on one end has chance and on the other a more consciously motivated performance and self-interested spectacle. Controversy, after all, can be a consciously wielded marketing tool for a film or a career. But what the controversy achieves, whether intentionally emitted or not, is the assurance of an uncensored event. To what extent such liveness can be controlled or managed is unclear and perhaps unknowable. It is however possible to identify the forms that it takes, the most common of which is the accidental, manifest in the accidental speech act, perhaps an excitable speech act that releases surprise into the air. In interviews, discussions, and the presentation and acceptance speeches of award ceremonies, the explosive comment appears to erupt like a buried mine accidentally stumbled upon rather than an intentional act. It is as though the comment and its effect surprise the enunciator most of all. The most notable festival in this regard is Cannes with its widely reported pranks, offensive opinions, and capers.

A recurring theme in the controversies of the Cannes film festival is sexism. In 2015, the festival organizers received criticism for having denied entry onto the red carpet to a group of women wearing flat shoes rather than the standard high heel. The happening was widely circulated on social media, with the British actress Emily Blunt—whose film *Sicario* (Denis Villeneuve, 2015) was in competition—contributing the view that "[e]veryone should wear flats, to be honest. We shouldn't wear high heels" (Furness 2015). However days later the festival's artistic director, Thierry Frémaux, addressing an audience at a Women in Motion discussion, announced that the festival was being treated unfairly for "heelgate" and for its limited selection of female directors for the main prize, attempting to deflect questions of sexism onto the Oscar awards (Webb 2015). Two years prior to this, in 2013, Roman Polanski's comments to journalists before the premiere of his film *Venus in Fur* that gender equality is "a great pity," and that "trying to level the genders is purely idiotic" caused a wave of commentary that rippled through press reports (Pulver 2013). It is difficult to assess whether this commentary has any correspondence with the controversy of the previous year in which there were no female directors selected for competition to win the *Palme d'Or*, and it was noted that only one woman had been awarded the prize in 64 years. At the screening of Michael Haneke's *Amour* (2011), the red carpet ceremony was disrupted by "La Barb," a feminist activist group wearing beards and carrying signs bearing ironic messages of congratulation.

Two years earlier, and in a more pronounced fashion, Lars von Trier caused a major disturbance in his comments about Hitler during a press conference for his film *Melancholia* (2011). After being asked about his German roots, the director commented that he understood Hitler, and that despite having done some "wrong things," "I can see him sitting there in his bunker at the end [...] I sympathise with him, yes, a little bit" (Shoard 2011). Von Trier was asked by the festival organizers to provide an explanation, and in response the director offered a statement of apology. Once again, the festival director, Thierry Frémaux, felt the need to respond, banning von Trier from the remainder of the festival; all press engagements to promote *Melancholia* were canceled. The hangover of this incident continued with subsequent festivals; at the Berlin International Film Festival 2014, promoting his next film, *Nymphomaniac*, von Trier adopted his "persona non grata" T-shirt throughout. Of a different genre, and more widely reported, were Sharon Stone's comments at Cannes in 2008, dismissing the Sichuan earthquake as "karma" for the Chinese government's treatment of Tibet, seemingly less calculated than von Trier's sympathizing with Hitler. Each of these spectacles produced not only controversy, but more significantly, a sense of the event running live, a liveness guaranteed by speech acts misfiring. In a twist of J. L. Austin's speech act theory, the actors speaking out of role and in earnest, appear to be ventriloquized by the lines that they speak so that intention becomes an empty category (Austin 1975).[4] There is a further reversal if one considers the standard reportage of the red carpet "glamour" brought by actors and directors to the event set against their inability to "perform reliably" (or their reliable unreliability). The potential to read this as a distraction of sorts, generated by the apparatus of the media, is explored by Liz Czach, who asks whether "film festivals [can] emerge from under the media attention directed at celebrities and reinvigorate their reputations as film-centred experiences" (Czach 2010: 143). The film critic Jonathan Romney reads celebrity "shenanigans" as a type of attention-seeking. Reporting for the *Observer* newspaper on the Berlin International Film Festival 2014 and the actor Shia LaBeouf wearing a paper bag on his head, he notes wryly "these days, everyone's a performance artist" (Romney 2014).

If controversy is addressed here in terms of its structural function of rendering liveness as real time, there is a need to recognize the potential depoliticization of statements and acts through their perception as slapstick contingencies. The treatment of gender-related issues at Cannes is a case in point. The "prank" by Ukrainian journalist Vitalii Sediuk of crawling under the skirt of actress America Ferrera with his camera at Cannes in 2015, reported by Sky News online as "Man Dives Under Ugly Betty Star's Skirt" (Sky News 2014) received a mute response from the festival management, implying that it was not regarded as a serious transgression. However it is also important to note that controversies arise that do retain a sobriety. An event at the Istanbul Film Festival in 2015 demonstrates the point, when the screening of the film *Bakur* (Çayan Demirel and Ertuğrul Mavioğlu, 2015) was canceled by the festival organizers shortly before its premiere, on the grounds of it not having an appropriate certification. The film, a documentary set in the camps of the Kurdistan Workers Party (PKK), an organization banned by the Turkish government, was seen to be subject to state censorship in this act. This in turn prompted the withdrawal of many other films from the festival in protest and eventually the cancelation of the competition.

The singularity of the accident

"The accident always happens in the present," Sylvere Lotringer says (in conversation with fellow theorist Paul Virilio), "but is *untimely*" (Lotringer and Virilio 2005: 100), suggesting that it is a happening that appears to have no "place" in the event, that it throws continuous time out of joint. Yet, on the contrary, accidental occurrences secure the time of the festival as an unrepeatable event. What emerges from this accounting for the prevalence of the "accidental" in film festivals is the inseparability of structure from contingency, a pairing that is mutually constitutive. The accident cannot happen without an organized framework of the festival program to depart from. Conversely the festival is in need of disruption, otherwise its tightly ordered listings risk blending into the urban film programs of general city life that run continuously throughout the calendar year. The structuring agency of a festival requires, demands even, the accidental: in order for the festival of film to be a critical happening, an event in the year that matters, it needs to be a live event, and in order to demonstrate that liveness its mechanical smoothness needs moments of disruption.

Is it possible to be more precise about the nature of contingencies that disrupt? In Doane's account of the earlier period, both modernism and cinema are together characterized by "the contingent, the ephemeral, chance-that which is beyond or resistant to meaning" (Doane 2002: 10). Contingency enters the frame of early cinema to produce a moment that seems to empty a sense of meaning and continuity, that voids the doctrine of rationalism. This form of disruptive shock that suspends comprehension for an instant was described by the art historian George Kubler as an "actuality" in his famous book on *The Shape of Time* (1962). While he did not have cinema in mind when writing this, he nonetheless provides what is perhaps the finest description of the shock of actuality film when he writes that:

> [a]ctuality is when the lighthouse is dark between flashes; it is the instant between the ticks of the watch; it is the void interval slipping forever through time; the rupture between past and future; the gap at the poles of the revolving magnetic field, infinitesimally small but ultimately real.
> (Kubler 1962: 15)

The disruption here and in Doane's account is closer to a suspension of linear time than a moment of coming to presence; contingency is a momentary sink or collapse into non-meaning. It is a moment when the Lacanian real (that which is unthinkable and unrecognizable) appears to flash up into consciousness for an instant, potentially rupturing the striated fabric of the symbolic order, or Badiou's event when the excluded appears to challenge reality and rethink its basis.[5]

In contrast, a contemporary disruption is an assurance of the singularity of the event, securing the join where the diachronic line of a film festival's history meets the synchronic line of this particular festival. The model of the film festival allows contingency to be situated at the center of its ordered and manicured world for reasons different from those of modernism. Contingency is not a release mechanism from the rigid grids of rationalized order, nor is it the punctum-like point of an event that is resistant to meaning. Rather, contingency testifies to the event as a shared experience, a collective experience dependent on being at one place and at one time. Pursuing this line of thought, it is possible to see how the effect of disruptive contingencies is not solely in those moments but permeates the whole festival. In gathering the spatio-temporal coordinates of the moment, the disruption makes the experience of "Cannes 2015" singular in a way that colors the screenings themselves. Despite the fact that these are recorded and therefore fixed events, the viewing of the films is a live experience in the here and now. What is historical, we might venture, is not the film itself (although film has a claim of different sorts to history), but the act of viewing. The assembly of people before a film is a commitment to the now of viewing, to this moment, but it is only in the context of the film festival that this experience is framed in terms of an event. It is an event that stands out from the deregulated environment in which it exists, defying isolation, fragmentation, and, most importantly, deferral. The contemporary film festival, in a reversal of Kracauer's formulation, suspends our allegiances to other distractions, allowing a momentary focus on the occasion of the film itself. The film festival provides for a time that is not later, not whenever, not at home nor watching on a train on a mobile, but now. The misfiring acts that appear to disrupt its smooth operation actually emphasize the time of the festival as live and pertaining to a singularity that cannot be repeated. Events may be relayed later, reported to others, and broadcast in some form, but the festival time remains anchored in a finite present.

In conclusion, the model of the film festival (rather than particular film festivals) goes against the grain of a contemporary deregulation of time that has reconfigured the practices and rituals of everyday life. The cultures of film viewing evidence the force of deregulation in the transformations of the past two decades. It is now a common place of scholarship to assume that the activity of film viewing may be broken up, distributed across a number of days, inserted between a number of other activities. The pre-given unit of film as a product bought or hired, is made pliable, available as segments to be downloaded, tailored to service the temporal needs of the viewer. Time is no longer experienced as units of duration but a patchwork of activities many of which will be overlapping. A film festival, on the contrary, gathers together the time of the film and the time of viewing. In so doing, it re-institutionalizes the collective attention of film viewing, and re-centers the time of projection as a live event, a liveness underscored by the discussions that follow. This choreography of events compressed into the window that is the festival provides for its specific temporality. It is possible to read about it later, or the following day, or watch it on the news or catch-up channel, but to experience the actuality of the event with all of the historical resonance of that term, the festival demands that you are there within the fold of its moment.

An earlier and shorter version of this paper was published as "Film Festivals-Time-Event," in D. Iordanova and R. Rhyne (eds.) (2009) *Film Festival Yearbook 1: The Festival Circuit*, St Andrews: St Andrews Film Studies, pp. 40–46.

Notes

1 For an elaboration of method in media archaeology, see Parikka's *What is Media Archaeology?* (2012).
2 This approach is developed further by Zielinski in an ongoing project entitled "Variantology," which seeks to illuminate the secret relations between things that have been covered over by the classification of objects and practices as disciplines. See *Variantology 1* as an example of the heterogeneous nature of the project (Zielinski and Wagnermaier 2005).
3 For a further elaboration of "affective labor" within the film festival, see Chapter 11 in this book, by Liz Czach.
4 Judith Butler's *Excitable Speech: A Politics of the Performative* (1997) is an illuminating application of Austin's theory to the military and the law court.
5 The French psychoanalyst Jacques Lacan's concept of the real derives from a tripartite system of the imaginary, symbolic, and real that collectively describe psychical subjectivity. If the imaginary is the closest description that he offers to everyday consciousness, and the symbolic is the system of culture, laws, and institutions that is mediated by a subject's entry into language, the real is that which is excluded from the symbolic and impossible to think (natural disasters or war fall into this category). The event features in the work of French philosopher Alain Badiou as a rupture in the social fabric that allows what is missing from that system to appear momentarily. These moments or events, which can arise in the realm of politics or art or love, allow what Badiou calls truth to appear fleetingly.

References

Augé, M. (1995) *Non-Places: Introduction to an Anthropology of Supermodernity*, trans. J. Howe, London: Verso.

Austin, J. L. (1975) *How to Do Things with Words*, 2nd ed., Cambridge, MA: Harvard University Press.

Benjamin, W. (1955) "The Storyteller," in *Illuminations*, trans. by H. Zorn, London: Pimlico, pp. 83–107.

Butler, J. (1997) *Excitable Speech: A Politics of the Performative*, London and New York: Routledge.

Charney, L. (1998) *Empty Moments: Cinema, Modernity and Drift*, Durham, NC: Duke University Press.

Czach, L. (2010) "Cinephilia, Stars, and Film Festivals," *Cinema Journal*, 49(2), pp. 139–145.

De Valck, M. (2007) *Film Festivals: From European Geopolitics to Global Cinephilia*, Amsterdam: Amsterdam University Press.

De Valck, M. and S. Loist (2009) "Film Festival Studies: An Overview of a Burgeoning Field," in D. Iordanova and R. Rhyne (eds.) *Film Festival Yearbook 1: The Festival Circuit*, St Andrews: St Andrews Film Studies, pp. 179–215.

Doane, M. A. (2002) *The Emergence of Cinematic Time: Modernity, Contingency, the Archive*. Cambridge, MA: Harvard University Press.

Elsaesser, T. (2004) "The New Film History as Media Archaeology," *Cinémas: Revue d'études cinématographiques | Cinémas: Journal of Film Studies*, 14(2/3), pp. 75–117.

Elsaesser, T. (2005) "Film Festival Networks: The New Topographies of Cinema in Europe," in *European Cinema: Face to Face With Hollywood*, Amsterdam: Amsterdam University Press, pp. 82–107.

Furness, E. (2015) "Emily Blunt on Cannes Heels Row," in *The Telegraph online*, May 20, www.telegraph.co.uk/film/cannes-festival/emily-blunt-cannes-heel-row/ (November 2, 2015).

Gunning, T. (1990) "Non-Continuity, Continuity, Discontinuity: A Theory of Genres in Early Films," in T. Elsaesser and A. Barker (eds.) *Early Cinema: Space, Frame, Narrative*, London: BFI Publishing, pp. 86–94.

Huhtamo, E. and J. Parikka (eds.) (2011) *Media Archaeology: Approaches, Applications, and Implications*, Berkeley, CA: University of California Press.

Iordanova, D. (2009) "The Film Festival Circuit," in D. Iordanova and R. Rhyne (eds.) *Film Festival Yearbook 1: The Festival Circuit*, St Andrews: St Andrews Film Studies, pp. 23.39.

Kracauer, S. (1963) *The Mass Ornament: Weimar Essays*, trans. T. Y. Levin, Cambridge, MA and London: Harvard University Press.

Kubler, G. (1962) *The Shape of Time: Remarks on the History of Things*, New Haven, CT: Yale University Press.

Lazzarato, M. (1996) "Immaterial Labor," in P. Virno and M. Hardt (eds.) *Radical Thought in Italy: A Potential Politics*, Minneapolis, MN: University of Minnesota Press, pp. 133–146.

Lebeau, V. (2008) *Childhood and Cinema*, London: Reaction.

Lévi-Strauss, C. (1962) *The Savage Mind*, trans. G. Weidenfield and Nicholson Ltd, Chicago and London: University of Chicago Press.

Lotringer, S. and P. Virilio (2005) *The Accident of Art*, trans. M. Taormina, New York: Semiotext(e).

Parikka, J. (2010) *Insect Media: An Archaeology of Animals and Technology*, Minneapolis, MN: University of Minnesota Press.

Parikka, J. (2012) *What is Media Archaeology?* Cambridge: Polity.

Pulver, A. (2013) "Cannes 2013: Roman Polanski Says Fight for Female Equality is a 'Great Pity'," *Guardian*, May 25, www.theguardian.com/film/2013/may/25/cannes-2013-roman-polanski-female-equality (November 2, 2015).

Romney, J. (2014) "Berlin Film Festival Roundup," *Observer*, February 16 www.theguardian.com/film/2014/feb/16/berlin-film-festival-roundup-2014 (November 2, 2015).

Shoard, C. (2011) "Cannes Film Festival Bans Lars von Trier," *Guardian*, May 19 www.theguardian.com/film/2011/may/19/cannes-film-festival-2011-lars-von-trier-banned (November 2, 2015).

Sky News (2014) "Man Dives Under Ugly Betty Star's Skirt," May 17, http://news.sky.com/story/1263366/cannes-man-dives-under-ugly-betty-stars-skirt (November 2, 2015).

Trahair, L. (2007) *The Comedy of Philosophy: Sense and Nonsense in Early Cinematic Slapstick*, New York: State University of New York Press.

Vaughn, D. (1990) "Let There Be Lumière," in T. Elsaesser and A. Barker (eds.) *Early Cinema: Space, Frame, Narrative*, London: BFI, pp. 63–67.

Webb, B. (2015) "Cannes: Festival Boss Hits Back After Heelgate," *The Telegraph*, May 22, www.telegraph.co.uk/film/cannes-festival/general-delegate-hits-back-after-heelgate/ (November 2, 2015).

Zielinski, S. (2002) *Deep Time of the Media: Towards an Archaeology of Hearing and Seeing by Technical Means*, trans. G. Custance, Cambridge, MA: MIT Press.

Zielinski, S. and S. M. Wagnermaier (eds.) (2005) *Variantology 1: On Deep Time Relations of Arts, Sciences and Technologies*, Köln: Walther König.

Further reading

Butler, J. (1997) *Excitable Speech: A Politics of the Performative*, London and New York: Routledge. (An account of how speech misfires in various official contexts.)

Colman, F. (ed.) (2009) *Film, Theory and Philosophy: Key Thinkers*, Durham, UK: Acumen. (For further reading about the philosophy of Badiou and Virilio as they relate to cinema and the event.)

Harbord, J. (2007) "Contingency's Work: Kracauer's Theory of Film and the Trope of the Accidental," *New Formations*, 61, pp. 90–103. (On the prevalence of the accident in film and film theory.)

Hesmondhalgh, D. and S. Barker (2011) *Creative Labour: Media Work in Three Creative Industries*, Abingdon and New York: Routledge. (An elaboration of the concept of immaterial labor and the deregulation of work.)

Parikka, J. (2012) *What is Media Archaeology?* Cambridge, UK and Malden, MA: Polity. (An introductory account of archaeological method.)

5 Publics and counterpublics

Rethinking film festivals as public spheres

Cindy Hing-Yuk Wong

In *The Structural Transformation of the Public Sphere*, Jürgen Habermas traces the development of the new European bourgeois places and dialogues from the seventeenth to nineteenth centuries, focusing on the evolution of "the sphere of private people come together as a public" (1989: 27). For Habermas, the bourgeois public sphere was not a place but a conceptual and discursive forum for rational debate over private matters that have public relevance, mostly about "commodity exchange and social labor" (ibid.). While in theory, participation in such a sphere should be open to all, this emergent public sphere demanded time, education, and commitment; this identified it as a project of the European enlightenment, intertwining the public sphere with the growth of capitalism within nation-states and forces challenging the inherited public power of the Court. This public sphere took place, or, more precisely, germinated in settings such as coffee houses, salons, and *Sprachgesellschaften* (literary societies), developed with emergent communication media through newspapers. It declined, in Habermas' evaluation, with the spread of social welfare states and elite-dominated mass media consumption in late nineteenth and early twentieth centuries.

Despite limiting his project to the bourgeoisie and what he saw as an eventual negative transformation to an era of mass culture, Habermas' proposition has proven to be valuable and provocative in the examination of both other arenas of democratic participation and with regard to other media, including film, internet, and social media. However, film festivals represent an interesting challenge within this dialogue. This chapter explores the public sphere not as a commentary on social theory so much as a map for current and future questions for film festival studies.

Habermas' formulation has proven especially provocative in terms of those who disagree with its central relationship to structures of bourgeois power. Miriam Hansen (1991), for example, expanded this concept to examine a nascent immigrant- and women-based public sphere in the cinema of the early twentieth century. This came at a time when women moved out of private homes and into the workforce, participating in a communal viewing experience with strangers in nickelodeons. Here, Hansen defined the term "public" as "denoting a discursive matrix or process through which social experience is articulated, interpreted, negotiated, and contested in an inter-subjective, potentially collective, and oppositional form" (Hansen 1993: 201). While Habermas had discussed the importance of a "World of Letters" in the eighteenth century and its origin in the previous two centuries (Habermas 1989: 52), for Hansen, cinema was as relevant as constitutional law or *belles lettres*, articulating new dialogues, not merely mass consumption of elite products.

Confronting the bourgeoisie more directly, Oskar Negt and Alexander Kluge have posited contesting public spheres where "[t]elevision, the press, interest groups and political parties [....] fused into a general concept of the public sphere" (Negt and Kluge 1993: 65), while envisioning an alternative proletarian public sphere. Similarly, Nancy Fraser (1992) has asserted the value of conceptualizing multiple public spheres and has highlighted the significance of subaltern public spheres neglected by Habermas, converging with work by Mary Ryan (1990, 1992) and Joan Landes (1988), who have explored women's public worlds. In Fraser's later work, she also examines the idea of a transnational public sphere (2007), which should inform our own investigation on the transnational nature of global film festivals. Such debates continue to inform our understanding of film festivals, including those that shape "subaltern" cinematic cultures and have wider implications.

Finally, Michael Warner's rich examinations of publics and counterpublics (1992, 2002a, 2002b) provide an extremely fruitful set of concepts and questions for film festival studies. For example, his vision of a public as an aggregate of strangers formed in relation to the discursive construction of concatenations of texts provides new vantages on the relations of text, reception, and practice in film festivals. While I have discussed film festivals as subaltern public spheres elsewhere (Wong 2011: 159–189); here, I explore the viability of pushing theories and debates around this generative concept even further to reexamine film festivals and to link film festival studies to social theory.

In this endeavor, other scholars have used the concept of the public sphere in their works on film festivals and related media questions, while also drawing on the work of Hansen, and Negt and Kluge. Liz Czach (2010) discusses a cinephilic public sphere in film festivals, which resonates with Warner's idea of the public called up by texts (Warner 2002a: 61). Chris Berry situates the works of Cui Zi'en, one of the first Chinese gay filmmakers, in an "emergent public sphere" (2004: 198) of talk shows on gay topics and suggests that international film festivals provide spaces for this kind of work. Berry reminds us that the study of public spheres in film festival studies should go beyond the limited confines of film festivals themselves as well as grappling with transnational dimensions. Litheko Modisane (2010), by contrast, studies the production, text, and reception of a 1988 South African film, *Mapantsula*, an anti-apartheid film about a petty gangster, to understand how the different contexts the film created and encountered constitute different definitions of public sphere. By following one film and exploring its textual conventions and its multiple political contexts from the positionality of the different publics, Modisane provides a masterful interrogation of how film festivals constitute only one critical component of the variegated public spheres this film and South African politics traversed in the late twentieth century. Finally, it is important to recognize Douglas Kellner's long-term engagement with the concept of the public sphere and changing media in more general but illuminating terms (1989).

This chapter focuses on the potential of theories of public spheres in the study of both A-list film festivals[1] as "heirs" of the liberal bourgeois public sphere and alternative film festivals that address specialized populations and concerns and thus recreate publics and discourses. The chapter takes film festivals as loose structures with many components that allow a great deal of flexibility of production, text, and audience. This elasticity manifests itself in the diversity of film festivals and in varied (and at times contradictory) sections, agendas, and readings within individual festivals. The governmental, nongovernmental, independent, commercial, and transnational natures of film festivals also create different relations to public power and private interests within which public spheres emerge.

Following Negt and Kluge, Hansen, and Warner, I also pay close attention to agency and the active forces behind different aspects of film festival's operations, from production to readership. More importantly, I suggest how theories of public sphere can be applied to general processes through which film texts and knowledge are evaluated, circulated, exhibited, and endorsed in different film festivals and extra-filmic contexts, thereby illuminating a complex articulation of public spheres, of contestations as well as negotiations. Here, the chapter links the potential of various formulations of public sphere to both empirical and theoretical research.

Finally, the chapter raises the question of what film festival studies may contribute to larger debates about the public sphere. Film festivals are concrete events, encompassing both time and physical spaces that allow people to congregate. They provide cases to investigate the interaction between public spaces and public sphere—a problematic point in public sphere studies—and to show how film festival as "places" facilitate the creation of public sphere(s). At the same time, we understand that public sphere is *not* merely public space; different festival spaces also form complex interrelated public spheres that cross national boundaries and encompass virtual worlds.

While festivals need physical spaces to realize presentations and discussions, the public sphere is based on discursive construction. Habermas' spaces, whether coffee houses or salons, "were centers of criticism—literary, at first, then political" (Habermas 1989: 32) where "critical debate, ignited by works of literature and art, was soon extended to include economic and political disputes, without any guarantee [...] that such discussions would be inconsequential, at least in the immediate context" (ibid.: 33). With these debates, "institutionalized art criticism, the journals devoted to art and cultural criticism" arose (ibid.: 41). The development of the public sphere of letters underpinned the public sphere as political realm; more importantly, the public sphere offered the potential of emancipation from existing power structures. Cinema shares similarities with other literary cultural productions, and film festivals provide spaces for the exhibition of cinema and the creation of debates, of film criticism and film theories that in turn further the development and reproduction of cinema prestige and knowledge (cf. Wong 2011: 100–128). While film festivals do not challenge the power of the Court, they provide alternatives to mainstream commercial cinemas, whose influence worried Habermas. At the same time, the very diversity of film festivals, from the A-list national festivals, to regional festivals, thematic festivals, festivals that address identity politics, and festivals of resistance attest to their "situatedness" in myriad opposing public spheres within transnational links. Film festivals thus participate in the varied public and counterpublic spheres in the larger world, adding their own distinctive contributions to the discursive formation of the public spheres and to our conceptualization of them.

The A-list: the bourgeois festival and the public sphere

The now established European A-listed festivals, like Cannes, Venice, and Berlin, very much resemble the classic bourgeois public sphere of letters, even in their conditions of emergence, in negotiation with both government and private spheres. These events are semi-governmental, although they increasingly rely on private/corporate contributions and cooperation within a neoliberal regime. They are exclusive—and they are dominated by men in production, distribution, programming, and commentary—yet they also create wider open arenas for informed debate about cinema, including the politics represented in many of the film texts and issues raised by film programming.[2]

At the same time, many A-list festivals have close relationships with the global economic powerhouse we label as Hollywood, from the parades of out-of-competition European premieres of Hollywood films at Cannes to the incessant courting of Hollywood stars in Venice, Cannes, and Berlin. The Competition sections of these top festivals favor "art films"[3] over high-budget Hollywood films, but the festivals themselves pursue Hollywood stars for ambience and attraction. Some directors also go from the red carpet to the Hollywood lot. Nevertheless, in the festivals' very insistence on art cinema in their main competitions, the A-list festivals recall the erudite salon.

Yet, not unlike the emergent bourgeois public sphere, these festivals remain closely related to economics, through their emphasis on production, distribution, and markets. Simultaneous—albeit separated—markets have become extremely important features of key festivals, where participants conduct the business of cinema. On the surface, the market cannot be a public sphere; it is about buying and selling and is set apart from the festival by its lack of critical apparatus and its openness to all who pay a fee to participate. However, the films "exchanged" there are more than commodities.

The content of these films, like those in competition, oftentimes have the potential to instigate public debates when they travel to new places, encountering new audiences. At the same time, these markets fund future projects[4] and may expand the public sphere. As Warner has suggested, Habermas often conceals the actual foundations of the bourgeois public sphere, making the elucidation of multiple functions of power within film festivals even more important.[5]

At the same time, any examination of the films in competition reveals many works that tackle difficult issues within dialogues that go far beyond festivals, whether concerned with politics, social justice, gender and sexuality, or destructive conflicts. Film festivals do not create social issues, but in selection, screening, and reception, they galvanize debates. Mahamat-Saleh Haroun, for example, a Chadian filmmaker who has been educated in France and has won festival awards, screened *Grigris* in competition in Cannes in 2013. *Grigris* is a social crime film about petrol traffickers in Chad; in the press kit, Haroun states that "my role is to break social taboos in order to allow people to discuss them."[6] In late 2013, more journalistic coverage on petrol trafficking surfaced in major Western news sources like the *New York Times*, the BBC, and *Financial Times*. While I do not posit direct links between the film and the news, this is how discursive universes are constructed, processes in which festivals participate by content, publicity, audience, and discussion.

Perhaps nowhere are the ties of Habermas' public sphere and the A-level festivals more evident than in the relations of festivals and nation-states. For Habermas, the bourgeois public sphere emerged in advanced European states like the United Kingdom, Germany, and France, just as its decline was linked to new political formations in these states with converging elites using media to dominate rather than discuss. Similarly, as Marijke de Valck (2007) has insisted, film festivals started as national affairs. They screened films from specific nation-states, sometimes selected by governments to highlight the gems of that country's productions, until the late 1960s. Hence, since their inception, these national festivals have embraced some international inclusion, while never treating all countries equally. In programming, at least, these early film festivals risked being mere showcases of a nation's glory, rather than any kind of public sphere. This was epitomized in the fascist convergence that allowed Leni Riefenstahl's *Triumph of the Will*, celebrating the rise of Hitler, to win the Silver Medal at the Venice Film Festival, sponsored by Mussolini. However, since cinema is a creative medium that no one can totally control in its content or its reception, even films that questioned the status quo or the authority gained exposure in these events. One year after the exaltation of *Triumph of the Will*, Jean Renoir's antiwar, anti-fascism film *The Grand Illusion* won a Venice prize for the "best artistic ensemble."[7] Therefore when we talk about whether film festivals participate in and create public spheres, the response can be quite complex, complicated, and, at times, contradictory; it is exactly these qualities that make film festivals interesting contested arenas for competing public spheres.

Most European film festivals through the 1950s remained European affairs with Hollywood, dotted with Japanese and occasional Indian entries but indifferent to large areas of the world. If the public sphere embodies the possibilities of emancipation and resisting the powerful, early editions of festivals in Venice, Cannes, and Berlin embraced Hollywood but did not foster the creation of a global public sphere. Not until the 1970s, after the jolting events of May 1968, did European festivals start to make concerted efforts to include cinema from outside of Europe. Moreover, after the 1970s, films screened in these festivals were no longer chosen by the participating countries but by festivals' programmers; while identified by origins, these films are supposed to represent the best of international productions of the year. These films thus have been reframed as platforms to discuss and debate the important issues of the day, from artistic forms and styles to politics to labor issues; debate and discussion are carried out by the juries, the press, the critics, and movie audiences, from professionals to the varied amateurs who watch these films. Oftentimes, in a festival context, these films are shown with directors, actors, producers, and cinematographers answering questions from the press as well as the general viewing public. This intimacy, which is seldom present in a general screening at a mainstream cinema, evokes both Hansen's and Warner's visions of transient but intense public spheres where people, who seldom meet, could be in the same space to discuss. The press, fulfilling its role as producing publicity within the public sphere, helps raise these issues in other fora and settings; in this way, the public sphere of letters participates in creating a discursive universe. Since film festivals occur in real time and space, when explored through the prism of the public sphere they also generate contradictory conditions that facilitate new discursive formations. Cannes is not always a bourgeois public sphere. When the radical filmmakers closed the festival in 1968, for example, it became a counterpublic sphere. From its foundation in 1951, the Berlin International Film Festival was a Cold War icon and propaganda tool for the West to exhibit its democratic credentials to the East across the city. It was established partly by the US State Department with the cooperation of the state and city governments of Berlin; it recalls Habermas' example of the pre-bourgeois radiance of the king in its meanings more than any definition of public sphere. The first Berlin International Film Festival, soon nicknamed *Berlinale*, was a multinational event, but it pointedly excluded any participation from the Eastern Bloc. Yet, by 1958, German and Western journalists attending the Berlinale visited East Berlin as well as the "DEFA Studios in Babelsberg and followed up invitations to visit the East Berlin film club the 'Möwe'" (Jacobsen 2000: 87). Again, film festivals create the possibilities of the formation of a wider public sphere, even with a public that participates in propagandistic film festivals but goes beyond and transforms them.

The limits of national discourse and those who shape it become clear in the transnational expansion of film festivals. In 1960, for example, the Berlinale invited films from Japan, Pakistan, the Philippines, Korea, Thailand, and

India. But "[c]ontemporary critics were severe in their judgment of films from the so-called developing countries" (ibid.: 96). Indeed, Dora Fehling of *Der Telegraf* wrote

> The screen was simply flooded with experiments from countries with undeveloped film industries. They were harming themselves by presenting their local products for comparison. It was impossible not to be bored watching this completely uninhabited, overabundance of exotic images. Annoyance at so much wasted effort was only alleviated by pity for those who had been so ill-advised.
>
> (Ibid.)

Still, even though the above quote was hardly favorable, the very existence of these films in the Berlinale forced discussions of these texts.

Over the years, the definition of "international" has expanded and most film festivals actively solicit films from all corners of the world to the rapt attention of critics, cinephiles, and scholars. One can then argue that film festivals, at a very minimal level, have normalized the inclusion of films from all over the world as one of their practices.[8] At the same time, in many of the Western A-list festivals, these favorites, "negotiated" amid considerations of novelty, localized productions, and competition among festivals, have gained greater exposure and resonance with global political and economic transformations. Hence, China (Taiwan, Hong Kong), Iran, Romania, Israel, and Palestine have been recognized as voices through film festivals.

How does one conceptualize a global or transnational public sphere? While the classical bourgeois public sphere was nation-bounded, international film festivals combine both elements of the national and global public sphere. Cannes embodies the French bourgeois public sphere, which is a national sphere with traditional rational debate on the merits of cinema; at the same time, its embrace of a selective international gaze enriches its Frenchness. Indeed, if film festivals enable the production and exhibition of films that otherwise have few opportunities to be made and hear voices suppressed by national or other regimes, are they fomenting the development of local and global counterpublic spheres? Or is it a truly emancipatory public sphere if the cinematic voices are influenced by the funding agency, using criteria set up by them?

The exploration, then, of national context (both as imagined community and as changing political-economic unit) allows us to raise questions about those festivals that are central to the articulation of a global film festival network. Nancy Fraser has pointedly demanded a rethinking of transnational public sphere by "constructing broadly inclusive public spheres in which common interests can be created and/or discovered through open democratic communication" (Fraser 2005). Yet, in many cases, even this analysis leads us past contradictions to counterpublics, to which I now turn.

Alternative festivals and counterpublics

In relating A-list festivals in the European tradition to Habermas and his work, I am exploring a rich but limited dialogue. In both the diversity of responses to Habermas and other film festivals illuminated by these models, it is necessary to review multiple models and their variations before turning to more concrete materials. Negt and Kluge, in *Public Sphere and Experience*, for example, attacked the weakness of the bourgeois public sphere as not taking into consideration "substantive life interest" (1993: 63). Concerned with the "general horizon of social experience" (ibid: 66), they posed the proletarian public sphere as a counterweight to Habermas' bourgeois public sphere and its inheritance in German public television. They read their proletarian public sphere not as an empirical category, but as a conceptual and proactive one that signifies alterity to the existing conditions of capitalistic production and the spaces and opportunities offered in the experiential horizon of everyday life. Their theories remind us of the importance of studying the experiences of film.

Miriam Hansen's masterful study of working class and female audiences in early cinema found a public sphere in the nickelodeons. Her theories link Negt and Kluge's proletarian life experience to Nancy Fraser's idea about subaltern public sphere. Again, from this perspective, we might explore different screenings and events hosted by film festivals, including the diverse segments of A-list festivals; show how participants create public sphere by discussing issues relevant to their lived experiences; and the process within which that gives rise to enlightened, rational debates on often neglected issues.

Nancy Fraser, meanwhile, also noted that Habermas' public sphere excluded women and the working class. In film festival studies, I postulate that if the major A-list festivals should be seen primarily as embodying the bourgeois public sphere, then alternative film festivals, whether centered in women's festivals, ethnic festivals, or any festivals that promote the voices of subordinated classes or issues should be examined as subaltern festivals. Even within A-list festivals like the Berlinale, many sections and awards, from the Forum[9] to the queer Teddy Award[10] have different publics and impact compared to the main competition sections. The very contradictory tendencies within film festivals can give rise to a better understanding of how different public spheres—bourgeois, counter, and subaltern—either complement each other or demand their own "spaces" within negotiated contestations.

Finally, Michael Warner's idea of publics and counterpublics are relevant to the study of film festivals because of his insistence on using texts to understand the formation of publics. Warner's texts are not isolated pieces of film or criticism, but a "concatenation of texts through time" (2002a: 62). Therefore, film festivals constitute part of a long, continuous process of the formation and reproduction of public sphere. Warner's publics are segments of a mass population who find themselves sharing specific texts and discursive formations, yet do not have to really know each other. Another important feature in Warner's theory is that "publics are only realized through active uptake" (ibid.: 60). At film festivals, production and programming of film texts, participation in viewing, and active discussions and critique of these texts enable the formation and continuation of public spheres.

In general, while the A-list festivals evoke the classic bourgeois public sphere, with fissures of contradictions and counterpublics erupting from time to time, alternative film festival organizers and participants often see themselves as explicitly embodying counterpublic spheres. I have previously discussed festivals with Human Rights themes as well as LGBTQ themes as examples of this formulation (Wong 2011: 159–189), but even so did not exhaust the range of those that celebrate the idea of resistance nor examine if they occupy specific public spheres. In Europe alone, for example, we find the Subversive Film Festival in Zagreb, Croatia; the Festival Résistances in Foix, France; and the Bristol Radical Film Festival in the United Kingdom. In the United States, Social Uprising Resistance Grassroots Encouragement (SURGE) represents a traveling festival in Austin, Urbana, Portland, Los Angeles, Santa Fe, and Berkeley. Most of these festivals combine screenings with workshops, talks, and debates that go beyond the screenings of festivals in Locarno or Venice.[11] Their organizers use terms such as "oppositional cinema," "radical media project," "non-hierarchical," and "collective effort," and are explicit in distinguishing themselves from the mainstream film festivals.

The Subversive Film Festival was established in 2008 in Zagreb, Croatia. Besides showing films, it has invited noted leftist scholars, including Slavoj Žižek and David Harvey, as major "attractions" and it has included a book fair amid other events. The festival openly proclaims its anti-neoliberal, anti-capitalist stance, including a fairly detailed explication of why film is a tool for these leftist endeavors. The festival states:

> we continue to use film to question the situation in which these [Athens and Madrid] occupations occurred, but also in the context of the utopia of democracy. As with these events, so does the universal language of the art of film constantly and deeply change, breaking gender, racial, social and censorship boundaries.[12]

Words like revolution, barricade, guerrilla, activist, progressive are used liberally in all publications over the years. The festival organizers see the festival as interlocutor on these issues and provide spaces for the articulations of these struggles.

At the same time, extra-filmic components of the festival also invite and shape counterpublics. Thus, the Subversive Festival has addressed Croatia's recent entry into the European Union as "subordination." The six main topics of 2013 were democratization and participation, workers' struggles, sex and class equality, new economic models, common and public goods, and media and public sphere.[13] Undoubtedly, the Subversive Festival wears its counterpublic sphere credentials on its sleeves, embracing all global political struggles and putting them in the forefront for discussion. Thus, it can then be seen as forms of publicity in the public sphere.

Even so, such festivals have a mode of production whose visibility and analysis are just as important as the questions we pose to the more bourgeois events. Even subversives have official supporters, sponsors, and partners. These range from the city of Zagreb to the Croatian Audio Visual Center and Croatian Ministry of Culture. Corporations like DHL, Peugeot, and Press Clipping (a media firm) appear in their lists alongside the Zagreb Institut Français. At any point where we investigate film festivals through the lens of the public sphere, multiple structures exist within a single film festival—even in the Subversive Film Festival, with its proclaimed counterpublic intentions, contradictions guide us toward fruitful analysis.

Let me turn to another less vehemently oppositional forum to show how issues raised by Negt and Kluge, Hansen, Warner, Fraser, and even Habermas can shape analysis. In an ethnic film festival, like the Asian American International Film Festival (AAIFF), the audience forms a specific public through texts, as described by Warner. The audience at AAIFF may not necessarily know one another, like Warner's publics, but they definitely share concerns that are generated by specific texts. I will use the AAIFF, and more generally global diasporic Asian film festivals, to push further into the potential of using varied debates about the public sphere in understanding such events, both at the level of texts and in practices.

AAIFF: Asian American International Film Festival in New York started in 1978. CCTV (Chinese Cable TV), a New York Chinatown media organization, initiated the festival; Chinese American as well as recent Chinese immigrant media artists in New York joined CCTV to create a community media organization that primarily promoted community media access. It then changed its name to Asian Cinevision and started the AAIFF. As we see here, the mode of production can be intimately related to the public sphere itself.

The formation of this festival, of course, has a great deal to do with the political culture of the United States of the era, guided by the Civil Rights Movement and movements around ethnic identity, gender, sexuality, and identity politics in all its manifestations. The immigration reforms of the 1960s fostered the assertion of new multiple or "hyphenated" identities in the United States while questioning identification of variations on "European American" as unmarked Americans. These reforms facilitated the growth of new Asian immigrant populations, including Chinese and Japanese who had suffered specific discrimination that impugned their citizenship, joined by both renewed migration from Global Chinese and new migrants from South Korea, South Asia, Southeast Asia, and other areas. All these represent a potential foundation for diverse public spheres based on changing issues, civil rights, and identity politics in the United States, issues that also have the potential to reach beyond national borders.

Not only did Asian American film festivals emerge, but they became meshed as well in revindicative worlds of Chicano film festivals, Black film festivals, and Native American film festivals. New critical apparatuses, in turn, emerged around both community organizers and university professors in new programs and students who constituted educated counterpublics meeting in the spaces of films and discussion (Espiritu 2005).

Other forms of Chinese American cultural expressions were also claiming cultural spaces and forming public spheres in US societies in this time, including *The Woman Warrior* (1976) of Maxine Hong Kingston and angry Asian works like the inclusive and uterine anthology *Aiiieeeee! An Anthology of Asian American Writers* (Chin et al. 1975). Asian American theater also took shape as another active and interactive forum (Lee 2006). Universities started forming ethnic studies departments: University of California, Berkeley, founded its Ethnic Studies Department in 1969, including engagement with African Americans, Asian Americans, Chicanos, and Native Americans studies. These programs, in turn, became linked to new public voices and protests for change. Finally, working with the Corporation of Public Broadcasting, the National Asian American Telecommunication Association (NAATA) was formed in 1980 and subsequently, a West Coast Asian American film festival—the San Francisco International Asian American Film Festival—followed in 1986. Many others would emerge along this trajectory.

The Asian American International Film Festival thus participated, invigorated, and reproduced a debate about the existing United States bourgeois public sphere challenged by civil rights and ethnic identities. It delineated a group of texts, agents, and readings within this larger panorama as the foundation for a counterpublic. AAIFF has been and continues to be a festival run by educated and assimilated people with Asian immigrant roots as well as recent immigrants. Its community mission is to reach out to "Asian Americans" and to provide them with tools for self-expression within a commercial broadcasting environment that did not provide such spaces. This public sphere attracts other people who see themselves as part of the living communities of Asian Americans to whom they belong, like the publics in Warner's description. It also seeks to change them as informed viewers reflecting on the nature of their categorization and their roles in a larger society.

The first few festivals drew products and organizers primarily from Chinese and Japanese American communities, partly because of their long histories. The festival organizers nonetheless insisted on calling themselves Asian American, envisioning a new and political identity. However, despite this vision of inclusion, the early festival was run primarily by native-born Chinese Americans, such as Daryl Chin who, along with Jonas Mekas,[14] worked at *SoHo Weekly News* and was a reviewer of avant-garde and independent films. Other founders included other media artists like Christine Choy and educated migrants from Hong Kong like Danny Yung[15] and Tsui Hark. The Hong Kong New Wave also connected to these people, creating discourses generated by public spheres that crossed national boundaries and generated transnational discussions while making identities more diffuse.

The first AAIFF programs included mainly shorts and documentaries; organizers showed 30 films in five and a half hours. The organizers chose works from other Asian American media organizations, for example, from the West Coast in Los Angeles, or Visual Communication, which championed works that celebrated "Asian American" identities by asserting that Asian Americans are American and that their stories need to be told. One of the first nationally distributed Asian American feature films, Wayne Wang's *Chan is Missing* (1981), was first screened at AAIFF as a highly experimental film called *Fire Over Water*; the film was later totally re-narrativized into a more commercially viable art film. For two years in 1982 and 1983 there was also an Asian American International Video Festival, dedicated primarily to avant-garde works that demands a departure from straightforward affirmative pieces.

Like any vibrant public sphere, especially one that struggled between affirmation and more nuanced understanding of identity, there were also constant debates across form and identity-related content issues. For example, Daryl Chin notes:

> Being Asian American does not necessarily have to mean being an immigrant, dealing with "foreign" culture because one's home life is still derived from the old country, or living in a ghetto. [...] After the very first Asian American Film Festival, we asked ourselves whether or not a film qualified as Asian American just because the filmmaker happened to be Asian American. After looking at all the movies which came through the first festival, our decision was yes.
>
> (Chin 1987)

On the other hand, Chin also recognized that many examples of Asian American cinema have the best noble intentions, but they are "boring as hell" (Okada 2009). Dialogue on different aspects of AAIFF continues to evolve with the changing structures and contexts of the many public spheres in which it participates—immigrants, Asian American, gender, community activism, forms.

AAIFF and related events patterned new pedagogies of "Asian Americanness." In the 1990s, for example, I worked with Philadelphia's Scribe Video and Asian Americans United to facilitate a film project in which Asian American high school students planned, filmed, and edited a 15-minute video about preoccupations in their lives: stereotypes, gangs, school, and their ability to talk and be heard. The film, *Face to Face: It's Not What You Think*, thus functioned both as documentary and pedagogy within the general goals of both organizations. It was screened, in turn, in festivals like the Chicago Asian American Film Festival and the San Francisco International Asian American Film Festival, affirming the process and product while opening up new audiences and questions (Wong 1997).

In fact, multiple publics have evolved in the varied events related to the AAIFF and the festival has participated in and engendered multiple public spheres. It has always been a community-based festival, but to broaden its reach, AAIFF now has a traveling festival through which institutions all over the country can request a package of the program to be shown in their own place at their own time. The most recent incarnations of the festival still are run primarily by Asian Americans, showcasing primarily Asian and Asian American themes, but offer a more expansive definition of Asian works made outside the United States as well as tackling questions that take different forms across these potential Asian arenas. Films from China or Japan are included, but their presence has diminished as works from South Asia and the Philippines have appeared more regularly. In 2013, screenings include classic films from Bollywood and the Taiwan new wave; *Linsanity*, which documents the fervor surrounding Chinese American professional basketball player Jeremy Lin; and the Centerpiece presentation, *Soongava: Dance of the Orchids*, introduced as the "the first Nepali film to spotlight LGBTQ issues."[16] In many ways, however, unless an emergent participatory community has a substantial educated group of diasporic people who understand their rights and seek public voices, this model remains dominated by now established Asian American perspectives intersecting with themes from other film festivals such as the exploration of sexuality and repression in the Global South or the search for novelty. Still, the mainstream cinema has not recognized many films shown at the festival, nor do they travel in the circuits of A-list or even so-called second-tier festivals (like Hong Kong, London, or South by Southwest). Yet, in terms of counterpublic spheres, size and reach are never the most important measurements. As the texts have become ever more diverse, a larger public, in Michael Warner's sense, has also formed, including people with or without Asian immigrant roots who have familiarized themselves with texts that have circulated in the public sphere for at least two or more generations. It is this generative possibility of the public sphere that allows festivals like AAIFF to continue to thrive.

Conclusions

The brief theoretical citations to intense and complex debates over public spheres that I have provided here, along with examples from film festival studies that might pattern future investigations, remain evocative more than comprehensive. As I have shown, Habermas' formulation of the bourgeois public sphere, despite significant objections, remains an important lens through which we might pose issues for film festival research. Not only the suggestive qualities of the original text but the critical responses to it from Fraser, Negt and Kluge, Warner, and others allow us to analyze issues of text, reading, audience, and power behind the scenes that constitute film festivals as events and integrate them into changing social and cultural worlds. In particular, I have argued that major film festivals—especially the European A-list festivals, although not limited to them—can profitably be read through the heritage of previous bourgeois worlds, especially if we highlight the foundations of economic power and the strategies of cultural domination that emerge at points of contradiction within these complex, multilayered events. By contrast, rich theories of alternative/counterpublics, and the thread many of these analyses share with regard to the creative potential and demands on emergent publics, force us to engage even more complex issues of specialized festivals in their social and cultural contexts and their participation in wider festival networks and practices.

Nevertheless, it is important not to treat the generative idea of the public sphere as a recipe book for festival analysis but as a theoretical debate in which festival studies can actively engage. The primacies of text, on the one hand, and business, on the other, within a world centered on discourses allows us to question both the complexities of power behind the screen and connections across multiple mediations in contemporary public spheres. The realities of festivals as places, as concatenations of texts and audiences, also enrich studies of publics and counterpublics, especially as key issues combine and separate in such rich texts and combinations. Finally, the questions of the limits of public spheres, especially as we move beyond a national frame (but do not escape it) seem paramount in film festivals as a whole and offer different nuances on transnational texts, connections, audiences, and debates that I have tackled at greater length in my monograph. Above all, it seems valuable that the intersections of film festival studies and elaboration and debates over the public sphere promise both important perspectives in our shared subject and important contributions from film festival studies to wider debates of social and cultural theory worldwide.

Notes

1 A-list film festival is an unofficial designation of FIAPF (International Federation of Film Producers Associations) endorsed Competitive Feature Film Festivals. They are generally recognized as the most prestigious film festivals today.
2 There are other A-list festivals that are very different from Cannes, Berlin, and Venice that have less global impact. The Shanghai International Film Festival, for example, is a newcomer to the A category. Yet it has been known very much as an arm of the Shanghai government and its business interests (Ma 2012). Chris Berry (personal communication) has raised many interesting points. He asserts that while many in the West may find the Shanghai festival antithetical to what a proper film festival should be, the major *raison d'être* of the Shanghai festival can be seen as one that answers primarily to its local Shanghai, Chinese constituents.
3 Many festivals exhibit cinema that can be considered as "second cinema" (art cinema) in Solanas and Getino's definition of Third Cinema (1985).
4 For an in-depth discussion of the role of film markets at festivals see Chapter 12 in this book by Tamara L. Falicov.
5 These contradictions are also visible in the associations that have formed around these A-list festivals. The International Federation of Film Critics Associations (FIPRESCI) is closely related to the public sphere generated by film festivals, as it endows critic prizes to the films shown at over 60 festivals. Very often the prizes

are linked to humanitarian concerns and help raise the profile of such issues. On the other hand, the FIAPF is an organization for film producers, therefore, its primary allegiance is to people providing resources to cinema, and it creates rules to govern the conducts of film festivals and has little *direct* connection with the public sphere.

6 Press Kit *Grigris*, interview with Mahamat-Saleh Haroun, www.festival-cannes.com/assets/Image/Direct/048180.pdf (December 1, 2013).

7 The propaganda minister of Nazi Germany, Joseph Goebbels, identified the film as Public Enemy #1 and the very survival of an original negative was in question until a copy was exchanged between Russia and the Cinémathèque in Toulouse in the 1960s.

8 We must be well aware that the whole continent of Africa is scarcely represented or represented through co-produced films rather than local developments like Nollywood.

9 "The International Forum of Young Cinema" started as an alternative program to the main competition of the Berlinale in 1969. After much soul searching of the festival, not unlike those of Cannes 1968, the Forum was integrated into the Berlinale fold and became an official, yet independently curated section in 1971.

10 The Teddy Award (1987) is the oldest award of an A-list festival, given to an LGBTQ-themed film across all sections of the Berlinale (www.teddyaward.tv).

11 There are also discussions at these festivals too, but they are primarily about cinematic issues.

12 www.subversivefestival.com/filmskil/5/42/en/feature-competition (January 21, 2014).

13 www.archive.subversivefestival.com/subff2013/txtl/1/186/en/forum (November 2, 2015).

14 Another important Lithuanian immigrant artist, sometimes called the father of American avant-garde.

15 Danny Yung became an important dance theater director when he returned to Hong Kong.

16 AAIFF catalog, www.asiancinevision.org/soongava/ (January 21, 2014).

References

Berry, C. (2004) "The Sacred, the Profane, and the Domestic in Cui Zi'en's Cinema," *Positions: East Asia Cultures Critique*, 12(1), pp. 195–201.

Chin, D. (1987) "After Ten Years: Some Notes on the Asian American International Film Festival," in The 1987 Asian American International Film Festival, catalog.

Chin, F., J. P. Chan, L. Inada Fusao, and S. Wong (eds.) (1975) *Aiiieeeee! An Anthology of Asian-American Writers*, Garden City, NY: Anchor.

Czach, L. (2010) "Cinephilia, Stars, and Film Festivals," *Cinema Journal*, 49(2), pp. 139–145.

De Valck, M. (2007) *Film Festivals: From European Geopolitics to Global Cinephilia*, Amsterdam: Amsterdam University Press.

Espiritu, Y., Le (2005) "Asian American Panethnicity: Contemporary National and Transnational Possibilities," in N. Foner and G. M. Fredrickson (eds.) *Not Just Black and White: Historical and Contemporary Perspectives on Immigration, Race, and Ethnicity in the United States*, New York: Russell Sage Foundation, pp. 217–234.

Fraser, N. (1992) "Rethinking the Public Sphere: A Contribution to the Critique of Actually Existing Democracy," in C. Calhoun (ed.) *Habermas and the Public Sphere*, Cambridge, MA: MIT Press, pp. 109–142.

Fraser, N. (2005) "Transnationalizing the Public Sphere," *republicart*, www.republic art.net/disc/publicum/fraser01_en.htm (December 6, 2013).

Fraser, N. (2007) "Transnationalizing the Public Sphere: On the Legitimacy and Efficacy of Public Opinion in a Post-Westphalian World," *Theory, Culture & Society*, 24(4), pp. 7–30.

Habermas, J. (1989) *The Structural Transformation of the Public Sphere: An Inquiry into a Category of Bourgeois Society*, trans. by T. Burger, Cambridge, MA: MIT Press.

Hansen, M. (1991) *Babel and Babylon: Spectatorship in American Silent Film*, Cambridge, MA: Harvard University Press.

Hansen, M. (1993) "Early Cinema, Late Cinema: Permutations of the Public Sphere," *Screen*, 34(3), pp. 197–210.

Jacobsen, W. (2000) *50 Years Berlinale: Internationale Filmfestspiele Berlin*, Berlin: Nicolai.

Kellner, D. (1989) *Critical Theory, Marxism and Modernity*, Cambridge: Polity Press.

Kingston, M. H. (1976) *The Woman Warrior: Memoirs of a Girlhood Among Ghosts*, New York: Vintage.

Landes, J. B. (1988) *Women and the Public Sphere in the Age of the French Revolution*, Ithaca, NY: Cornell University Press.

Lee, E. K. (2006) *A History of Asian American Theatre*, New York: Cambridge University Press.

Ma, R. (2012) "Celebrating the International, Disremembering Shanghai: The Curious Case of the Shanghai International Film Festival," *Culture Unbound: Journal of Current Cultural Research*, 4, pp. 147–168.

Modisane, L. (2010) "Movie-ng the Public Sphere: The Public Life of a South African Film," *Comparative Studies of South Asia, Africa and the Middle East*, 30(1), pp. 133–146.

Negt, O. and A. Kluge (1993) *Public Sphere and Experience: Toward an Analysis of the Bourgeois and Proletarian Public Sphere*, trans. by P. Labanyi, J. O. Daniel, and A. Oksiloff, Minneapolis, MN: University of Minnesota Press.

Okada, J. (2009) "'Noble and Uplifting and Boring as Hell': Asian American Film and Video, 1971–1982," *Cinema Journal*, 49(1), pp. 20–40.

Ryan, M. P. (1990) *Women in Public: Between Banners and Ballots, 1825–1880*, Baltimore, MD: Johns Hopkins University Press.

Ryan, M. P. (1992) "Gender and Public Access: Women's Politics in Nineteenth-Century America," in C. Calhoun (ed.) *Habermas and the Public Sphere*, Cambridge, MA: MIT Press, pp. 259–288.

Solanas, F. and O. Getino (1985) "Towards a Third Cinema," in B. Nichols (ed.) *Movies and Methods: An Anthology*, 1, Berkeley, CA: University of California Press, pp. 44–64.

Warner, M. (1992) "The Mass Public and the Mass Subject," in C. Calhoun (ed.) *Habermas and the Public Sphere*, Cambridge, MA: MIT Press, pp. 377–401.

Warner, M. (2002a) "Publics and Counterpublics," *Public Culture*, 14(1), pp. 49–90.

Warner, M. (2002b) *Publics and Counterpublics*, New York: Zone Books.

Wong, C. H.-Y. (1997) "Community Through the Lens: Grassroots Video in Philadelphia as Alternative Communicative Practice," unpublished PhD dissertation, University of Pennsylvania.

Wong, C. H.-Y. (2011) *Film Festivals: Culture, People, and Power on the Global Screen*, New Brunswick, NJ: Rutgers University Press.

Further reading

Calhoun, C. (ed.) (1992) *Habermas and the Public Sphere*, Cambridge, MA: MIT Press. (In this collection scholars from various academic disciplines assess and critique Habermas' foundational theory of the bourgeois public sphere.)

Habermas, J. (1989) *The Structural Transformation of the Public Sphere: An Inquiry into a Category of Bourgeois Society*, trans. T. Burger, Cambridge, MA: MIT Press. (Habermas' book on the bourgeois public sphere is the foundational book which all further conceptions of alternative public spheres refer back to.)

Negt, O. and A. Kluge (1993) *Public Sphere and Experience: Toward an Analysis of the Bourgeois and Proletarian Public Sphere*, trans. by P. Labanyi, J. O. Daniel, and A. Oksiloff, Minneapolis, MN: University of Minnesota Press. (Negt and Kluge offer a critique of Habermas' theorization of the bourgeois public sphere and argue for the consideration of a proletarian public sphere.)

Warner, M. (2002) *Publics and Counterpublics*, New York: Zone Books. (Warner introduces the concept of the (queer) counterpublic, which is particularly useful for studying identity-based or community-oriented film festivals associated with social movements.)

6 Fostering art, adding value, cultivating taste

Film festivals as sites of cultural legitimization

Marijke de Valck

As the introductory chapter to this volume showed, film festivals come in many sizes and shapes, and they address different stakeholders on the basis of different priorities. Among such variety, however, there is one thing all film festivals have in common: they screen films. To understand the ontology of film festivals, it is therefore essential to zoom in on film festivals as particular sites of exhibition and determine what sets them apart from other modes of screening and watching film. What differentiates a festival screening from a theatrical release? Are films screened at festivals appreciated differently than when shown elsewhere? And how does the existence of festivals as an exhibition circuit influence filmmakers? In this chapter we will use a cultural socio-logical approach to elucidate what structures and principles underlie the existence and dynamics of an exhibition circuit composed of film festivals. The work of French sociologist Pierre Bourdieu will be central to our discussion. Scholars working on film festivals have frequently turned to Bourdieu, and in particular to his concept of symbolic capital, to explain how festivals function as sites of cultural legitimization (e.g., Czach 2004; De Valck and Soeteman 2010; Elsaesser 2005). In two recent articles I have extended these approaches to discuss how processes of commercialization affect contemporary film festivals (De Valck 2014a, 2014b). This chapter draws on Bourdieu and festival scholars' uses of his work to elucidate how such theoretical frames can further our understanding of film festivals.

The discussion is divided in three sections, each taking a key Bourdieuian concept as its focal point. The first section, "Field," deals with festivals' posi-tions in what Bourdieu calls the "field of cultural production" (see his collec-tion of essays on the field of cultural production, published in English in 1993). The section frames festivals as being rooted outside the mainstream commercial movie industries—driven as they are by box-office receipts—and consequently explains how film festivals have incorporated artistic norms and principles of evaluation as their main model. The second section, "Capital," then elaborates on the process by which festivals confer value upon the films that show at them. Selection for a competition, sidebar, tribute, or retrospective brings cultural recognition to the artifact and its maker, while winning an award bestows the ultimate form of prestige. Finally, the last section, "Habitus," will argue that film festivals not only provide cultural consecration but also sustain the system of cultural legitimization at film festivals, by producing filmmakers that make films specifically for the festival circuit and by cultivating the audiences that are interested and capable of consuming these works. Each concept is explained using one or more concrete examples from recent festival history.

Field

Bourdieu distinguished between different "fields" in society, such as the political, juridical, economic, religious, scientific, and cultural fields, which share invariant properties, but also have their own sets of values and principles (Bourdieu 1996). He further subdivided the cultural field into the subfields of restricted production and large-scale production (ibid.: 217). Restricted or small-scale production has a relatively large degree of autonomy, such as in poetry circles. Poets operate in a small market where fellow poets dominate the audience of public readings and make up a significant part of the modest sales (Craig and Dubois 2010). Achievements are assessed and careers made in reference to the aesthetic norms of the poets' internal community. With large-scale production, on the contrary, a mass and thus general audience is targeted, and profitability of the product typically outweighs aesthetic considerations. In Hollywood, for example, test screenings of movies and television series are a common tool to gauge audience interest, and the results may be used to change the product before its release.

The two subfields should not be taken as fixed categories, but rather be seen as the poles on a sliding scale, each characterized by a different principle of hierarchization: the autonomous principle for restricted production and the heteronomous principle for large-scale production. The autonomous principle involves internal hierarchization, largely following its own norms and sanctions, while the heteronomous principle implies external hierarchization, importing values from outside fields, most notably economic ones. At this pole, cultural products are considered not so different from other goods in the marketplace; they are measured on their commercial success or social notoriety, and it is recognition by the general public that makes artists renowned. Hollywood stardom, for example, is determined by popularity with audiences. At the autonomous pole, on the other hand, prestige is linked to appreciation by peers or experts from within the field. What public audiences think matters significantly less.[1] Poets, in this vein, are made by peers, not a general public. There is a continuous struggle between the different logics in the cultural field, and cultural works produced at the heteronomous side of the spectrum are often not considered as art, but labeled as entertainment or popular culture instead.[2]

Cinema originated as a technical novelty at fairs and traveling expositions, a realm of popular arts and commercial culture. Cinema was thus not considered as an art form from the beginning. Initially, the so-called "cinema of attractions" (Abel 1994; Gunning 1994) aimed at entertaining its audiences with trick films and comics, and caused widespread amazement about the new medium's power to capture real life with actuality filmmaking. It was only after a decade of experimentation that this cinema of attractions developed into a coherent form of narrative cinema. However, even this narrative cinema, it is argued, continued to rely on spectacular attractions (Abel 1994: 156) and was targeted at a broad public. The mode of exhibition also changed. With the move to permanent venues—nickelodeons in the US and, some years later, cinema palaces in Europe and the US—the activity of distribution was detangled from exhibition. Or at least it was in a procedural sense; as distribution was quickly recognized for its strategic value, existing film companies expanded to control all elements in the film business: production, distribution, and exhibition. The big companies that emerged as a result, like Pathé and Gaumont in France and Warner Brothers and Paramount Pictures in the US, used this vertical integration to inflict Machiavellian booking techniques, and so they came to dominate their domestic markets.

When the Venice Film Festival was founded in 1932, the choice to have it act under the umbrella of the Arts Biennale was a strategic one. By aligning cinema with the high arts, the festival created a new international space for the celebration of cinema as artistic achievement, a space where films were not simply hawked or offered as cheap entertainment for the masses, but showcased and judged on aesthetic merits. The question then emerges: why was such a space needed? There were several conditions that together created a historically opportune moment for festivals to take roots (see De Valck 2007: 23–25), but considering this chapter's interest in exhibition, we limit ourselves here to the weakening competitive position of European cinemas and industries.

In the late 1920s and early 1930s the American movie industry was in full transition to "the talkies." As Donald Crafton argues in his study on this transition, "[s]ound enabled the American film industry to solidify its power as the leading exporter of entertainment" (1999: 418). While small countries struggled with the disadvantage of small home markets, the domestic market in the US was the biggest in the West, and was shielded from competition by tariffs and other protectionist measures (De Grazia 1989: 58). The American movie industry, moreover, targeted a broad mass audience, and its universal stories, melodramas, and the message about an "American dream" not only enchanted its own domestic "melting pot" population but proved popular across borders as well. European film industries, on the other hand, were largely inwardly oriented, while European nations appeared too preoccupied with their nationalist agendas. When another World War broke out on the European continent, the various national film industries were damaged, and the American film industry was prone to capitalize on its initial advantage with innovative methods of production, distribution, and marketing. The phenomenon of film festivals, which went through its first boom in the immediate postwar period on the European continent, offered a novel way to try and beat such American media imperialism: by presenting cinema as art instead of commodity, and by introducing film festivals as alternative sites of exhibition.[3]

So what did it precisely mean that cinema was included in, or at least associated with, the realm of high arts at festivals? From a cultural sociological perspective, one of the most significant effects concerns the different set of norms and principles that were applied, compared to film's position in the regular exhibition market. Bourdieu has brilliantly described the conditions under which in the second half of the nineteenth century a particular idea of culture, free from the influence of market and politics and opposed to the "false" world of the bourgeoisie, emerged in the literary field in France. Rebelling against the structural subordination to the tastes of the new self-made men in power at the time, writers like Flaubert, Balzac, and Baudelaire sought to free themselves from dependence on audience demand or state patronage. They invented the notion of "art for art's sake," of art that was made with a pure concern for aesthetics that would become the norm in the modern literary field and high culture in general.[4] A side effect was that this art was unsellable at the market. Bourdieu writes:

> The symbolic revolution through which artists free themselves from bourgeois demand by refusing to recognize any master except their art produces the effect of making the market disappear. In fact they could not triumph over the "bourgeois" in the struggle for control of the meaning and function of artistic creativity without at the same time eliminating the bourgeois as a potential customer.
>
> (1996: 81)

This notion of art for art's sake informed the norms and principles driving the new film festival phenomenon. In Venice, Cannes, Locarno, Berlin, Karlovy Vary, and other early festival events, cinema was attributed a *hybrid* identity. Festivals were, on the one hand, positioned as an art form and aligned to the ideology of art for art's sake, with ample attention for the aesthetic quality of the films shown. On the other hand, they carried the burden of cultural and national representation, which pointed to the geopolitical agendas at stake in the organization of festivals (see Fehrenbach 1995; Moine 2012). Because of the gathering of international film professionals, moreover, festivals also developed as important events for the industry, adding a market function. Although cinema was far from free from the influence of market and politics at film festivals, the emphasis on aesthetics was crucially different from cinema's position in the mainstream distribution and exhibition contexts.

The European film festivals that were founded in the immediate postwar period can thus be understood, among other reasons, as response to the American domination of European cinemas. With their support of film festivals, European nations and film industries promoted an alternative for commercial exhibition of film that hinged on the recognition of film as art. The festival-as-exhibition-site differs from commercial theaters first in its appreciation for artistic achievement; films are not screened as part of a business undertaking, but because they are considered important or worthy to be shown. In other words, festival screenings typically serve a *cultural* purpose, not an economic one. Second, festival exhibition is realized under different conditions. At festivals the films enjoy very limited availability, being programmed for one to three screenings per festival, while movies may run several weeks in the same permanent cinema theater, depending on box-office success. Third, where commercial cinema owners depend on revenues from ticket sales and food and beverages, festivals have additional sources of income, such as subsidies, sponsorship, and merchandise, and thus can program more autonomously than those cinema owners. In recent years it has become more common for film festivals, in particular less prestigious ones, to pay screening fees to producers (Peranson 2008), but the amount concerned is still modest and cannot be considered as an economically viable distribution model on its own.[5] So, although money is increasingly involved, festival exhibition remains predominantly tied to autonomous modes of organization: films are screened for cultural reasons, and their exhibition does not generate (a significant) profit.

Capital

Bourdieu not only described the conquest of autonomy in the field of cultural production in the nineteenth century, he also analyzed the historical formation of a bohemian artistic identity, showing how the archetype of the poor artist dedicated to his/her art was created at that time (1996: 55). The Romantic idea that artists are exceptionally gifted, have particular sensitivities, and operate in a magical-like sphere that remains untouched by the mundane practices of economic and social life is in fact contradicted by Bourdieu's research. He explains how social structures, dispositions of people, and competition between agents underlie the cultural field. The organization of the cultural field thus functions, he demonstrates, like all other social fields with rules, discourses, and institutions that can be distinguished and analyzed. With what is arguably his best-known concept, "capital," Bourdieu fleshes out a theory of different rewards that drive social agents. At the heart of Bourdieu's sociology is the belief that all social agents are motivated by personal gain and, more specifically, a wish to occupy the best position in their field. To this aim, agents follow the rules of the game in the field they occupy and pursue accumulation of particular forms of capital that enable them to advance their position. When asked what sets his theoretical approach apart from certain economic methods, Bourdieu elaborates on his notion of capital. He states:

> A general science of the economy of practices that does not artificially limit itself to those practices that are socially recognized as economic

must endeavor to grasp capital [...] in all of its different forms, and to uncover the laws that regulate their conversion from one into another.

(Bourdieu and Wacquant 1992: 118)

Bourdieu distinguished between different types of capital: economic capital, social capital, cultural capital, and symbolic capital (see Bourdieu 1986; Webb et al. 2002). Economic capital refers to money, assets, and other economic resources. Social capital involves access to resources based on one's network and relationships. Cultural capital determines a person's social status in society (class) and is formed by knowledge, skills, education, attitudes, and taste. Symbolic capital, finally, points at the resources available to one on the basis of prestige, honor, and recognition. All manifestations of capital serve as "the energy of social physics" (Bourdieu 1990: 122) and are used by groups and individuals to advance their positions. What counts as legitimate capital is determined by the norms in those social spaces, but everyone is driven by at least one form of capital. So, while avant-garde artists would typically treat monetary motivations (economic capital) with disregard, they do pursue the symbolic capital (the artistic recognition and prestige) that can advance their ranking in the restricted field of cultural production.

With this Bourdieuian frame in mind, film festivals can be understood as places where filmmakers can acquire symbolic capital. This is significantly different than the mainstream film industry, which revolves predominantly around economic capital. In commercial filmmaking, box-office results determine a film's success and directly impact on actors' careers. Their fee, for example, increases with more box-office hits to their name, and will decrease again when such performance is discontinued. Hollywood has the highest paid actors in the world, with salaries running into eight figures for top-billed actors and actresses.[6] While it is true that contemporary film festivals can be considered a part of niche economies that replicate the Hollywood blockbuster and star model on a smaller scale (De Valck 2014a; Perren 2001/2002), the money involved in quality cinema, independent cinema, world cinema, global art cinema, and other niches is very modest in comparison, and, ultimately, does not constitute the key asset driving the people involved. The main capital in these niches is symbolic: prestige, honor, and recognition. As noted before, film festivals operate on a different model than commercial exhibition sites and their (autonomous) programming choices are based on the strength of the stories and aesthetic qualities rather than (expected) popular success. Because of such emphasis in selection criteria, film festivals are able to offer what is called cultural legitimization: selection by a festival brings cultural recognition to the film and its makers, because it serves as hallmark of quality. Below we will also see that the possibility of converting the symbolic capital acquired at festivals into economic capital is a key attraction of certain festivals.

First let's take a closer look at how the principle of cultural legitimization works on the festival circuit. Thomas Elsaesser argues that:

one of the key functions of the international festival becomes evident, namely to categorize, classify, sort and sift the world's annual film production. The challenge lies in doing so not by weeding out and de-classifying, or of letting the box-office do its brutal work, but rather by supporting, selecting, celebrating and rewarding—in short, by adding value and cultural capital at the top, while acting more as a gentle gate-keeper than a bouncer at the bottom.

(2005: 96)

Film festivals typically program films that will not survive the prerogatives of a commercial release on their own: foreign language films, world cinema, art cinema, documentaries, and other noncommercial genres. These are typically films without well-known actors, often dealing with serious themes, produced on small or medium budgets, and without the financial resources to compete with Hollywood's marketing machine. At film festivals, these films are not simply screened and left to popular vote; they are embedded in a rich discursive context that encourages discussion, reflection, and engagement with the films' content and aesthetics. Films can be presented as part of a themed program, for example, highlighting new talent or indicating interesting developments from a certain regions and well-known (new) waves. Film screenings may be attended by the director, who gives an introduction to the film and stays on to take questions afterward. Festivals produce and facilitate extensive writings on the films shown: directly, in the form of catalog texts and dailies; and indirectly, by accrediting and servicing the press. In addition, there may be talk shows or special events. Most importantly, festivals feature competitions, for which films are selected, and can win prizes. A prize or award is the most tangible form of symbolic capital. Moreover, competitions and their prizes have the necessary news value to attract film critics, who will write and report on the festival's program from an expert position that can amplify the cultural legitimization that is already offered by festival selection.

In his study on the economy of prestige, James English observes how cultural prizes have taken a flight since their inception in the nineteenth century. Prizes are particularly suitable to confirm the autonomy of the arts, but as cultural quality and value are subjectively asserted, the authority by which an award has been conferred can easily be disputed, and give occasion to alternative prizes. English writes:

> [N]ew prizes would emerge to compete with established ones, to try to tarnish them or at least to steal some of their luster, and that all prizes would struggle to defend or improve their positions on the field of cultural production.

(English 2008: 53–54)

In Bourdieu's theory of fields, all competitions epitomize power struggles. Who is in a position to speak on behalf of the field? Who can attribute value?

Being an official manifestation of value, prizes and awards function as regulators and gatekeepers of the field of cultural production. Bourdieu insisted that cultural and symbolic capital are typically misrecognized as capital, and that we tend to consider people's aesthetic achievements, their intellectual capacities, and their taste for art as inherent qualities and not as something that is acquired in a competition, inherited from family, or learned at school (Webb et al. 2002: 152). English emphasizes how prizes and prestige can become the object of public contestation. He argues, "each new prize that fills a gap or void in the system of awards defines at the same time a lack that will justify and indeed *produce* another prize" (ibid.: 67).

The logic of proliferation that English describes can also be argued to drive the expansion of the festival circuit. The number of film festivals has grown exponentially, especially since the 1980s. The process of differentiation, with which evermore narrowly specialized events are founded, is a major factor for festival proliferation. Most of the (new) festivals award prizes to generate news value and attract press, and the proliferation of festivals in this way contributes to the proliferation of cultural prizes. Such a massive increase requires any researcher of a specific film festival event to critically reflect on Bourdieu's concept of capital. Clearly, not all festivals are able to bestow prestige or offer cultural legitimization in equal manner. The festival system is heavily tiered, and only a limited number of festivals have the authority to bestow globally recognized prestige. The list of most important festivals includes the well-known festivals in Cannes, Berlin, and Venice in Europe, Sundance and Toronto in North America, and Hong Kong and Busan in Asia. Winning an award at the Cannes film festival is the most prestigious honor a filmmaker can receive, while at the bottom of the incessant festival supply there are plenty of events that may not distribute any symbolic capital at all.

Bourdieu's interest in different forms of capital included attention for the conversion of one form into another, and considering festivals' diverse identities and ranking, it is worthwhile to briefly discuss how the notions of capital are utilized in festivals-as-exhibition sites, and how they connect festivals to other (exhibition) circuits. First, some festivals maintain strong relations with the commercial film industries. Sundance is a quintessential example; it is Hollywood's presence, and the lure of independent, indie, and corporate exchange that has become Sundance's main forte. Second, there is the possibility of festival exhibition as a stepping-stone to theatrical release. This pertains to a small selection of the films programmed at film festivals, and prestigious prizes enhance the chances of a successful release. For example, *La Vie d'Adèle*/*Blue Is the Warmest Color* (Abdellatif Kechiche, 2013) enjoyed wide theatrical distribution after winning the *Palme d'Or* in 2013—in addition to touring the festival circuit—and has achieved good box-office results.[7] In other words, symbolic capital can be converted into economic capital. In this particular example there are two vital ingredients driving the success. Clearly, the Cannes award had a major impact, but the buzz of winning the world's most prestigious accolade was amplified by various "scandal" discussions in the press that covered the film's taboo-breaking topic and aesthetics—in particular the explicit lesbian sex scenes—and the publicly fought-out clash between the director and one of the film's leading actresses. It seems fair to say that festival acclaim nowadays is a prerequisite for art cinema distribution. One only has to sample some art houses and look at the promotional posters to see how central film festivals have become to contemporary art house programming. Virtually each and every poster will feature one or several festival logos, highlighting the film's selection for a prestigious competition and/or the festival prizes won. An empirical study by Stephan Mezias and colleagues notably shows that the impact varies depending on the festival and nomination. Studying the top three European film festivals, they found that best picture films generate a larger increase in audience attendance than other nominations, and films nominated at Cannes receive a much greater increase than those nominated in Berlin and Venice (Mezias et al. 2011: 193). However, most film festivals do not offer a way into theatrical exhibition at all, and neither do they offer opportunities to cross over into the mainstream. In other words, many films screened at festivals have no circulation outside the festival world.

Third, we may ask, does the capital conversion also work the other way round? Can economic capital be translated into symbolic value? The historical relations between Hollywood and festivals show that, although strained, the collaboration is mutually beneficial (Jungen 2014). While it is true that Hollywood does not need the prestige of festival selection—they rely on marketing and sales practices instead—and typically the big companies shy away from participation in official programs to avoid the critical press that comes with festival competitions, blockbusters are often screened as an out-of-competition festival event, using festivals' momentum and gathered press corps for promotional aims. This way, Hollywood product may take advantage of festivals' prestigious atmosphere, which can render some standing and a sense of exclusivity to the next entertainment vehicle without actually engaging in the tricky process of cultural legitimization. Among the big Hollywood productions that had their world premieres in Cannes as out-of-competition events are: *Mad Max: Fury Road* (2015), *The Great Gatsby* (2013), *Madagascar 3: Europe's Most Wanted* (2012), *Pirates of the Caribbean: On Stranger Tides* (2011), and *Wall Street: Money Never Sleeps* (2010). Festivals, in their turn, profit from such arrangements as well; the launch of one of Hollywood's potential seasonal blockbuster hits guarantees media attention. Moreover, the Hollywood stars that travel to festivals to promote their film add glamour. The quintessential red carpet ritual would be less significant if the celebrities from the realms of entertainment and popular culture would not share the privilege of mounting the stairs with competition participants and future laureates.

Habitus

With Bourdieu's concept of symbolic capital we were able to frame (certain) festivals as important sites of cultural legitimization and show how they function as gatekeepers in the field of cultural production. However, festivals not only act as gatekeepers, but as tastemakers, and it is Bourdieu's notion of habitus that is particularly well suited to explain the dynamics behind tastemaking and festivals. The concept of habitus encompasses the way socialized norms influence individuals' behavior and thinking. Bourdieu can be seen as a constructionist–structuralist; not only does he pay attention to objective social structures, he distinguishes schemata or incorporated structures (thoughts, feelings, actions) that people have about these structures and which are used to shape and sustain them. Habitus then refers to the largely unconscious functioning of systems, rules, categories, laws, and values in society. What people believe to be common sense, the natural or necessary order and proceeding of things, is in fact a largely arbitrary set of arrangements held up by the beliefs and practices of people.

Jen Webb, Tony Schirato, and Geoff Danaher underline the relevance of the concept for understanding the behavior of artists:

> Habitus is important in making sense of what artists do and how they understand themselves and their field, because artists compete for, and take up, positions on the basis of two important structures: the *objective* structures (the field and its institutions) which make positions available; and the *incorporated* structures (the habitus), which predisposes individuals to enter the field.
>
> (Webb et al. 2002: 173)

How do film festivals influence the behavior of filmmakers? Following Bourdieu, there are two structuring logics that together determine which positions are available to filmmakers. For circuits outside the mainstream film industries, film festivals occupy nodal roles in both instances, as gatekeepers and as tastemakers. Festivals' gatekeeping function refers to the *objective* structures; filmmakers have to "pass" festivals in order to find exposure (exhibition opportunities), recognition (assessed as worthy enough to be shown), and ideally also prestige (selection for esteemed programs, prizes, or other honors). As tastemakers, film festivals are in addition part of the *incorporated* structures that contribute to upholding the belief in art cinema's autonomous values and thus to continuous production and reproduction of the "game" of art cinema (Bourdieu 1993: 167). Festivals, using Bourdieu's words, "ensure the reproduction of agents imbued with the categories of action, expression, conception, imagination, perception, specific to the 'cultivated disposition'" (Bourdieu 1996: 121).

In his study of the Edinburgh Fringe Festival (the renowned international theater festival), Wesley Shrum argues that "taste in high arts is mediated by experts, whereas taste in low art is not" (1996: 40). Building on Bourdieu's theory of distinction and the class dimensions of questions of taste (Bourdieu 1984), Shrum emphasizes the role of experts in the field of restricted cultural production. Its system of symbolic consecration is supported by a system of education and semi-institutional circles that hold authority positions. Examples are museums, galleries, literary magazines, and also film festivals. Because of the work of film festivals,[8] certain aesthetic dispositions regarding cinema are continuously confirmed, and thus filmmakers are predisposed to produce films *in* certain traditions and *for* the festival exhibition circuit. Moreover, at festivals audiences are incessantly stimulated to appreciate cinema as art form and develop more refined film preferences than are associated with mainstream commercial cinema. This is particularly relevant for young people. Festivals thus are in Bourdieu's words part of "a system for reproducing the producers of a determinate type of cultural goods, and the consumer capable of consuming them" (Bourdieu 1996: 121). Film festivals do so by cultivating certain tastes.

A good example of a filmmaker with a clear festival flavor and career is Apichatpong Weerasethakul.[9] Weerasethakul premiered with his debut feature *Dokfa nai meuman/Mysterious Object at Noon*—a semi-documentary in which different Thai citizens contribute to a chain story—at the International Film Festival Rotterdam in January 2000. The film had its North American premier at the Vancouver International Film Festival in October of the same year, where it won a special citation Dragons and Tigers Award. It subsequently embarked on a packed festival tour, collecting a number of other awards on its way.[10] After this successful debut, Weerasethakul continued to build his reputation at international film festivals with a distinct voice and original style. In 2002 Weerasethakul received the *Prix Un Certain Regard* in Cannes for *Sud sanaeha/Blissfully Yours*. He officially entered the ranks of established filmmakers with his third feature, *Sud pralad/Tropical Malady*, which was selected for the Cannes competition in 2004. Despite initial poor reviews in the trade papers, the film was honored with the Jury Prize, and the filmmaker has enjoyed a steady favorable reception in the global press since. *Sang sattawat/Syndromes and a Century* (2006) premiered in Venice. In 2010, Weerasethakul reached the zenith of festival acclaim with a *Palme d'Or* for *Loong Boonmee raleuk chat/Uncle Boonmee Who Can Recall His Past Lives*. In 2012 he returned to the Cannes competition with *Mekong Hotel*.

When Weerasethakul won the *Palme d'Or* he was the first Asian filmmaker since 1997 and the first Thai filmmaker ever to receive this honor. With his previous feature films Weerasethakul had acquired a strong cinephile following on the international film festival circuit, who appreciated the way his work was rooted in Thai regional culture and interlaced its loose stories with autobiographical components and gently exposed political sensibilities. Above all, film critics have praised his idiosyncratic film style. "Dreamlike" is one of the adjectives most often chosen to describe the sensation of watching Weerasethakul's films (Sicinski 2011: 27). While his slowly paced and associative films can pose a challenge, even to cine-literate viewers, and the pronunciation of his name is notoriously difficult, Apichatpong's public performances disclose a tight match with the in-crowd of the global art cinema scene. During these appearances Weerasethakul is knowledgeable, eloquent, and very funny. While his protagonists may dwell deep in the forests of peripheral Thailand where they encounter ghosts and enchanted animals, the director is clearly at home in the cosmopolitan world of international cinema. As an American art school graduate,[11] who refers to Federico Fellini, Jean-Luc Godard, Francis Ford Coppola, Manoel de Oliveira, and Maya Deren as his inspiration (Weerasethakul 2011: 27), Weerasethakul shares a certain cinephilic disposition with the professionals of the festival circuit.

Weerasethakul's Western education is not immediately apparent when watching his work. His distinct film style is not reminiscent of Western traditions, and his artistic choices, such as the emphasis on rural Thai settings and quiet protagonists, seem to forecast peripheral reception. When one looks closer, however, the Thai director is manifested as someone astutely aware of contemporary art cinema norms and festival practices. His unique style and artisanal film practice beckon a reading in terms of creative authorship that fits the art for art's sake ideology like a glove. And Weerasethakul fulfills the role of disinterested or naïve artist perfectly in his public appearances. On the occasion of the first Busan Cinema Forum, for example, he jokes about his initial ignorance of production matters.

> Working in 35mm pushed me to work with more crew and link us to the commercial facilities in Thailand. First I called the camera rental company. A receptionist asked what company I was calling from. I said I called from myself. She was confused and we had an awkward discussion. I understood then that I had to have a company to establish an account, to have a discount, to deal with tax issues, and so on. So I started a company, registered it under my name, followed by the names of my sister, my brother, and my mom.
>
> (Weerasethakul 2011: 31)

Weerasethakul moreover seems to have fully grasped that as a Thai film artist, his best chances for funding and exposure are to be found through the international film festival circuit. On this circuit there is strong interest in world cinema, original voices, and topical issues, interests that Weerasethakul's oeuvre meets. As Bill Nichols argued, festival audiences are attracted to discovering unfamiliar countries through cinema. "An encounter with the unfamiliar, the experience of something strange, the discovery of new voices and visions serve as a major incitement for the festival-goer," he writes (Nichols 1994: 17). With this in mind, Weerasethakul's preference for Northern Thai forests fits the taste of global festival audiences better than if he had used the well-known imagery of Southern beaches; the unknown seems more authentic and is more exciting for an audience craving the unfamiliar. In a similar vein, Weerasethakul's use of enchanted animals and ghosts solicits reflection on the cultural meaning of such imaginary, while also functioning as an authorial signature. In addition to reading along the lines of world cinema and auteur cinema, the films address issues with sociopolitical relevance, and the homoerotic elements resonate particularly well with progressive festival publics.

This is not to say that Weerasethakul's films are very popular. Although he has received widespread critical acclaim[12] and has a dedicated cinephile following on the festival circuit, to appreciate his work, one needs to be well-versed in art cinema aesthetics. It is crucial to note that this is exactly the tool that festivals offer; they foster cinephilia and nurture the appreciation of a certain art cinema tradition. To repeat Bourdieu's formulation: festivals produce the consumers capable of consuming these cultural goods, by cultivating the tastes of festival visitors and providing them with frameworks for understanding unfamiliar works. The significance of the festival setting in finding audiences for the more difficult, obscure, peripheral, and divergent films is apparent when we observe that even with prestigious accolades, Weerasethakul's films unfortunately have not performed very well in other exhibition venues.

Summary

In this chapter I have worked with Bourdieu's concepts of field, capital, and habitus to shed light on the foundation and dynamics of film festivals as particular exhibition sites. We have seen how film festivals were established in response to Hollywood's domination of European cinemas, and where their commitment to foster film as art originates. We elaborated on the ways in which festivals can add value, and function as influential sites of cultural legitimization. To the function of gatekeeper, finally, we added the role of tastemaker, to indicate festivals' contribution to a certain cultivated disposition that produces and reproduces both the filmmakers creating the films screened on the festival circuit and the audiences flocking to festivals to watch them.

Bourdieuian approaches can generate valuable knowledge and perspectives on film festivals. They are particularly useful for studies that seek to explain why festivals matter, and may serve to ground festivals' functioning in the larger context of the arts world. Bourdieu can also be a starting point to explore how (part of) the festival circuit interrelates with commercial filmmaking, the field of large-scale production. He has been criticized, though, for neglecting the rise of the cultural industries (Hesmondhalgh 2006: 217), and theoretically such studies would benefit from combination with other research traditions. Considering the diversity within the festival world, each research project ought to start with an assessment of the particular position and context of the festival(s) under scrutiny. Even if a festival is not a gatekeeper or tastemaker, and its prizes do not generate substantial symbolic capital, Bourdieu's understanding of (power) relations and principles in the cultural field can offer a frame to start and analyze that festival's specific dynamics.

To end this piece two remarks must be made. First, Bourdieu's work is extremely rich and his writing notoriously complicated. Here I have merely scratched the surface of his legacy. For more comprehensive accounts of his complex theory of practice I refer to the suggested readings, which include two of Bourdieu's books and some excellent introductions and anthologies that have been published. Second, Bourdieu's conception of agency and structures is dynamic. Therefore, although the social dynamics and principles described in this chapter certainly have firm grounding in recent and present society, they are not immune to change. Particularly significant seems to be how in recent years the festival scene has witnessed a growing concern with monetary matters. Screening fees have become more common, for example, and a substantial number of new festivals have begun awarding cash prizes.[13] For the moment it seems the most important festivals still rely on the prestige of their prizes, and festivals that lure directors and producers with money are taken less seriously as recognition of aesthetic accomplishment. The encroachment of symbolic capital's autonomy at festivals is pronounced though, and bears further scrutiny in the coming years, for it might demand a change in the theoretical frames we bring to bear on film festivals-as-exhibition sites.

Notes

1 Bourdieu further divides the autonomous pole into the avant-garde—committed to experimentation—and the conventional—also referred to as authorized, bourgeois or consecrated—based on current conventions. At the heteronomous pole he distinguishes between the popular—aiming to please a predefined (mass) audience—and the commercial—striving to maximize economic profit. Neither of these positions, however, is stable. What is an avant-garde piece of art at one point in time can acquire commercial value later. Think for example of the Impressionist paintings used as iconic images on merchandise for sale in museum stores today.

2 A well-known example of such struggle is the auteurist turn in film criticism in the 1950s and 1960s. Originating in France and associated with the *Nouvelle Vague* film critics writing for *Cahiers du Cinema*, this new approach distinguished quality on the basis of a director's personal vision and style. Notably, Hollywood directors were able to assert such personal vision and style, despite working within the constraints of an entertainment industry.

3 For a study of the legitimation of film as art form in the United States, also see Bauman (2001).

4 It must be noted that the rebellion in nineteenth-century France was not only against bourgeois art, but also to "realist" or social art, which opposed bourgeois art as well. What counts as avant-garde or pure artistic taste, however, is a dynamic development. Both realism and sociopolitical engagement are included as valued aesthetic approaches in various (high) art forms in later periods.

5 This may be different for certain small independent films that can reach more audiences through (specialized) festival circuits than with a limited theatrical release.

6 See for example Forbes annual overview of Hollywood's top paid actors and actresses. For summer 2013: www.forbes.com/sites/dorothypomerantz/2013/07/16/robert-downey-jr-tops-forbes-list-of-hollywoods-highest-paid-actors/ and www.forbes.com/sites/dorothypomerantz/2013/07/29/angelina-jolie-tops-our-list-of-hollywoods-highest-paid-actresses/ (March 21, 2014).

7 For information on box-office results, both domestic and worldwide grosses, see Box Office Mojo www.boxofficemojo.com/movies/?page=main&id=bluewarm.htm (March 21, 2014).

8 Film festivals are among the institutional and semi-institutional circles fostering and promoting art cinema. Film criticism in newspapers, magazines, and blogs also plays a role, as well as film archives and art houses.

9 In addition to his film productions, Weerasethakul also makes media art installations.

10 *Mysterious Object at Noon* won the Grand Prize (Woosuk Award) at the Jeonju International Film Festival, second prize and the NETPAC, Special Mention Prize at the Yamagata International Documentary Film Festival. The film was screened at many other film festivals, including the London Film Festival, the Singapore International Film Festival, and the Hong Kong International Film Festival. Source: www.kickthemachine.com/works/misterios_object_at_noon.html (March 21, 2014).

11 Weerasethakul has a master's degree in fine arts (filmmaking) from the School of the Art Institute of Chicago from 1997.

12 In a poll about the best films of the past decade (2010) among 60 well-known curators, historians, festival programmers, and archivists by TIFF Cinematheque curator James Quandt Weerasethakul's *Syndromes and a Century* came out on top. *Tropical Malady* ranked sixth, *Blissfully Yours* thirteenth. See https://web.archive.org/web/20131219010622/http://blogs.indiewire.com/thelostboy/tiff_cinematheque_names_best_of_decade (November 3, 2015).

13 Examples are the Abu Dhabi International Film Festival, Dubai International Film Festival, and the Tribeca Film Festival.

References

Abel, R. (1994) *The Ciné Goes to Town: French Cinema, 1896–1914*, Berkeley and Los Angeles, CA: University of California Press.

Bauman, S. (2001) "Intellectualization and Art World Development: Film in the United States," *American Sociological Review*, 66(3), pp. 404–426.

Bourdieu, P. (1984 [1979]) *Distinction: A Social Critique of the Judgment of Taste*, trans. R. Nice, Cambridge, MA: Harvard University Press.

Bourdieu, P. (1986) "The Forms of Capital," in J. Richardson (ed.) *Handbook of Theory and Research for the Sociology of Education*, New York: Greenwood, pp. 241–258.

Bourdieu, P. (1990) *The Logic of Practice*, Cambridge: Polity Press.

Bourdieu, P. (1993) *The Field of Cultural Production: Essays on Art and Literature*, ed. R. Johnson, Cambridge: Polity Press.

Bourdicu, P. (1996 [1992]) *The Rules of Art: Genesis and Structure of the Literary Field*, trans. S. Emanuel, Stanford, CA: Stanford University Press.

Bourdieu, P. and L. L. D. Wacquant (1992) *An Invitation to Reflexive Sociology*, Chicago, IL: University of Chicago Press.

Crafton, D. (1999) *The Talkies: American Cinema's Transition to Sound, 1926–1931*, Berkeley, CA: University of California Press.

Craig. A. and S. Dubois (2010) "Between Art and Money: The Social Space of Public Readings in Contemporary Poetry Economics and Careers," *Poetics*, 38, pp. 441–460.

Czach, L. (2004) "Film Festivals, Programming, and the Building of a National Cinema," *The Moving Image*, 4(1), pp. 76–88.

De Grazia, V. (1989) "Mass Culture and Sovereignty: The American Challenge to European Cinemas, 1920–1960," *The Journal of Modern History*, 61 (March), pp. 53–87.

De Valck, M. (2007) *Film Festivals. From European Geopolitics to Global Cinephilia.* Amsterdam: Amsterdam University Press.

De Valck, M. (2014a) "Film Festivals, Bourdieu, and the Economization of Culture," *Canadian Journal of Film Studies*, 23(1), pp. 74–89.

De Valck, M. (2014b) "Supporting Art Cinema at a Time of Commercialization: Principles and Practices, the Case of the International Film Festival Rotterdam," *Poetics*, 42, pp. 40–59.

De Valck, M. and M. Soeteman (2010) "'And the Winner is…': What Happens Behind the Scenes of Film Festival Competitions," *International Journal of Cultural Studies*, 13(3), pp. 290–307.

Elsaesser, T. (2005) "Film Festival Networks: The New Topographies of Cinema in Europe," in *European Cinema: Face to Face With Hollywood*, Amsterdam: Amsterdam University Press, pp. 82–107.

English, J. (2008) *The Economy of Prestige: Prizes, Awards and the Circulation of Cultural Value*, Cambridge, MA: Harvard University Press.

Fehrenbach, H. (1995) "Mass Culture and Cold War Politics: The Berlin Film Festival of the 1950s," in *Cinema in Democratizing Germany: Reconstructing National Identity after Hitler*, Chapel Hill, NC and London: University of North Carolina Press, pp. 234–259.

Gunning, T. (1994) *D. W. Griffith and the Origins of American Narrative Film: The Early Years at Biograph*, Chicago, IL: University of Illinois Press.

Hesmondhalgh, D. (2006) "Bourdieu, the Media and Cultural Production," *Media, Culture & Society*, 28, pp. 211–231.

Jungen, C. (2014) *Hollywood in Cannes: The History of a Love-Hate Relationship*, Amsterdam: Amsterdam University Press.

Mezias, S. J. Strandgaard Pedersen, J.-H. Kim, S. Svejenova, and C. Mazza (2011) "Transforming Film Product Identities: the Status Effects of European Premier Film Festivals, 1996–2005," in B. Moeran and J. Strandgaard Pederson (eds.) *Negotiating Values in the Creative Industries: Fairs, Festivals and Competitive Events*, Cambridge: Cambridge University Press, pp. 169–196.

Moine, C. (2012) "Festivals de cinéma et politiques culturelles dans l'Europe de la guerre froide: diversité des enjeux et des acteurs," *Territoires contemporains*, 3, http://tristan.u-bourgogne.fr/CGC/publications/Festivals_societes/C_Moine.html (November 3, 2015).

Nichols, B. (1994) "Discovering Form, Inferring Meaning: New Cinemas and the Film Festival Circuit," *Film Quarterly*, 47(3), pp. 16–30.

Peranson, M. (2008) "First You Get the Power, Then You Get the Money: Two Models of Film Festivals," *Cineaste*, 33(3), pp. 37–43.

Perren, A. (2001/2002) "Sex, Lies and Marketing: Miramax and the Development of the Quality Indie Blockbuster," *Film Quarterly*, 5(2), pp. 30–39.

Shrum, W., Jr. (1996) *Fringe and Fortune: The Role of Critics in High and Popular Art*, Princeton, NJ: Princeton University Press.

Sicinski, M. (2011) "Dreaming in Cinema: Capturing the Imagination of Apichat-pong Weerasethakul," *Cineaste*, 26(2), pp. 26–29.

Webb, J., T. Schirato, and G. Danaher (2002) *Understanding Bourdieu*, Los Angeles, CA: Sage.

Weerasethakul, A. (2011) "Superabundance," in Y.-K. Lee (ed.) *Conference Proceedings of Busan Cinema Forum: Seeking the Path of Asian Cinema: East Asia*, Busan: Busan International Film Festival, pp. 30–35.

Further reading

Bourdieu, P. (1990) *In Other Words: Essays Towards a Reflexive Sociology*, trans. M. Adamson, Stanford, CA: Stanford University Press. (In this collection of lectures and interviews Bourdieu answers frequent questions about his work and explains its principles and main results. Originally published in 1987.)

Bourdieu, P. (1998) *Practical Reason: On the Theory of Action*, Stanford, CA: Stanford University Press. (With an emphasis on class, cultural capital, time, power, and morality this collection of conference presentations tackles some of Bourdieu's main findings. Originally published in 1994.)

Brubaker, R. (1985) "Rethinking Classical Theory: The Sociological Vision of Pierre Bourdieu," *Theory and Sociology*, 14, pp. 745–775. (Early article that positions the work of Bourdieu within classic social theories.)

Swartz, D. (1998) *Culture and Power: The Sociology of Pierre Bourdieu*, Chicago, IL: University of Chicago Press. (Solid introduction to the work of Bourdieu that does a good job explaining his complex theories to readers unfamiliar with his work. Focuses on questions of culture and power.)

Wacquant, L. (2006) "Pierre Bourdieu," in R. Stones (ed.) *Key Sociological Thinkers*, London: Palgrave Macmillan, pp. 215–229. (Concise and general overview of the life and work of Bourdieu. Originally published in 1998.)

Part III
Method

Introduction

Skadi Loist

Like any form of media research, film festival studies is topic-driven, and the approach taken entirely depends on the given research question. As we have seen in the previous part, the complexity of the festival world has led to a highly interdisciplinary arsenal of theories being employed in festival studies. Methodological approaches also draw on a number of various disciplines and research schools, even though they have seldom been as explicitly discussed as their theoretical companions: they range from participant observation and (auto)ethnography to qualitative methods such as textual and discourse analysis, and interviewing in media industries research, to quantitative data gathering and statistical analysis in management. The three chapters in this part turn to explicitly engage the question of method and methodology, while approaching them from different angles.

One of the main determinants for the methodological approach being taken is the historical horizon of the research question. Researchers interested in the contemporary workings of the festival circuit have the clear advantage of potentially being able to collect material and data directly during the festival. Historical research questions, on the other hand, are to a large degree framed by the materials that are available in archives. Depending on the status and organizational context of the festivals, it differs greatly what kind of records—festival catalogs; organizational, legal, and fiscal records; submissions; films; and festival ephemera—are kept and to whom they are accessible (Barnes 2016). Ger Zielinski discusses these problems of archival research for film festival studies in his chapter in this section. By using the example of LGBT/Q film festivals, he adds another layer of potential contextual problems that come with changing politics and histories of community-based activist events.

In Chapter 7, Toby Lee turns to contemporary festival research and describes the classic ethnographic approach of going into the field and doing participant observation. Drawing on her own fieldwork at the Thessaloniki International Film Festival, she describes what it means to immerse herself in the festival context, following spontaneous and intuitive connections rather than a purely functional route of prescribed festival tasks. This account also reminds us that film festivals cannot be divorced from their spatial, temporal, and cultural contexts.

In the last chapter of this part, Diane Burgess and Brendan Kredell delve into a conversation about how best to tackle the complexities of film festival research without falling into binary traps. Instead of upholding an arbitrary theory versus practice binary, or an insider/outsider divide that seems to collapse easily in the light of multiple positionings of actors on either side of the divide, one could instead try "surfing binarisms," as Tom Boellstorff has called it (2010: 222). Thus Burgess and Kredell emphasize the importance of a nuanced research approach, which includes a careful reflection on positionality. Similar sentiments have been discussed in media industry studies and production studies, which also pay close attention to the self-reflexive discourses of those industries (Caldwell 2009; Loist 2016).

These discussions on positionality within knowledge production of such an interdisciplinary and global field as film festival studies also remind us to not only consider the researcher's status in relation to the festival industry but also within language and taste cultures. Linguistic barriers hindering individual researchers in comparative and transnational research can for instance be compensated by collaborative projects. The proximity of the researcher to their research object also plays a role in relation to activist, ethnic, and identity-based film festivals and their communities. As becomes obvious in Lee's case study, the situated knowledge of the researcher vis-à-vis the political and community contexts needs to extend to particular political, activist, and aesthetic languages in order to avoid rash, simplistic generalizations.

Last but not least, a slow move in film festival studies toward quantitative data analysis should be mentioned. While most of the existing festival research employs qualitative, textual, ethnographic, and archival methods, there is a discernible tendency toward quantitative methods in recent years. Qualitative methods are very useful for nuanced discussions and the drive to theorize larger mechanisms. Questions relating to audience research or the business side of global film circulation within festival studies, however, benefit from quantitative data. Yet, as the festival circuit is an unwieldy field of diverging interest groups without coherent regulation, hard data are very hard to come by. Thus, studies collecting and analyzing quantitative data are only beginning to appear.

References

Barnes, H. L. (2016) "The Data-Driven Festival: Recordkeeping and Archival Practices," in A. Vallejo (ed.) *Documentary Film Festivals: History, Politics, Industry*, New York: Columbia University Press, in press.

Boellstorff, T. (2010) "Queer Techne: Two Theses on Methodology and Queer Studies," in K. Browne and C. J. Nash (eds.) *Queer Methods and Methodologies: Intersecting Queer Theories and Social Science Research*, Burlington, VT: Ashgate, pp. 215–230.

Caldwell, J. T. (2009) "Cultures of Production: Studying Industry's Deep Texts, Reflexive Rituals, and Managed Self-Disclosures," in J. Holt and A. Perren (eds.)

Media Industries: History, Theory, and Method, Chichester: Wiley-Blackwell, pp. 199–212.

Loist, S. (2016) "Film Festival Research Workshops: Debates on Methodology," in A. Vallejo (ed.) *Documentary Film Festivals: History, Politics, Industry*, New York: Columbia University Press, in press.

7 Being there, taking place

Ethnography at the film festival

Toby Lee

In a 1994 essay on the emergence of new Iranian cinema on the international film festival circuit, Bill Nichols observes that, as festival-goers, we learn to digest new, foreign cinema by reading it in terms of the norms and conventions of the international film festival. By discerning in it the patterns and formal elements that we have grown accustomed to seeing in the context of international festivals, we make the foreign familiar by—paradoxically— plucking it from its local context and inducting it into our global network. However, Nichols ends his essay by pointing to the inadequacy of such familiarization or knowledge, warning that:

> [b]eyond it lie those complex forms of local knowledge that we have willingly exchanged for the opportunity to elect Iranian cinema to the ranks of the international art film circuit. Hovering, like a specter, at the boundaries of the festival experience, are those deep structures and thick descriptions that might restore a sense of the particular and local to what we have now recruited to the realm of the global.
>
> (Nichols 1994: 27)

While Nichols was writing about the process of watching and understanding a film, his observations could easily be applied to the process of researching and understanding a film festival. Since the emergence of film festival studies, a dominant concern within this field of research has been to examine the festival in terms of "the realm of the global," i.e., to focus on the participation of festivals in larger networks of media, people, ideas, and capital (Stringer 2001; Elsaesser 2005; De Valck 2007; Iordanova and Rhyne 2009), and methodologically this has meant an emphasis on systemic approaches to the global festival circuit. As a counterpoint to this tendency, this chapter explores how we might access the "deep structures and thick descriptions" that surround and give meaning to a festival, in order to get "a sense of the particular and the local," and to understand how the festival is actually experienced, on the ground and in real time. In particular, I use my own ethnographic research on the Thessaloniki International Film Festival as an example, to see how the methodological tools of anthropology—ethnographic fieldwork, participant observation, and sustained engagement on a smaller scale—might allow for a better understanding not only of film festivals as culturally, politically, and economically embedded social experiences, but also of the larger transnational networks in which they participate.[1]

Ethnography: definitions and practices

Nichols' use of the term "thick description" is a direct reference to anthropologist Clifford Geertz, whose original articulation of this concept is helpful in clarifying the contours of ethnography as a methodology, which admittedly can be hard to pin down. As any anthropologist would readily attest, ethnographic fieldwork often resembles an ad hoc process, with the researcher improvising on-the-spot responses to unexpected circumstances and tricky interactions—playing different social roles as needed, listening to whoever is willing to talk, following one lead to the next, and trying to piece together a coherent picture out of what seem to be loose threads and dead ends. In trying to formulate a working definition of ethnographic fieldwork out of this hodgepodge of practices, I turn to Geertz' seminal discussion of ethnography and its epistemic parameters:

> From one point of view, that of the textbook, doing ethnography is establishing rapport, selecting informants, transcribing texts, taking genealogies, mapping fields, keeping a diary, and so on. But it is not these things, techniques and received procedures, that define the enterprise. What defines it is the kind of intellectual effort it is: an elaborate venture in [...] thick description.
>
> (Geertz 1973: 6)

By "thick description," Geertz means the act of illuminating the countless "webs of significance" (ibid.: 5) that connect social actors to each other and that allow any social object or action to take on shared meaning among them. Whatever the object of research—be it a particular practice, a ritual, or an entire film festival—Geertz states that the job of the ethnographer is to try and understand the various contextual "webs" that shape how that object is perceived and experienced. Some examples of such "webs" might be shared cultural heritage, social conventions, political histories, economic structures, transnational networks, hierarchies of value, or ideologies. Ethnography as an endeavor aims to shed light on these contexts or frames that structure social and cultural significance.

For Geertz, this is only possible through a process that he describes as "microscopic" (ibid.: 21). In his understanding, the ethnographer does not take on these larger "webs of significance" from the top down, but rather by approaching such broader structures "from the direction of exceedingly extended acquaintances with extremely small matters" (ibid.). In other words, ethnography is humble work: spending significant amounts of time in a place, with a people, doing what can often seem to be rather insignificant. Sharing a coffee or a meal, making small talk, observing everyday tasks, participating in menial work, common practices, routines—such "microscopic" practices often constitute the day-to-day work of the ethnographer, what Geertz refers to as "deep hanging out" (Geertz 1998, 2001). For most anthropologists, it is only through such extended engagement on the level of the everyday that we are able to understand the diverse ways in which larger structures or networks are actually taken up, resisted, or otherwise put to use in lived experience.

In my ethnographic research on the Thessaloniki International Film Festival, as both an annual event and a cultural institution functioning year-round, I largely took the approach of "deep hanging out." Over 22 months between 2005 and 2010, my primary methodology was sustained participant observation. For this, I occupied a number of different roles: as a volunteer assisting in various departments during the ten days of the festival each November, a volunteer researcher or coordinator for various festival programs and publications, an audience member and festival-goer, a filmmaker and dilettante programmer, and sometimes as simply an anthropologist-observer, gratefully tagging along or sitting in on meetings and trying my best not to appear too out of place. Occupying these various roles gave me the opportunity not only to observe the festival from within, but also to experience firsthand some of the many different publics addressed by the festival, by being a part of them. This pushes against a tendency within film festival studies to focus on the discourse produced by or around the festival, or on larger festival structures, programming, or the festival circuit, which runs the risk of relying too heavily on institutional rhetoric or the declarations of festival directors, programmers, and critics. The methodology of year-round participant observation allowed me a closer look at the complex and meaningful micro-interactions that take place within the wider social space of the festival, and it also helped to create a sense of social familiarity that facilitated more intimate conversations with fieldwork subjects, which I supplemented with formal interviews.

The main portion of my fieldwork (2008–2010) was greatly shaped by a decision I made early on concerning the direction of my research. Having started by spending time in the festival's main offices in Athens, I quickly realized that I was less interested in what would usually be considered the "center" of the institution—the offices, the core staff, the work of the festival director, programming decisions—and more interested in what might be considered its "periphery," where the festival interacts with other institutions, businesses, and individuals, and with its public. At the festival headquarters in Athens, much of the activity resembled that of any other film festival: watching screeners of films, reviewing other festival programs, contacting filmmakers or sales agents, writing press releases. In late 2008, in the context of the economic, social, and political crises that were beginning to unfold in Greece at the time, the goings-on inside the festival offices seemed of less relevance than how the festival was functioning in a broader social and cultural field. Thus a large part of my research focused on the relationship between the festival and other players in this field, such as the Ministry of Culture, the Greek Film Center, other film festivals in Greece, filmmakers, distribution companies, local businesses, the Thessaloniki Cine Club, the Film Department at the Aristotle University of Thessaloniki, and cultural initiatives and programs in Thessaloniki, both public and private. I spent a great deal of time away from the festival itself, sitting in on meetings; hanging out and chatting with people in their offices, over coffee, or in their homes; attending screenings, press conferences, protests, and other events.

As I developed close relationships over time with people in the field, learning about their deeply personal ties to the festival, the dynamic between individual and institution also became an important part of my research. People's personal histories of involvement with the festival, their loyalties, and their professional, political, and emotional investments all put flesh on the bones of institutional structures. This is tricky terrain, where the personal and the political are mapped onto each other, and in learning to navigate it, I not only became acutely aware of the intensely political nature of social life in Greece, but also had to become a political being myself, carefully considering my alignments, how they might be perceived, and what doors would open or close accordingly. Although my position as a foreign academic afforded me some neutrality, there were still moments when my inquiries were met with silence or politely declined; in some cases, these silences were telling in and of themselves, and I learned to listen for them and to incorporate them, when possible, in my analyses. As an academic, I also shared a connection with the considerable number of scholars who work in or around the festival, and an important part of my fieldwork comprised long conversations with these fieldwork subjects, colleagues, and friends.

In contrast to research that focuses primarily on organizational structures, programming patterns, or institutional discourse, this more intimate and "microscopic" ethnographic research yields a different kind of knowledge of the festival, as it is actually lived and experienced by individuals. In addition, fieldwork requires the researcher to be deeply embedded in the complex and constantly shifting social and cultural contexts that constitute her "field," in which the festival itself is embedded. For this reason, ethnographic research allows a real-time understanding of how festivals themselves shift in response to changing contexts, and sometimes in unexpected ways, as I quickly learned in the case of the Thessaloniki festival.

Unexpected encounters, significant webs

During my time in the field, I also spent a great deal of time with people and in places that initially seemed to have no direct relationship to the film festival at all but that, in retrospect, I can see as having helped build a foundation for making sense of the specific contexts in which the festival takes on "particular" and "local" meaning. These contexts—social, political, economic—constitute the "webs of significance" that Geertz understands as shaping or framing our perceptions and experiences of an object, an event, or a practice. These "webs" can seem countless, often entangled, and it is not always clear to the ethnographer which are most relevant to her research. We begin with a certain set of assumptions about how best to frame or contextualize our object of study, but often we end up in a very different place. In an essay on the ethnographic process, Ruth Behar discusses this aspect of ethnographic fieldwork, characterizing it as an exercise in the unexpected. Recounting how she first came to ethnography, she writes:

> I was seduced by the notion of fieldwork, the idea of going some place to find a story I wasn't looking for. Of course, ethnographic journeys are always taken with the knowledge that the "field" has already been theorized by precursors of various sorts. But the beauty and mystery of the ethnographer's quest is to find the unexpected stories, the stories that challenge our theories [...]. We go to find the stories we didn't know we were looking for in the first place.
>
> (Behar 2003: 16)

Behar's description of the ethnographic journey, as encounters with the unexpected in a theorized terrain, is an apt description for my own experience in the field. When I started my research on the Thessaloniki festival, I assumed that the most important "webs" for me to explore were the global circuit of international film festivals, transnational media economies, and practices of cosmopolitanism, since these seemed to provide the main contexts in which film festivals were being understood at the time. However, not long after I began the main portion of my fieldwork, the unexpected erupted, drastically changing the context of my research.

On the evening of December 6, 2008, a few months after I had arrived in Greece, a 15-year-old boy was shot and killed by police gunfire in a central neighborhood of Athens. What ensued was an unprecedented explosion of public protest and collective rage. For weeks following the shooting, the streets of Athens and cities across the country were filled with thousands of protesters marching against the shooting. While some of the protests were peaceful, many ended in rioting and violence, with vandalism of both public and private property, hundreds of arrests, and bloody clashes between protesters and riot police. State buildings and police stations were firebombed, cars and dumpsters burned in the streets, and the government struggled to keep the situation in check, eventually being ousted in emergency elections.

While the police shooting of an innocent teenage boy is tragic and unjust, clearly it was not in and of itself the sole reason behind such civil unrest and destruction. As the protests continued and grew in intensity, it soon became clear that the shooting had a larger social significance, beyond the problem of police brutality. The incident also unleashed underlying social frustrations that had been building up over years as a response to government financial scandals, rampant clientelism, and what was generally acknowledged to be a much larger culture of corruption and lack of transparency that characterized the Greek state. There was also a simmering dissatisfaction, particularly among younger generations, with a lack of earning power and the growing sense of limited professional horizons—early indications of the economic crisis that would soon overwhelm the country. This financial and professional uncertainty, together with the entrenched corruption in the public sector, had led to an underlying sense of frustration with and distrust of the state, which was seen as having abused the country's finances for the benefit of the elite few, and in the process having failed to provide for its citizens' economic and social welfare. The shooting of the teenage boy was a lit match in this larger tinderbox of social discontent, which exploded in public expressions of collective fury.

Of course, Greece is no stranger to protest. In a country where political graffiti is ubiquitous, and where national holidays mark historical dates of uprising and resistance, public protest can be so common as to sometimes seem commonplace. But the sustained unrest of 2008 and 2009 was different. It felt unusual in its ferocity, but more importantly, in the kinds of public discourse that grew around and from it. The marches, occupations, and riots were accompanied by an ever-growing discourse that aimed at collective action and fundamental change in the political and social status quo. In the months following the shooting, as this discourse of civic rights and responsibilities was emerging in the press and online, I noticed that the same themes were dominating my everyday conversations with friends, fieldwork subjects, and even passing acquaintances. Nearly everyone I knew or spoke to was affected in one way or another by the political, social, and economic instability. Conversations and interviews would inevitably turn to a discussion of the "uprising," the ongoing strikes and protests, and the shortcomings of the state. Some would talk about the lack of transparency and accountability in government and the public sector; others spoke about the need for renewed civic participation and a sense of responsibility for collective welfare. As the months passed, protests over the shooting morphed into protests over the state's handling of the economic crisis, the bailout by international lenders, and relentless austerity measures.

As part of my fieldwork, I spent a great deal of time absorbing the tumultuous social climate, trying to understand the complicated politics and histories of the present situation, which was itself continuously changing. Large portions of my day were dedicated to reading newspapers and blogs; watching the news; talking politics with informants, friends, neighbors, strangers; attending marches, protests, sit-ins, and occupations. More and more, this ethnographic work led me to think about the proper role, function, and reach of the state, both in relation to its citizens and in a larger transnational sphere, as well as the right of citizens to make claims on or demands of the state and its assets. In many ways, this felt far from my main research topic, the film festival, and I often wondered if all the time I was spending away from the festival, researching ongoing political and economic developments and the resulting social unrest, was leading me too far astray. At the same time, however, it felt important, and even unavoidable, to try to get a handle on this shifting social, political, and economic terrain in which I found myself embedded.

In fact, I was soon to learn that these questions concerning the relationship between the state and its citizens were not that far from my research topic after all. As the crisis worsened and the civil unrest continued, this turbulence began to affect the field of public culture, and more specifically the Greek film world. In a very practical sense, the Thessaloniki festival as an organization was affected by the political and economic upheavals because of its close relationship to the state; although technically it is a legally independent entity, it did receive the majority of its annual funding from the Greek Ministry of Culture, and the position of festival director is largely considered to be a kind of political appointment, with each change of government bringing with it a new director and new key staff.[2] With the unfolding economic catastrophe and the shrinking of state budgets, festival staff began to worry that they would be cut or their contracts not renewed, and those who continued to work for the festival had to wait months for paychecks. However, at the same time that this atmosphere of fiscal restraint was taking over, the festival was also preparing for its fiftieth-anniversary edition in November 2009, with a full slate of lavish celebrations, VIP guests, commemorative publications, and special programs and exhibitions. The incongruity between the severity of the national economic crisis and the extravagance of the festival's celebrations provoked sharp public criticism, all the more serious precisely because of the state funding that made up over two-thirds of the organization's annual income: it was public money that was being used. Against the backdrop of crisis and the newly current discourse of state accountability, these criticisms of the festival took on the much larger set of meanings, tensions, and grievances that were dominating public discourse at the time.

In addition, the preparations for the fiftieth-anniversary edition were also disrupted by a boycott of the festival by Greek filmmakers, who were withholding their films from the festival as a protest against the state. In the months leading up to the November festival, a group of over 200 Greek directors, producers, and screenwriters came together to protest what they considered to be a dysfunctional national film policy and the state's mishandling of public funds set aside for the support of Greek cinema. Their demands included an overhaul of the existing film legislation and state funding structures, and increased government support for domestic film distribution. They vowed to withhold their films from the 2009 Thessaloniki festival unless their demands were met, or unless the festival organizers joined their movement by completely reorganizing the fiftieth edition to resemble more of a protest than a celebration. Neither happened, and the 2009 festival took place with most Greek filmmakers, and Greek films, abstaining. The filmmakers' absence turned a spotlight on the connection between the state and the film festival as an institution of public culture. By choosing the festival as the primary site of their protest against state policies, the filmmakers cast the festival as a space of the state and attempted to redefine their own relationship to the state through the festival.

In articulating their positions, the filmmakers relied heavily on a rhetoric of state responsibility and citizens' rights, closely resembling the larger protesting public of Greece post-December 2008; according to them, it was the responsibility of good government to ensure the health of independent Greek film production, distribution, and exhibition. This was part of a larger conversation taking place at the time around the proper role of the state in cultural production and the right of citizens to demand state support for public culture. In the press and in conversations with people working in or otherwise connected to cultural fields, a common point of concern were the major problems within the Ministry of Culture and the severe challenges faced by dysfunctional cultural institutions and initiatives: not only the lack of adequate state funding, but also overgrown and convoluted bureaucratic structures, the apathy of cultural administrators, and the static introduced by personal ambition and party politics. Underlying these concerns was the assumption that the state is, or at least should be, responsible for public culture in Greece. Cinema, theater, opera, dance, orchestras, archaeological heritage, visual arts, architecture—all of these cultural fields were assumed to fall under the jurisdiction of the Ministry of Culture, and the state was held responsible for the health of these various fields, financially, legally, and administratively. The debate over the film festival in the months leading up to its fiftieth-anniversary edition was ultimately political and civic.

To the casual festival-goer, none of this turbulence was particularly visible during the 2009 festival. To an impressive extent, the festival organizers were able to keep these tensions and controversies under control; there was generally little noticeable disturbance in the programs and festivities, and very few references to the crisis or the absent Greek filmmakers in the discursive output of the festival itself—in its publications, its daily newspaper, on its website, in its press releases, on its own dedicated television channel. In fact, on the surface, and especially to the foreign observer, the 2009 festival edition was a great success, with international luminaries such as Werner Herzog in attendance, favorable reviews in foreign press, and increases in ticket sales and in the number of participating industry professionals. However, the picture was quite different for the ethnographer who had spent over a year immersed in the "microscopic" process of trying to understand the festival's immediate social, cultural, and political contexts, or local "webs of significance." From this perspective, the Thessaloniki festival could be seen in terms of its position within the larger debate on the relationship between the state, citizens, and public culture. In this sense, the festivals' fiftieth-anniversary edition was marked by precariousness and contestation, caught up in the instability of the conditions "on the ground."

Publishing the past, remembering in the present

As an example of this ethnographic process and perspective at work in my research on the Thessaloniki festival, we can take as our starting point a book: a special retrospective volume published by the festival to commemorate its fiftieth anniversary—*50 Years of the Thessaloniki Film Festival: 1960/2009* (Thessaloniki International Film Festival 2009). The ethnographic exploration of a text in the context of a film festival is something that anthropologist Daniel Dayan explicitly addresses in an essay on the Sundance Film Festival. Noting the sheer volume of printed materials generated by, around, and about the festival, Dayan writes of his methodology:

> Observation and interviews were obviously helpful, but the festival's most striking and to me most unexpected feature concerned the role of print. [...] My principal task as ethnographer was unexpected. I could not just ignore these masses of paper, reject this unwanted information, nurture the dream of a face-to-face Sundance. [...] Being in Park City made no difference: I had to read.
>
> (Dayan 2000: 52)

While I agree with Dayan that the discursive output surrounding a festival is an important element in how the festival is constructed, perceived, and experienced, I would argue that, for an ethnographer, the "reading" of a text goes well beyond the paper and the printed word. In the case of the 2009 Thessaloniki festival's commemorative volume, my reading of this particular text began long before a single word was written, and my analysis focuses less on what is written in the book than on how it is being read and put to use by others.

My involvement with the volume began in January 2009, as the festival was moving into full gear in its preparations for its jubilee edition. Since I had arrived in Greece, I had become friends with Athina Kartalou, head of festival publications and a film studies scholar herself, who invited me to be a part of the research team for the book. She told me how she envisioned the book: a large, full-color, coffee-table tome that would chronicle the history of the festival, edition by edition, with detailed information about each year's programming, plenty of accompanying photographs, and special sections for more anecdotal information. Over the following months, as I attended editorial meetings and worked in archives and libraries together with the small group of researchers that Athina had assembled, I observed how the institutional history of the festival was being constructed. Later that year, at the presentation of the book that took place during the November festival, I was able to see how this history was then taken up by the public and used to reflect on the present.

Some of the main issues that emerged in the process of working on the publication were questions of the authorship, as well as the publics, of history:

by whom, and for whom, history is produced. When Athina first described to me the idea for the publication, she referred to the book using the word *lefkoma*, which translates in English to "scrapbook" or "album," and from the first organizational meeting, this was the word used among the group to refer to the publication. The model of a scrapbook complicates the idea of authorship because, unlike a written history or memoir, it functions more as a collection of traces of the past than as an overarching historical narrative, and each of those traces might have its own complicated history of authorship. At the same time that the scrapbook represents a highly subjective, curatorial act, it also allows its creator or compiler to claim a certain objectivity, deferring the responsibility of authorship to the multiple authors, cited or not, of the scrapbook's constituent elements.

The discussion that took place during the first editorial meeting pointed to these questions of authorship, objectivity, and subjectivity. During this initial discussion concerning the larger shape and function of the publication, everyone quickly agreed that the *lefkoma* would have to be as thorough and objective as possible. For the film historians in the group, it was a question of scholarship—they wanted the volume to serve as a resource and reference for other scholars who might be interested in the festival and its history—while others felt that anything perceived as subjective or editorializing would have political implications. The concern for objectivity was illustrated most clearly in the debate over the publication's introductory text. The head editor had brought with her examples of retrospective publications from other festivals and cultural organizations; flipping through them, we noticed that they all contained a long opening text, either synthesizing the history of the organization or offering an analysis or interpretation of that history. We tried to think who would be the best person to write such an introductory text for the *lefkoma*; someone suggested Despina Mouzaki, the current director of the festival, as a logical choice, while others suggested Michel Demopoulos, the previous director, since he had led the festival for nearly 15 years and had been responsible for transforming it into the institution as it exists today. But the head editor deemed both inappropriate—they were too polarizing, she argued, because of their political affiliations. One of the researchers suggested that we ask one of the more established critics or film historians, but the editor replied that even they would not be "neutral" enough; she argued that anyone with enough authority and experience to qualify to write such an introductory text would either have a particular point of view or would at least be accused of having one, and she did not want anyone to accuse the festival or the editorial team of pursuing a larger agenda or ulterior motive with the book. In the end, it was decided that there would be no such text at all; apart from the formalities of opening remarks by the director and a short text describing methodology, structure and abbreviations, there would only be photographs and information about each festival edition in the form of data points. In the quest for absolute objectivity, or at least the appearance of it, the group went so far as to erase authorship completely, or at least attempt to.

However, despite this concern for "objectivity," it was also clear from our first meetings that the very nature of the group's work was interpretive. Even in simply deciding what information to present, in what form, the group would be determining how the history of the festival would be structured, and how, through that particular version of its history, the institution would be perceived and understood. Meeting periodically over a period of a few weeks, the group discussed for hours: how the different editions of the festival should be presented; if the festival's chronology should be divided into "eras," by decade, by director, or at all; if anecdotes and "unofficial" stories should be included, or only the bare facts about each year's programming, and which facts; if equal attention should be given to the sidebar events, exhibitions, master classes, and Industry Center activities; and which members of the festival programming and organizational staff from each edition should be included. In debating which elements to include in the book, and how, the editorial team was actually debating how to define the festival itself. Thus, even in these early stages of conceptualization, there was a clear tension between the ideal of objectivity and the necessary subjectivity of the editorial process—a tension that centered on the question of authorship, the particular positions from which this history was being authored, and how these positionalities determined the shape of that history.

In October 2009, after all the research and most of the editorial work had been completed, I caught up with Athina on the status of the project. She said that the book was almost ready to print; the only task remaining was a final, detailed examination, particularly of the photographs and the anecdotal information, to make sure that everything was in order politically. When I asked her what exactly they would be looking for in the material, she specified: names that should not be mentioned and some that should, people who should not appear next to each other in photograph arrangements, stories that should be left out. She would be setting aside a few days especially, to work closely with the editors on this. Athina was known for having an acute sense of political dynamics and was highly attuned to both micro-politics, on the one hand, and larger party and cultural politics, on the other. Combing through the *lefkoma* material in this way, she was adjusting it to a very particular public—one familiar with and sensitive to different moments of controversy or conflict in the festival's history—with an eye to how this version of the festival's past would navigate the political dynamics of the present. In this respect, the editorial approaches to authorship and to the public converged; in both cases, the goal was to revisit history while avoiding offense and conflict.

During the official book launch, however, it was precisely a history of conflict that became the focal point of the discussion. On the penultimate day of the 2009 festival, a group of "experts" was gathered in front of an audience to present and discuss the volume. Among the packed audience was the usual army of journalists, photographers, and videographers, and in the front of the room sat a panel of notable historians, critics, writers, and filmmakers. While the event began predictably, with an initial discussion of the historiographical merits of the *lefkoma*—its objectivity, its thoroughness, its methodological rigor—the conversation soon took a different, less expected direction: namely, a focus on conflict as an important part, perhaps even the most important part, of the festival's history. For example, Ilias Kanellis, a journalist and magazine publisher sitting on the panel, spoke at length about the book's anecdotal sections, stating that what interested him most was not the descriptions of major cinematic events, but rather "the secondary events, apart from cinema—the heckling, the protests, the complaints" (Kanellis 2009). He then went on to read entries from these sections, most of which had to do with moments of conflict: the public's disapproval of and vocal negative reactions to particular films or jury decisions, filmmakers refusing to accept prizes for political reasons, complaints about the festival's lack of organization, rumors of the festival perhaps being moved to Athens, and even the establishment of the first "anti-festival" in 1961, when two directors whose films were not chosen by the pre-selection committee organized screenings of their films in Thessaloniki at the same time as the festival. The speaker was careful to point out that he considered these moments of conflict as "important not just for the study of film history, but for the study of the social history of our country over the last fifty years" (ibid.).

Similarly, another panelist, historian Antonis Liakos, focused his comments on conflict, collectivity, and resistance. He began by talking about the festival as part of a larger "education" that his generation received through cinema: "The film festival, the films, the cinema clubs, the journals—it was all a learning context, which shaped a whole generation" (Liakos 2009). For him, the history of the festival was intertwined with the larger social history of Greece:

> One could say that the festival follows and is a counterpart to the history of Modern Greek society. First of all, starting from the 1960s, it's been a field of communication, of mutual recognition, of socialization, a field which connects the '60s, the sudden opening of that period, with later the period of the dictatorship, the rise of the public, its autonomous role, the role of the "second mezzanine"—all of these elements that bring together the festival-as-institution with the festival-as-public. And it's also a point of resistance; it prepared the way for the climate that would develop later, the climate of resistance. The relationship between the festival and the resistance during the years of the dictatorship is a very important part of the history of this festival. At the same time, the relationship between filmmakers and the festival is also very important. In a way, the festival resembles a kind of Roman democracy, in which the public engages in discussion with the patricians, the plebeians with the patricians, the filmmakers with the Ministry of Industry, the juries with the film critics. And to tell you the truth, I'm glad that this dynamism manifested itself this year as well, with this separate festival of the [boycotting] filmmakers in Athens. I'm glad in the sense that these moments of opposition show that the festival is still alive.
>
> (Ibid.)

Here, the history of the festival is presented as a history of collective action, of public conflict, debate, and resistance. The term "second mezzanine" refers to the practice of festival-goers in the upper balcony of the cinema who vocally, and sometimes violently, let their opinions be known. The practice of the second mezzanine first arose during the Greek military dictatorship (1967–1974), at a time when the ticket prices for festival screenings varied according to the category of the seating; thus the upper balcony was usually full of youth and students, who could only afford the cheapest tickets. The "second mezzanine" was famous for interrupting screenings, and sometimes even stopping them altogether, with their jeers, heckles, or ironic applause. Particularly in the 1970s, during and immediately following the dictatorship, many of the second mezzanine's reactions were politically motivated—thunderous applause and, in later years, audience awards for films that were considered politically, socially, or formally progressive; and loud disapproval for films that were thought to be supported by the state or too commercial, sometimes even leading to physical violence and police intervention.

In the 1980s, the second mezzanine reached a fever pitch—according to some, it devolved into a kind of hooliganism—but the practice had died down by the early 1990s, when the festival was radically restructured to resemble more closely the international film festivals of Western Europe, a move that was part of a larger effort to "modernize" and "Europeanize" the country by bringing it more in line with developing EU cultural policies and the global cultural economy. But still today, for many festival-goers of that generation, and even of younger generations who were too young to have experienced it directly but are familiar with the lore, the second mezzanine is a well-known and fondly remembered part of the festival experience, representing a level of audience engagement and critical interaction that many feel no longer exists among the festival public. By referring to the second mezzanine, the historian was evoking this particular history of the festival, which he then extended and elaborated through references to resistance under the junta, the "Roman democracy," and the actions of the filmmakers protesting the Ministry of Industry in the 1970s. This was a history of the festival centered on conflict, collective action, and a critical public, and he extended it to the present moment, to encompass the actions of the protesting filmmakers, who organized a special week of screenings to show their films in Athens, just a few days before the start of the Thessaloniki festival that they were boycotting. In this view of the festival, conflict was not something to be avoided, but rather a positive sign of "dynamism" and vitality, an indication that the festival was still a space for social and political action.

In the commemorative volume, moments of conflict from the festival's history are not entirely avoided; it does include references to the "second mezzanine," the various anti-festivals, and tensions between filmmakers and the state. But in the book, these moments of conflict—described "objectively" and listed in the volume's uniform bullet-point lists—are neutralized, subsumed in a larger flow of facts and data. In contrast, nearly all of the panelists highlighted this sense of conflict, presenting it as the defining characteristic of the festival's history. While the volume's editorial team was actively trying to avoid potential conflicts, stressing objectivity and even authorlessness and attempting to weed out anything that might be too contentious, these panelists saw contention as not just necessary, but even desirable. They were not idealizing conflict simply for the sake of conflict itself; rather, they saw that conflict as indicative of a lively, dynamic, and vital public sphere. For them, the debates, fights, oppositions, and controversies were an integral part of the festival's social, political, and cultural significance. Throughout its history, the film festival provided the occasion for this kind of gathering, this critical collectivity, and created a space where the members of a critical and diverse public could engage and interact with each other. The book launch served as a site for remembering that history, reclaiming it and connecting it to the present moment. This emphasis on publicness, and more specifically on a critical publicness or collectivity, can be understood in relation to the larger civic discourse that was growing at the time in Greece. In this sense, the festival's fiftieth-anniversary retrospective publication was being used to reflect on what was happening in the present moment.

Being there

What is revealed in this example of "ethnographic reading"—a process that involves the "microscopic" work of ethnographic research, as well as an awareness of the larger social and political contexts, both historical and in the present day, in which the festival is situated—is a way of understanding the film festival that is grounded in lived experience over time. The complex negotiations that went into the making of the commemorative volume, and by extension the construction of the festival's institutional history, do not appear in any written form, nor are they preserved in any archives. Only through the ethnographic work of "being there" (Geertz 1988) can the researcher get a sense of the tensions underlying the editorial process, and most importantly a sense of what did not make it into that history, what was left out, and why. Similarly, being immersed in the turbulent social and political life of Greece over an extended period of time yielded an intimate understanding of the larger "webs of significance" that shaped how people were experiencing the festival. In the context of the country's current crises and their historical resonance, the festival became a site of resistance, of engaging critically with the state, and remembering collective political action. Again, the discussion that took place during the book launch and its gestures toward a renewed sense of critical collectivity are not preserved in catalogs, programming notes, newsletters, or trade press reviews. Likewise, the protesting filmmakers and the questions raised by their boycott were largely absent in the discursive output around the festival, especially in the foreign press. Ethnographic research gives us a view onto such ephemeral, invisible, or silent moments; a "thick" understanding of the deep structures that give them meaning; and what they reveal about the festival as social experience.

What I am advocating is not a return to a simplistic "village ethnography," an old-fashioned insistence on an idealized notion of place in which locality, community, and culture are bounded and conflated. As a discipline, anthropology has been thinking critically about ethnography in relation to place, locality, and the "field" for decades (Appadurai 1991; Augé 1995; Clifford 1997; Gupta and Ferguson 1997). The result of such disciplinary reflection has not been to jettison ethnographic fieldwork, but rather to crack open notions of place and to think in terms of how locality is conditioned by global structures, and vice versa. In the context of the Thessaloniki film festival, the informed ethnographer asks how the festival functions as a node in a global network, serving to connect Thessaloniki to a larger transnational circuit of "global cities" and media events, but just as importantly also serving as a point of resistance or breakdown in that transnational flow. For example, as we saw during the book presentation, the transformations that the festival underwent during its internationalization in the early 1990s in many ways represented a move toward Europeanization and cultural integration with the EU; however, on another level, they were experienced by many locals as a loss—a loss of community, of a form of collective engagement. As film festivals continue to proliferate and to resemble each other—in their programming, their rhetoric, their structures—it becomes all the more important to take a close look at the concrete ways in which this global network actually takes place, in particular places and at particular times. If, as many scholars would argue, film festivals are increasingly important social, political, and economic spaces, then ethnography is an invaluable tool for examining, understanding, and representing the festival as rich, lived experience.

Notes

1 This essay is adapted from parts of my PhD thesis, "Public Culture and Cultural Citizenship at the Thessaloniki International Film Festival," which explores the relationship between state, citizen, and public culture during a period of acute social, political, and economic crisis (Lee 2013). Research for this project was made possible by generous support from the Social Science Research Council, the Fulbright Foundation, and the Minda de Gunzburg Center for European Studies at Harvard University.

2 Since 2012, with the near-bankruptcy of the Greek state, the festival has stopped receiving funding from the Ministry of Culture. Instead, it now survives primarily on EU grants and private sponsorships, and its annual budget is a fraction of what it was in 2009. As of July 2015, festival staff were still trying to prepare for the next edition; however, with the turmoil of the July 5 referendum, capital controls, and the new bailout agreement, it was unclear if the festival would have the resources it needs to continue.

References

Appadurai, A. (1991) *Modernity at Large: Cultural Dimensions of Globalization*, Minneapolis, MN: University of Minnesota Press.

Augé, M. (1995) *Non-Places: Introduction to an Anthropology of Supermodernity*, trans. J. Howe, London: Verso.

Behar, R. (2003) "Ethnography and the Book that Was Lost," *Ethnography*, 4(1), pp. 15–39.

Clifford, J. (1997) *Routes: Travel and Translation in the Late Twentieth Century*, Cambridge, MA: Harvard University Press.

Dayan, D. (2000) "Looking for Sundance: The Social Construction of a Film Festival," in I. Bondebjerg (ed.) *Moving Images, Culture and the Mind*, Luton: University of Luton Press, pp. 43–52.

De Valck, M. (2007) *Film Festivals: From European Geopolitics to Global Cinephilia*, Amsterdam: Amsterdam University Press.

Elsaesser, T. (2005) *European Cinema: Face to Face With Hollywood*, Amsterdam: Amsterdam University Press.

Geertz, C. (1973) *The Interpretation of Cultures: Selected Essays*, New York: Basic Books.

Geertz, C. (1988) *Works and Lives: The Anthropologist as Author*, Stanford, CA: Stanford University Press.

Geertz, C. (1998) "Deep Hanging Out," *The New York Review of Books*, 45(16), pp. 69–92.

Geertz, C. (2001) *Available Light: Anthropological Reflections on Philosophical Topics*, Princeton, NJ: Princeton University Press.

Gupta, A. and J. Ferguson (1997) *Culture, Power, Place: Explorations in Critical Anthropology*, Durham, NC: Duke University Press.

Iordanova, D. and R. Rhyne (eds.) (2009) *Film Festival Yearbook 1: The Festival Circuit*, St Andrews: St Andrews Film Studies.

Kanellis, I. (2009) author's field notes, November 21.

Lee, T. (2013) "Public Culture and Cultural Citizenship at the Thessaloniki International Film Festival," PhD thesis, Cambridge, MA: Harvard, Department of Anthropology.

Liakos, A. (2009) author's field notes, November 21.

Nichols, B. (1994) "Discovering Form, Inferring Meaning: New Cinemas and the Film Festival Circuit," *Film Quarterly*, 47(3), pp. 16–30.

Stringer, J. (2001) "Global Cities and the International Film Festival Economy," in M. Shiel and T. Fitzmaurice (eds.) *Cinema and the City: Film and Urban Societies in a Global Context*, Oxford: Blackwell Publishers, pp. 134–144.

Thessaloniki International Film Festival (2009) *50 Chronia Festival Kinimatografou Thessalonikis: 1960/2009 [50 Years of the Thessaloniki Film Festival: 1960/2009]*, Thessaloniki: Ianos.

Further reading

Bazin, A. (1955) "Du Festival considéré comme un ordre," *Cahiers du Cinéma* 8, 48. (An early, playful ethnographic treatment of the Cannes Film Festival.)

Hansen, M. (1993) "Unstable Mixtures, Dilated Spheres: Negt and Kluge's *The Public Sphere and Experience*, Twenty Years Later," *Public Culture*, 5(2), pp. 179–212. (A theoretical discussion of the public sphere as a space of conflict or contestation.)

Schwartz, V. (2007) *It's So French! Hollywood, Paris, and the Making of Cosmopolitan Film Culture*, Chicago, IL: University of Chicago Press. (Contains an ethnographically inflected history of the Cannes Film Festival, locating that particular history in a larger transnational political and economic context.)

Warner, M. (2002) *Publics and Counterpublics*, New York: Zone Books. (Provides a useful framework for thinking about dynamic and oppositional spaces of public discourse and practice, of which film festivals can be seen as an example.)

8 On studying film festival ephemera

The case of queer film festivals and archives of feelings

Ger Zielinski

Introduction

Permit me to start this chapter with a short anecdote regarding a curious situation that made me think hard about the nature of ephemera in archival research on film festivals.

While working on my doctoral dissertation, I encountered many boxes of file folders at Toronto's Canadian Lesbian and Gay Archive for flyers, posters, programs, and newspaper clippings that mentioned the festivals that I was studying at the time. The volunteer archivists at such community centers tend to be professional librarians who provide their expertise pro bono. They kindly offered me coffee and cookies along with any new folders that I desired to inspect. In one folder I came across a simple black and white facsimile of a call for submissions to what would have been the city's first gay film festival in 1981, along with a street address. This was a fascinating find and left me with such questions as: Did it ever take place? Who organized it? What titles were screened? Where were the screenings? Did it take place in public or in someone's home? I photocopied the sheet and then started my detective work. I searched online digital newspaper databases for mention of such an event between 1980 and 1982, checked municipal records for permits, and queried activists and filmmakers who surely would have known of it, if not been participants. All of this was to no avail. I visited the address and discovered that the previous building at that location, well situated in the Gay Village, had been razed and left as a vacant lot.

All of this added more mystery to the inquiry. The Toronto International Film Festival's Film Research Library, like most other cinematheque libraries and archives, excluded such festivals. The community archive had highly constricted space, no newspaper mentioned the event, and people's memories of a possible event over two decades ago were foggy. I was left at a point of unknowing and had to continue with other pressing research in order to move my project along. I am still unsure whether the festival took place or was merely a fleeting desire before its time. The anecdote, however, does present many of the elements that are common when researching community festivals: most typically work on shoe-string budgets, without proper records or space for archives, often run by volunteers who each have a relatively short tenure at the festival. In this case, I noticed the piece of ephemera—the call for submissions—that addressed me from decades ago. Its promise compelled me to consider ways to determine its value as a historical artifact in piecing together the history of the festivals in one city.

In this chapter I address important methodological and epistemological questions on the value and use of ephemera that arise in research on film festivals, but particularly in the case of identity-based community festivals.[1] My case study here regards the increasingly globalized lesbian and gay film festivals, and I concentrate my attention on the special ephemeral documents that these festivals produce. For my larger theoretical framework, I draw on Michael Warner's theory of publics and adapt it to the experience and constitution of festival-goers as intersecting counter/publics and engage Ann Cvetkovich's concept of an archive of feelings (2003) in the context of the lived festival. I address below the question of the use, value, and limitations that ephemera present to the scholar researching film festivals, historical and current. Moreover, I will argue that the festival programs of films not only borrow from queer histories and posit new queer pasts and futures, but that the festivals themselves also produce new affective ephemeral material that is folded back into queer cultural experience.

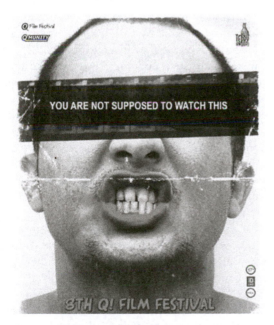

Figure 8.1 Poster of the Q! Film Festival, Jakarta. Courtesy of the festival.

> The poster is from the traveling Q! Festival based in Jakarta, Indonesia, and vividly commands festival-goers to perform a daring defiance or transgression by attending and seeing clandestine or forbidden films: "You are not supposed to watch this!" The festival itself receives threats from hostile groups opposed to its queer themes (Zielinski 2012).

Ephemera and archives

Conventionally, ephemera might occupy a few folders but are rarely the priority of the typical archive. The fleeting nature of ephemera leaves them prey to the charge of being merely contingent and unruly, beneath the value of serious documents such as correspondence, financial statements, or internal operating records. However, depending on the objective of the research and the nature of the cultural formation at the heart of the study, ephemera may play such an important role that it would be irresponsible for a scholar to overlook them. In the case of certain festivals with low funding and no archives, ephemera might be the sole remaining material evidence of the festival, save interviews with its organizers or participants.

Etymologically, we may trace the word "ephemera" via Medieval Latin to denote something (typically a fever) lasting one day back to Ancient Greek prefix and preposition *epi* (on) joined to *hemera* (day), resulting in "ephemera" (*epi-hemerai*, *ephemeros*). Events, and festivals in particular, bristle in ephemera in the form of publicity oriented to those outside of the event, but also other types oriented to those at the event itself. Through its careful selection, design, placement, and frequency, it is used to help craft the self-definition or identity of the event itself. For example, posters suddenly appear at chosen points throughout a city, as a part of a media campaign to inform city denizens of the coming festival, while a related campaign may be pursued on social media to promote awareness to possible festival-goers anywhere in the world. The standard process for creating such ephemera involves the festival organizers, a special committee dedicated to publicity and advertising (including identity branding), and an invitation to selected designers or filmmakers to create the publicity ephemera for the festival. The festival must then authorize the various ephemera as officially representing the event.[2] In general terms, this is how the festival negotiates and agrees to the advertising and publicity ephemera that are in turn representative of the festival itself. In effect, the festival is responsible for the audiovisual ephemera that it selects to represent itself, and this can certainly affect the way people outside of the festival understand it and ultimately who attends.

Established festivals are afloat in the production of ephemera, printed but also in various other media and formats, including printed posters, buttons, pens, program guides, trailers, t-shirts, and coffee mugs, among other items. Earlier editions of any festival generally have fewer ephemera available to researchers as very little is collected in larger archives, beyond the occasional personal collection; the material disperses and becomes lost as time charges on. Without a doubt, any systematic attempt to collect all ephemera would surely overwhelm even the largest cinematheque or archive. The film festival researcher rarely has the luxury of finding a single archive that could serve the project in its entirety; cinematheques and film museums, however long-standing, avoid any concerted effort at collecting film festival ephemera, save the occasional program guide or poster, since their mandate aims elsewhere. The festivals themselves often serve the purpose of an archive of their own ephemera, if they have the space to store the material, notion to collect it, and have taken the extra effort to retain it.[3] Evidently, film festivals are very much focused on the annual event, and once it is over, that year's ephemera is completely redundant, exhausted of its use-value, and regularly disposed of.

Much of my research has concerned film festivals that emerged from related social movements, which means that if community-oriented archives exist and are accessible, they become a part of the research. They are volunteer-run archives that attempt to collect a wide variety of material associated with various facets, in my case, of LGBT communities. My research brought me to Brooklyn's Herstory Lesbian Archives, San Francisco's Gay Lesbian Bisexual Transgender Historical Society, the Canadian Lesbian and Gay Archives in Toronto, and Montreal's *Archives gaies du Québec*, among others. While such community archives are important, they are also very limited by their small budgets and spaces. They may contain exceptional pieces of ephemera from, say, heated campaigns or protests that took place in each respective city.[4]

Ephemera as a term is employed in a number of ways in cinema studies, so it is important to clarify its meanings and how it relates to the study of festivals. Rick Prelinger coined the phrase "ephemeral film" for the sorts of films that he collected (Cook et al. 2015); his archive brought together a wide variety of ignored genres, such as industrial, instructional, and educational films, as well as advertisements, all of which had a short duration of use-value.[5] The more standard name used for ephemeral film today is "orphan film."[6] These film "genres" until recently have escaped film studies but have become increasingly important in the making of documentary films and other types of films that attempt to reference and comment on the past through found footage. Those who make use of such archives and films range from students to well-established filmmakers to television producers, commercial to independent, including, for instance, German filmmaker and television producer Alexander Kluge and experimental filmmakers Mike Hoolboom and Matthias Müller. With the Prelinger Archives, among others, we have the notion of an archive of films whose original use-value has been exhausted, and the films themselves are largely ignored as objects of study. Naturally, in the context of events and festivals, television and video advertisements and especially festival trailers fall under the category of ephemeral films and eventually orphan films, once the festival ends. Sometime after the event, festival-goers may re-watch the trailer that they had seen at a festival and recall various moments from the festival: its programs, its parties, its hype, and so forth. Film critics, who are often compelled to attend many screenings, often speak of trailers and posters from various editions of festivals, and the editions themselves, as a sommelier appreciates a list of wines. These ephemera are crucial to a study of how any festival presents itself to the world and operate mnemonically to cue memories.

Furthermore, there are also two specialized archives of print ephemera. The John Johnson Collection of Printed Ephemera, held in the Bodleian Libraries at the University of Oxford, primarily specializes in nineteenth century print culture. The second is the Ephemera Society of America, dedicated to preserving assorted ephemera of the United States. Both of these collections are in the process of being digitized and made accessible online, which has led to an even more vigorous re/circulation of digital representations of their ephemera on new platforms. These collections would be very useful to historians of visual culture who are studying the circulation of printed posters, photographs, and advertising in the nineteenth century and the constitution of publics.

In the context of LGBT historiography, for example, ephemera and abandoned private collections of letters and photographs have played a crucial role in the attempt to write histories of nearly-erased lives. They are the fragments that are put together speculatively to invite imagined yet plausible life stories as a retrieval. In his essay "Looking at a Photograph, Looking for a History," art historian David Deitcher addresses this issue as he describes how he sifts through piles of old discarded photographs in antique shops and flea markets (Deitcher 1998). Such photographs would be, technically, a sort of private ephemera from discarded personal collections, and as private these items are generally not reproduced as multiples on a large scale. The task of the historian in this case is to imagine plausible personal gay and lesbian histories that were never written down.[7] Festival research is less challenging in this respect, however older defunct festivals do rely more on historical archival work than ethnographic and sociological methods, such as in-depth interviews and participant observation, which would be more readily appropriate and available to researchers working on current film festivals.

Ephemera, film festivals, and festival publics

A handful of scholars have written on film festivals and their production of ephemeral texts. The associated theory of publics plays a strong role here in how festival publics are constituted through the production and circulation of ephemeral texts by and on the festivals.

As an important early contribution, cultural anthropologist Daniel Dayan's study of the Sundance Film Festival approaches the festival as a social construction, as he introduces his text:

> [a]nthropologists try to identify performances, to coin names to designate them, to unravel the scripts they perform. They try also to identify rules, to propose a grammar of encounters, a rhetoric of gatherings. The following paper tries to identify some of the rules that define what we call a film festival.
>
> (Dayan 2000: 43–44)

Figure 8.2 Poster of identities—Queer Film Festival. Courtesy of identities.

> Vienna's long-standing identities festival reveals itself through a close-up that troubles gender and sexual presuppositions, even as its title remains curiously vague—what identities?—but suggestive of an embrace of a plurality of identities. This is a common motif across gay and lesbian culture, from the early "inverts" and androgynes.

Dayan addresses the roles of the films, genres and boundaries, of the market, and of filmmakers and the audience. He notes,

> [o]bservation and interviews were obviously helpful, the festival's most striking—and to me most unexpected feature concerned the role of print [...] a Niagara of printed paper was spelling out meanings, offering captions, telling and retelling daily events until they reached a stable, paradigmatic form.
>
> (Ibid.: 52)

Another innovative scholar in the area is film historian Julian Stringer, who takes a rhetorical analysis approach toward film festivals in order to uncover their unique "festival-image" from careful analysis of how their program guides and websites reveal a certain signature of the festival and how festival ephemera are used as tools for creating an identity for the institution (Stringer 2008). To this approach to ephemera, I would add the concept of publics and their formation in the context of film festivals and their related events.[8]

While there are several theories of publics, for the purposes of this chapter I have chosen the work of Michael Warner to provide a useful framework through which to consider festivals, their ephemera, and the formation of their publics (Warner 2002).[9] An interesting illustration of the process of constituting a public is the inauguration of San Francisco's Frameline festival, the longest-running lesbian and gay film festival in the world. In 1977 a group of gay filmmakers based in San Francisco decided to make their screenings public instead of only showing each other's work to one another in private. The filmmakers were uncertain that anyone outside of their circle of friends would have any interest in their films, and so saturated the Castro area with posters (Wiegand 2003). They held their public screenings in the two community centers, and thereby opened the event to new, contingent stranger relations. Much to their surprise, the event generated a very enthusiastic response and public, and the festival commonly known as Frameline was born.[10]

Although publics may rely on various institutions and media for communication, they have no institutional being and are virtual entities. One institution may dissolve, and another or others may replace it, perhaps retaining parts of the earlier public; this also involves a competition for constituting

Figures 8.3–8.6 Screengrabs of Frameline festival trailer. Co-Directors Bill Weber and David Weismann, Courtesy of Frameline: the San Francisco International LGBTQ Film Festival.

> Here we have Frameline effectively reinhabiting old forms of spectacle and camp wit. The trailer brings to life a parody of Busby Berkeley's film form and dance routines with dancing drag queens and voiceover that teases the viewer to "get out and see a movie, duh!" Camp wit is a very old cultivated sensibility and practice in gay culture, among others, that Susan Sontag famously tried to characterize in her well-known essay "Notes on 'Camp'" (Sontag 1967).

new publics (also known as "outreach") and maintaining the already established festival-going public through various festival initiatives, including its own publicity, advertising, programming, perceived identity, and so forth. In the case of LGBT film festivals, we notice festival-goers tend, in general, to be a smaller sampling of the larger LGBT community. New York City provides a compelling example with its three somewhat competing, somewhat parallel LGBT film festivals, but each distinguishes its own distinct festival signature or identity, effectively presenting its festival-idea. The New York Gay Film Festival was the largest in the world and appealed to a broad popular section of the LGBT community with its emphasis on accessible narrative feature films. MIX NYC: New York Queer Experimental Film Festival, founded in 1987, still maintains its specialization in experimental film, installation, and performance art. Moreover, MIX has inspired the formation of several related festivals, such as MIX Brazil, MIX Mexico, and MIX Milan, which also put their programming emphasis on queer experimental media art. The interest in experimental or artists' film and video attracts a very narrow public, one that is open to formally playful and innovative work. The collapse of the New York Gay Film Festival led to the formation of the third annual LGBT film festival in 1988, named NewFest,[11] which actively expanded its constituency and distinguished itself from the defunct festival through its name, logo, and stylistic changes in posters, as well as its change in organizational structure and community involvement.[12] NewFest's innovations and deliberate expansion of roles for a greater diversity of community members led to the formation of new festival-going publics.

A festival's circulation of ephemeral texts is itself a diffusion to strangers and has a special temporality. In most cases the temporality of circulation has a well-defined punctuality, setting a rhythm as well as expectations. In the life of any city, examples would include cycles in annual events such as carnivals and film festivals, the printed press, regular television programming, monthly film screenings, and so on. Film festivals participating in the international circuits must also obey temporal constraints placed on them by those circuits,[13] and must effectively fit in with the scheduling among the other players, if they want to be considered truly "international."[14] Apart from the temporal aspect of the calendar and the festival's relationship to others, each edition of the festival has its own particular daily temporality, i.e., the number of screenings per day, the number of days of the whole festival, and the number of repetitions of the films in the programming.[15] Festival ephemera is produced alongside this process, through announcements, posters, websites, television commercials, among others, throughout the year, and culminates in the event of the festival itself. For the purposes of the study of festivals these ephemera become useful to the researcher in piecing together not only the past editions of festivals, but also ones currently under observation.

Community-oriented film festivals are organized around some claim to group identity, whether sharply or hazily defined, and are highly sensitive to their public's opinions. Praise and complaints are circulated throughout the festival and may have significant effects on the organization, its structure, its programming, its self-presentation, and its future livelihood. In the case of annual LGBT film festivals, the idea that the film festival presents is carried in the prose and images that it generates and circulates through various media. It may aim to appeal to young radical artists (MIX NYC), middle-aged middle-class professionals (NewFest), devoted cinephiles, occasional cinemagoers, exclusive or overlapping publics.

Warner posits an alternative to the presupposed reading-public model for publics.[16] Warner contends that a public is poetic world-making or autopoetic,[17] which he combines with his notion of counterpublic. This involves the festival presenting its own style and way of seeing the world, particularly through its ephemera and programming, which in turn attracts or constitutes its festival-going public.

According to Warner, some of the important performative elements include such markers as "the pragmatics of its speech genres, idioms, stylistic markers, address, temporality, mise-en-scène, citational field, lexicon, and so on" (Warner 2002: 114). The dominant theories of the public sphere take public address to be a type of rational-critical dialogue with its circulation flows as rational discussion, that is to say, they put the emphasis on persuasion over poiesis. Warner finds fault in these theories for their entire reliance on the framework of theories of language in as much as it systemically delegitimizes all publics or counterpublics that follow modes other than the rational-critical (ibid.: 115). This works well with his analysis of the history of the gay and lesbian movement, as it diverged from its radical anti-assimilationism and

Figure 8.7 Logo of Queer Lisboa festival. Courtesy of the festival.

> The motif of the "*queer* duck," namely someone who stands out or is a little odd, has gone global in spite of its origin in the foreign English language. Lisbon's festival is one of many to make use of such a playful shibboleth and suggests an implicit claim to an alliance with international LGBT networks and culture. The symbol should be legible to those with knowledge of that international culture and likely familiar with the English language. The festival-going public grasps its playful meaning, an act which lends a possible shared recognition among the festival-goers in relation to the identity of the festival.

began to harmonize with the state through a discourse of legal rights. It is precisely that tension between the assimilationists and anti-assimilationists in the case of the gay and lesbian movement that creates a similar tension between public and counterpublic. The aim for a wider public through assimilation, and its associated condition of homonormativity,[18] may marginalize those legitimate concerns of the counterpublic, much closer to the radical historical origins of the movement.

Variety in publics follows from modes of address, style, spaces of circulation, e.g., gay community newspapers and festival catalogs, which Warner names subpublics or specialized publics. Borrowing from Nancy Fraser's (1992) work on subordinated social groups, Warner extends it to include alternative publics or subaltern counterpublics (ibid.: 118). Accordingly, a counterpublic includes two characteristics: it has an awareness of its own subordinate status, whose discourse out of context, or in the "wrong" social context, may inspire hostility; and second, that which nevertheless must still come into being through the address to indefinite strangers. For example, from Eve Kosofsky Sedgwick, Warner chooses the example of "the closet" which only exists within a (presupposed) heteronormative discourse but could not exist in a queer counterpublic. Within a condition of *homonormativity*, however, there may be different types of "closets," perhaps BDSM,[19] transgender, bisexual, or downlow,[20] among others.[21] Identity is conferred on members through their participation in their respective counterpublic. Warner notes the promise of the counterpublic in the poesis of scene making and its transformative intent, producing change in some sense. Agency is attributed to counterpublics as they strive for and attain the rational-critical mode of discourse, the mode most favored by the state and based on the model of private reading and decoding. Moreover, counterpublics do not lend the reader model such privilege, but rather they often hold such values as, for example, embodied sociability and performance over print, e.g., carnivals, BDSM, and public sex practitioners. It is precisely when a counterpublic adapts itself to engage the state on its own terms, namely through rational-critical discourse that it forsakes its earlier transformative ethos and becomes a social movement. The tension or play between contemporary publics and historical or marginalized counterpublics in the LGBT scenes is particularly noticeable at the related film festivals with respect to taste cultures, programming, self-definition, or identity, and is well represented in the ephemera circulating throughout the festival itself.

Ephemeral archive of feelings

As discussed above, festivals generate significant amounts of prose: program guides, posters, advertising, journalist reportage, and so on (Dayan 2000; Elsaesser 2005). I contend that this should be extended to the larger sense of text to include many other types of audiovisual documents, much of them ephemera, beyond print media. The festival produces its own ephemeral,

Figures 8.8–8.11 Screengrabs of MIX NYC 2009 trailer. Courtesy of MIX NYC: New York Queer Experimental Film Festival.

MIX's rather audacious 2009 trailer "I want to go into the closet with you" bends the idea of the closet back upon itself in a way that would surely amuse the late Eve Kosofsky Sedgwick, who addressed the motif of the closet very seriously in her pioneering books on literary and queer theory (Sedgwick 2008). The performative act of coming out of the closet is parodied and playfully rehabilitated for sexual pleasure far from its historical origin in secret private shame. MIX festival puts the emphasis on experimental film and revives early gay liberation's very pro-sex stance, albeit adapted to contemporary queer culture. The trailer presents itself from a staged domestic private space to the festival-going public in the cinema with the presupposition that the figure of the closet would be intelligible to the members of the audience. Evidently, it would be hard to imagine the same figure employed in a trailer for another type of festival successfully without major adaptation.

archival materials that intimate its ethos and even internal contradictions, its principles of programming, and its social and political contexts.

In LGBT film festivals, viewers experience a play of presence and absence at the event, namely at the screenings, waiting in line, and so forth, through the fleeting mechanisms of resemblance, empathy, identification, memory, recollection, repulsion, disidentification, and so on. The festival itself takes

Figures 8.12–8.13 Festival poster of Mezipatra Queer Film Festival, 2009. Courtesy of STUD Brno; Mezipatra Queer Film Festival, Brno, Prague.

The Czech Republic's touring Mezipatra festival's 2009 poster by Jan Kolar startles the viewer with its faux bullet holes perched on a street. The poster in fact won design awards (Drachovska 2009). The bold crosshairs on the poster provide a focus, even a target, that the mock bullet holes make clear. This campaign took place during a period of years where violence erupted at similar festivals in Eastern Europe, namely Sarajevo in 2008, St. Petersburg in 2008, and Belgrade in 2009.[22] The poster intimates the danger of visibility itself, being seen, becoming a target.

place as a constellation of sites producing ephemeral heterotopic space for the duration of the event. The traces of ephemera—posters, guides, notes, trailers, and so on—serve as mnemonic tokens. Through repetition during the festival, meanings and feelings have been generated. We start to learn the festival's brand with the first print or online ad, poster, or radio mention.

Festival ephemera have found ways to reference the affective histories of AIDS, the culture wars, gender struggle, LGBT movement, but also pop culture—films and television, especially via celebrity and camp culture associated with certain films.[23] Moreover, queer art house auteurs, e.g., Chantal Akerman, Rainer Werner Fassbinder, and Pedro Almodóvar, among others, find their films cited in text or image, most often for selected retrospectives of their work. Another important source is queer cultural history itself, along with its specialized motifs and signs, including more ephemeral gestural tropes associated with queer bodies, as José Muñoz might call it (Muñoz 1996). While program guides and posters do carry with them affective dimensions,

Figure 8.14–8.16 Side by Side Festival logo and posters for the St. Petersburg 2011 and Moscow 2012 festival editions. Designer Dasha Zorkina. Courtesy of Side by Side LGBT International Film Festival.

Russia's innovative touring Bok-o-bok (Side by Side) festival had been making a name for itself on the international circuit, and in 2009 the queer cultural festival took place in St. Petersburg with invited guests from many countries participating. The title conveys a sense of solidarity but is purposefully vague on the main issue. However, the so-called anti-homosexual propaganda law came into force first in St. Petersburg but now also applies to the entire Russian Federation, so any such public signage today would be illegal. In this image appear not only the rainbow motif, addressing an emergent global collectivity, akin to similar festivals elsewhere in the world under difficult conditions, but also an androgynous couple rendered in stick-figures. Under a separate law the festival is now labeled a "foreign agent" by the Russian government due to international funding and has further restrictions on what it may do (Loist and Zielinski 2012).

so do various digital manifestations, trailers, and ads. The festival ephemera culls together elements excerpted from previous years or films from the current one.

Ann Cvetkovich's concept of an *archive of feelings* posits a new way to think of archives and the constellation of audiovisual culture, especially in the absence of long recorded pasts and archives. LGBT film festivals themselves afford a compelling possibility as a living networked archive of feelings as their films move from festival to festival over the year. Cvetkovich thinks her concept through in the analysis of a selection of individual films and their contingent relationship to popular culture and personal histories. She writes,

> These documentaries use the power of visual media to put the archive on display, incorporating a wide range of traditional and unorthodox materials, including personal photographs, videotapes from oral history archives, innovative forms of auto-documentary, and "archival" footage, including clips from popular film and television. Film and video can extend the reach of the traditional archive, collating and making accessible documents that might otherwise remain obscure except to those doing specialized research.
>
> (Cvetkovich 2002: 109)

Figure 8.17 Poster for Q! Film Festival 2007, Jakarta and Bali. Courtesy of the festival.

> This figure shows another poster from Jakarta's Q! Festival. As a single, isolated poster it appears to wish for and anticipate diversity in a very broad sense, idealized or otherwise. The festival is largest in Asia and held in Indonesia, a relatively socially conservative country, but whose population is large enough to secure some relative freedom for this successful touring festival.

Figures 8.18–8.23 Screengrabs of Miami Gay and Lesbian Film Festival 2007 trailer, O-TV Creative Services.

The Miami LGBT Film Festival's trailer with Anita Bryant is one of the most poignant trailers for any festival. It remobilizes activist energies from the 1970s with some camp humor and biting irony intended for its local Florida audience. Sources include police camera footage of the raid of a gay bar and paddy wagon, television footage of Anita Bryant, the infamous anti-homosexual advocate, former beauty queen, and Florida oranges mascot, as well as video images of a subsequent pride parade to bring the short trailer to triumphant closure. The rather long trailer recalls the difficult historical challenges and presents a rather triumphant or at least defiant call to arms to the audience to both remember their past and continue the struggle.

Cvetkovich seeks out and finds a new sort of archive for which no conventional archive has existed. Her films depend in part on found material, both image and sound, that resonate with queer histories. She posits, furthermore, that:

> [l]esbian and gay history demands a radical archive of emotion in order to document intimacy, sexuality, love, and activism, all areas of experience that are difficult to chronicle through the materials of a traditional archive.
>
> (Ibid.: 110)

Queer film festivals are both composed of and actively produce overall ephemeral archives of feelings through the event and its ephemera. Moreover, such

Figure 8.24 25—A Brief History of the Festival (Marc Huestis, 2001).

Huestis' celebratory documentary (2001) on the twenty-fifth anniversary of Frameline is clearly an ephemeral film and required viewing for anyone researching Frameline or LGBT film festivals for its rich history of the festival. The filmmaker is also one of the co-founders of the festival who has spent most of his life in San Francisco with the Castro district as his base. The autoethnographic portrait reflects on the festival's origin and development through many debates and crises in the historical context of the culture wars, identity politics, and AIDS that affected members of the LGBT community in the United States very directly. The film recounts the history from the 1970s to the early 2000s through modes of testimony, talking-head interview, limited reenactment, and found footage. The film was not conceived for distribution or exhibition outside of the anniversary edition of the festival itself. Its emotional tone varied widely according to the issues being addressed, from poignant to light and playful.

"affective power" of queer archives is especially felt, without much surprise, at LGBT film festivals. The festival's programs of films, videos, and other work, mobilize life histories through found images, music and sound, interviews, or scripts and actors. While the programming of any festival, its selection and sequencing of films, also plays an extremely important role in bringing the festival into being as an event, I would argue that festivals and festivality[24] exceed their programming and are beyond the mere sum of their individual films.

Queer film festivals are awash in ephemera—a "Niagara of printed paper" and more—that in part work to constitute the festival public but also provide a partial mirror-like reflection strewn with affectively charged fragments and citations of queer cultures and pasts.

Concluding remarks

Research on film festivals, both those long ceased and those continuing today, depends on access to festival organizers or festival-goers, if possible, but also on access to documents associated with the festival. These documents include the festival's ephemera, which intimate how a festival presents itself to the world and attracts festival-goers to thereby constitute its publics. A new festival in a city or a new festival director may take special care in developing a strong campaign to show what the festival intends to deliver and what may have changed. Posters may work to reveal the limits of local censorship laws or cultural taboos. They may also make reference to selected local shared or imagined international histories of the community. In the case of lesbian and gay film festivals, I have shown how the ephemera borrow from, circulate within, and contribute back in turn to an archive of feelings that depends on the lived histories of the larger community but also its local manifestations. This reflexive circulation of texts, meanings, and experiences can also apply to other types of community film festivals, in particular, well beyond the case studies here.

Notes

1 I wish to thank Dorota Ostrowska for inviting me to share earlier versions of this research with her keen graduate students in 2012 and 2013 at Birkbeck College, University of London, and also T. L. Cowan for the opportunity to speak on archival research to her enthusiastic students at Eugene Lang College, The New School, New York City in 2012. I greatly appreciated the spirited discussions.

2 The issue of labor in the running of festivals is rarely addressed, and so much of the work done at small and large festivals is volunteer, including pro-bono work of designers, among others (see Loist 2011).

3 One important archive proves to be the exception to the rule, namely the MIX Collection, which holds paper and media files of the MIX: New York Lesbian and Gay Experimental Film and Video festival (1987–2001) in the downtown collection of the Fales Library and Special Collections at New York University. Its various collections can be searched online at www.nyu.edu/library/bobst/research/fales/.

4 For example, I could not ignore the material recurring in all the above archives concerning the protests against the release of the controversial film *Cruising* (William Friedkin, 1980) that swept across North America and Western Europe in the early 1980s. However, community archives certainly do not have the space to store program guides and posters from every edition of the local queer film festival.

5 The collection was sold to the Library of Congress and has been made available online at archive.org as the Prelinger Archives.

6 The website of the annual Orphan Film Symposium broadens the category to include other films such as educational, ethnographic, industrial, government, experimental, censored, independent, sponsored, obsolescent, small-gauge, silent, student, medical, unreleased, and underground films, kinescopes, home movies, test reels, newsreels, outtakes, fringe television, among others. There is a clear mixture of films intended for public use and those made for internal use by organizations or private domestic space, say, of the family. While Prelinger's term puts the emphasis on the relatively short duration of intended use-value of the film, the term "orphan" intimates the abandoned sense of the films that have fallen from use and circulation for whatever reason (Prelinger 2009).

7 Other approaches that attempt to address the reticence in historiography often created by the taboo expressions of sexuality would include the innovative work of art historian Gavin Butt on Andy Warhol and the artist's reworking of his own image in the early 1960s New York art scene. Butt's study centers on the study of that elusive and ephemeral form of speech called gossip (Butt 2005).

8 For example, this would include what Thomas Elsaesser discusses as the festival's capacity to serve as an "agora" where public debates take place (Elsaesser 2005).

9 Since the emphasis in this chapter is on methodology, please see Chapter 5 in this book by Cindy Hing-Yuk Wong on the use of the theories of publics in film festival research, which includes a section on Warner.

10 Frameline's official name is the San Francisco International LGBTQ Film Festival, while "Frameline" refers to the umbrella organization that houses the festival, distribution and production initiatives. See Zielinski (2009a) for a brief historical overview of this and other related festivals.

11 The full name of this festival is NewFest: New York's Annual LGBT Film Festival.

12 See Gamson (1996) for a study of the relationships between the festivals.

13 For an important article on the concept of film festival circuits, see Iordanova 2009. See also Chapter 3 in this book by Skadi Loist on the festival circuit.

14 See also Chapter 4 in this book for Janet Harbord's take on time and temporality of the festival.

15 The unique, complicated temporality of film festivals has been discussed by others, for example Elsaesser 2005.

16 See Chapter 5 in this book by Cindy Hing-Yuk Wong for a detailed discussion of public sphere theory.

17 His use of the term poetic comes from the Greek concept of *poiesis* as an activity oriented toward some end, but also in contrast to *praxis* as an activity as an end in itself.

18 "Homonormativity" is a neologism discussed by Lisa Duggan (2003) to indicate a similar marginalizing effect within the LGBT community as "heteronormativity" applied to all those bodies that exceed heterosexuality. Duggan's concept also hints at the process of mainstreaming of the lesbian and gay movement with middle-class values at the expense of the rest. For a critical survey of the related discourse, see Sullivan (2003).

19 "BDSM" stands for bondage and domination and sadomasochism.

20 The term "downlow" ("DL") means a discreet gay male who can still pass for heterosexual among heterosexual people.

21 Symptoms of homonormativity would include the chilling effect of increased respectability in various areas of gay and lesbian culture. The modes of address, for example, have shifted, as the frank "body language" used in advertising for gay sex services was toned down during the 1990s as middle-class senses of propriety and discretion and fear of losing advertising revenue became stronger (Sender 2004).

22 John Greyson's highly poetic essay film *Covered* (2009) addresses the events and their historical context of the Queer Sarajevo festival and is available to view at https://vimeo.com/6308870 (Zielinski 2012).

23 Karl Schoonover's essay (2015) on the post-human motifs in festival posters provides a rare serious engagement with the ephemera of LGBT film festivals.

24 I proposed the neologism "festivality" at the 2010 SCMS conference in Los Angeles after noticing colleagues grasping for some word that could mean "festivalness" or "festivality"—already in use in French (*festivalité*), but apparently with the slight pejorative sense of "festivalization" or "spectacularization" of local culture. Evidently, festivality need not be value-ridden but a statement on the fact or nature of festivals and their culture.

References

Butt, G. (2005) *Between You and Me: Queer Disclosures in the New York Art World, 1948–1963*, Durham, NC: Duke University Press.

Cook, S., Bartolomé Herrera, B., and Robbins, P. (2015) "Interview with Rick Prelinger," *Synoptique*, 4(1), pp. 165–191.

Cvetkovich, A. (2002) "In the Archives of Lesbian Feelings: Documentary and Popular Culture," *Camera Obscura*, 17(1), pp. 106–147.

Cvetkovich, A. (2003) *An Archive of Feelings: Trauma, Sexuality and Lesbian Public Cultures*, Durham, NC: Duke University Press.

Dayan, D. (2000) "In Quest of a Festival," in I. Bondebjerg (ed.) *Moving Images, Culture, and the Mind*, Luton: University of Luton Press, pp. 43–52.

Deitcher, D. (1998) "Looking at a Photograph, Looking for a History," in D. Bright (ed.) *The Passionate Camera: Photography and Bodies of Desire*, New York: Routledge, pp. 23–36.

Drachovska, B. (2009) "Festival Mezipatra představuje nový grafický vizuál," *Czech Design*, September 21, www.czechdesign.cz/temata-a-rubriky/festival-mezipatra-predstavuje-novy-graficky-vizual (November 4, 2015).

Duggan, L. (2003) *The Twilight of Equality? Neoliberalism, Cultural Politics, and the Attack On Democracy*, Boston, MA: Beacon Press.

Elsaesser, T. (2005) "Film Festival Networks: The New Topographies of Cinema in Europe," in *European Cinema: Face to Face With Hollywood*, Amsterdam: Amsterdam University Press, pp. 82–107.

Fraser, N. (1992) "Rethinking the Public Sphere: A Contribution to the Critique of Actually Existing Democracy," in C. Calhoun (ed.) *Habermas and the Public Sphere*, Cambridge, MA: MIT Press, pp. 109–142.

Gamson, J. (1996) "The Organizational Shaping of Collective Identity: The Case of Lesbian and Gay Film Festivals in New York," *Sociological Forum*, 11(2), pp. 231–261.

Greyson, J. (2009) *Covered*, video, http://vimeo.com/6308870 (March 15, 2014).

Huestis, M. (2001) *25—A Brief History of the Festival* (Marc Huestis, USA 2001, 60 min).

Iordanova, D. (2009) "The Film Festival Circuit," in D. Iordanova and R. Rhyne (eds.) *Film Festival Yearbook 1: The Festival Circuit*, St Andrews: St Andrews Film Studies, pp. 23–39.

Loist, S. (2011) "Precarious Cultural Work: About the Organization of (Queer) Film Festivals," *Screen*, 52(2), pp. 268–273.

Loist, S. and G. Zielinski (2012) "On the Development of Queer Film Festivals and Their Media Activism," in D. Iordanova and L. Torchin (eds.) *Film Festival Yearbook 4: Film Festivals and Activism*, St Andrews: St Andrews Film Studies, pp. 49–62.

Muñoz, J. (1996) "Ephemera as Evidence: Introductory Notes to Queer Acts," *Women & Performance: A Journal of Feminist Theory*, 8(2), pp. 5–16.

Prelinger, R. (2009) "Points of Origin: Discovering Ourselves Through Access," *The Moving Image*, 9(2), pp. 164–175.

Schoonover, K. (2015) "Queer or Human? LGBT Film Festivals, Human Rights and Global Film Culture," *Screen*, 56(1), pp. 121–132.

Sedgwick, E. K. (2008) *Epistemology of the Closet*, updated with a new preface, Berkeley, CA: University of California Press.

Sender, K. (2004) *Business, Not Politics: The Making of the Gay Market*, New York: Columbia University Press.

Sontag, S. (1967) "Notes on 'Camp' (1964)," in *Against Interpretation, and Other Essays*, New York: Delta, pp. 275–292.

Stringer, J. (2008) "Genre Films and Festival Communities: Lessons from Nottingham, 1991–2000." *Film International* 6(4), pp. 53–59.

Sullivan, N. (2003) *A Critical Introduction to Queer Theory*, Edinburgh: Edinburgh University Press.

Warner, M. (2002) *Publics and Counterpublics*, New York: Zone Books.

Wiegand, D. (2003) "Marc Huestis Grew Up Wanting to Be Either an Actor or President. Now the Filmmaker and Camp Impresario is Using His Showmanship to Promote Peace," *The San Francisco Chronicle*, July 16, Section D 1.

Zielinski, G. (2009a) "Queer Film Festivals," in J. C. Hawley and E. S. Nelson (eds.) *LGBTQ America Today: An Encyclopedia*, Westport, CT: Greenwood Press, pp. 980–984.

Zielinski, G. (2012) "On the Production of Heterotopia, and Other Spaces, in and around Lesbian and Gay Film Festivals," *eJump Cut* 54. www.ejumpcut.org/archive/jc54.2012/gerZelinskiFestivals/index.html (April 9, 2014).

Further reading

Cvetkovich, A. (2003) *An Archive of Feelings: Trauma, Sexuality and Lesbian Public Cultures*, Durham, NC: Duke University Press. (This book provides a good introduction to Cvetkovich's concept of archive of feelings and how it is applied to films and examples from popular culture. While her study concerns lesbians, it can be very useful to conceptualizing other groups.)

Stringer, J. (forthcoming) *Regarding Film Festivals*. New York: Palgrave Macmillan. (This is the revised and updated version of the author's PhD dissertation. Excellent introduction to rhetorical analysis and his concept of festival-idea, which are applied to program guides and other festival ephemera.)

Warner, M. (2002) *Publics and Counterpublics*, New York: Zone Books. (Warner's book posits an innovative theory of the public and introduces the concept of counterpublic. It is particularly useful to those studying identity-based or community-oriented film festivals associated somehow with social movements.)

Viewing suggestions

25—A Brief History of the Festival (Marc Huestis, USA 2001, 60 min.). Documentary on Frameline: San Francisco International LGBT Film Festival.

Acting Out: 25 Years of Queer Film and Community in Hamburg (Ana Grillo, Christina Magdalinou, and Silvia Torneden, Germany 2014, 85 min.). Documentary film on the Hamburg International Queer Film Festival.

Covered (John Greyson, Canada 2009, 15 min.). Essay film covering the violent disruption of the Queer Sarajevo festival, available online: https://vimeo.com/6308870.

Our Story—10-Year "Guerrilla Warfare" of Beijing Queer Film Festival (Yang Yang, China 2011, 45 min.). Documentary about the clandestine Chinese lesbian and gay film festival.

Queer Artivism (Maša Zia Lenárdič and Anja Wutej, Slovenia 2013, 96 min.). Documentary giving insight into the European queer film festival circuit by covering five festivals.

9 Positionality and film festival research

A conversation

Diane Burgess and Brendan Kredell

Introduction

Diane Burgess: This chapter grew out of several informal discussions regarding whether one needed to be an insider in order to speak with authority about how film festivals work. I had attended several conference presentations and kept hearing the same catchy pull quote from Mark Peranson's article "First You Get the Power, Then You Get the Money" (2009), which left me wondering what might happen as the number of dedicated film festival researchers continued to grow. Would these sexy catchphrases become floating signifiers, nodding to the intricacies of festival politics but with increasingly weak ties to their initial context(ual realities)? In thinking about the research process, Brendan and I concurred that the idea of access could be broken down into issues of position and perspective that influence a researcher's relationship with, and approach to, the object of study. Indeed, the more we grappled with the insider/outsider binary (that presumably divided us[1]), the more common ground we found as the binary dissolved into epistemological complexity. It is these questions of access, position, and perspective that guide our exploration of film festival research. In this chapter, we examine some of the challenges presented by festival research, from trying to get a handle on festival ontology to suggesting strategies for how novice researchers can devise a manageable project.

First, the roots of the aforementioned insider/outsider dilemma require a bit more elaboration. From critics to programmers, there has always been professional overlap between the festival circuit and academia. Many of the discipline's initial explorations of festival morphology came from scholars moonlighting as critics and programmers, while festival histories have been penned by journalists like Kenneth Turan (2002) and Brian D. Johnson (2000) or event co-founders like William Marshall (2005) and Lorry Smith (1999). Reaching back even further, in 1978's "Catch as Catch Cannes: The Moles and the Moths," published in *The Village Voice*, critic and theorist Andrew Sarris set out a basic taxonomy of his fellow festival attendees. From a historical perspective, the ethnographic approach has played an integral role in the development of the genre of film festival writing, to the extent that the insider voice is embedded as a central trope.

According to Richard Porton, in his introduction to *Dekalog 3: On Film Festivals*, his guiding principle in commissioning the anthology's contributions was "the importance of harnessing the personal (although hopefully non-narcissistic) voice" (2009: 1). What Porton sought from his contributors was the "somewhat jaundiced, but certainly not jaded view" of those with direct experience of the "ambivalent mixture of affection and informed revulsion" that the festival circuit inspires (ibid: 2). In other words, the specific cachet that would become the anthology's selling feature seems to emerge less from access to insider knowledge than from the experience of having one's cinephilic idealism repeatedly tempered by both the commercial realities of the film industry and the continuous onslaught of vacuous spectacle. Whether it is a perspective shaped by festival experience, or an interpretative advantage generated by insider access, my sense is that the researcher's relationship to film festivals has a significant impact on both the process and product of research.

Brendan Kredell: To be sure, there has been a historical intersection between the sets of people who study and write about film festivals, and the set of people who work (or have worked) at film festivals in some capacity. There is a significant amount of cultural work performed at film festivals that remains hidden from the attendees, and many of the issues addressed here and elsewhere in this book require a kind of specialized knowledge and privileged access that can come only with intimate knowledge of the inner workings of film festivals.

With that said, festivals are hardly unique in the way that they afford privileged access to a relative few but impact the lives of many more. Social scientists of many different stripes have grappled with the "positionality" of qualitative cultural research, but in general there is agreement that a binary "insider/outsider" approach to conceptualizing fields of cultural work is, at best, imprecise, and at worst it undermines the research by obscuring the more complex relationships of position and power that exist within any cultural field.

Here I agree entirely with Diane—I find it much more helpful to think critically about the positions within the field that each of us occupies as we conduct our research. A seasoned festival programmer is attentive to questions concerning the hierarchies of power within the festival world, and thus can address these issues with the benefit of the uniquely privileged position that working at a festival affords. Anthropologists and other qualitative researchers have observed that this "emic" approach—in which the perspectives and experiences of participants are foregrounded—is often used when conducting research in newer fields or those that have not been adequately theorized.[2]

As a field, film festival studies has moved beyond its initial descriptive and taxonomic phase. Since at least as far back as Bill Nichols' seminal essay "Global Image Consumption in the Age of Late Capitalism" (1994), we find evidence of an "etic" approach to festivals—an effort to apply existing conceptual schemes and critical models to the study of film festivals. As film festival studies expands in scope, examples of this type of work abound: scholars have situated the festival within the frameworks of network theory, cinema historiography, and urban development, to cite but a few examples.

Importantly, I do not mean to suggest that we should favor one approach over the other here; indeed, the rejection of the "insider/outsider" binary is a recognition that a synthetic approach to the study of festivals is the most fruitful. Instead, I want to encourage students coming to the academic study of film festivals for the first time to consider the variety of approaches that one might take. Many studies begin from a perspective internal to the festival, but this need not mean that working at a festival is a prerequisite for writing about the cultural work of film festivals.

Defining the object of study

DB: OK, but leaving aside questions of professional access and interpretive advantage, can we even have a theory of festivals? Or is a synthetic approach to festivals a reflection of ontological uncertainty, resulting in an etic approach that is, at best, piecemeal? Getting a handle on the film festival as an object of study can be difficult. A film festival comprises an exhibition space; an event; and an institution with links to civil society, cinema culture, the film industry, and to other festivals. Faced with a global proliferation of film festivals that range from red carpet extravaganzas to cinephilic showcases to targeted niche events, film festival scholars have found a singular definition of their object of study to be elusive. In the introductory essay of *Screen*'s 2011 film festivals dossier, David Archibald and Mitchell Miller note the diversity of institutional models and presentation modes that fuel debate regarding the fundamental attributes of the festival format.[3] Similarly, in the introduction to her book, *Film Festivals: Culture, People, and Power on the Global Screen*, Cindy Wong spends several pages detailing the myriad types of events that emerged globally following World War II, and then shifts her focus from individual operational footprints to shared interests in exploring canon, cultivating talent, and contributing to "the wider construction of film as a field of knowledge" (2011: 15). However, in the midst of variable potential approaches to defining festivals, the search for generalizable characteristics may yield a tacit assumption of sameness when it comes to the operational dynamics of festival space.

The notion of shared interests implies common or compatible goals, which may lead to the conclusion that festival organizers are chasing an ideal model. For instance, Wong asserts that "Cannes obviously does not represent all festivals, [but] it remains the one festival that all other festivals look to" (ibid.: 22). The perception of an "accepted formula" is also reflected in Hannah McGill's observation that "most of the world's smaller festivals [strive] to emulate the velvet-roped, red-carpeted, celeb-infested, A-list big boys" (2011: 284). As the former artistic director of the Edinburgh International

Film Festival, McGill presents an insider's perspective on the application of generalized models by funders and journalists. An interesting tension arises between perception and experience as she recounts "weeping tears of rage" when confronted with press accounts of "the troublesome 'competition'" with Cannes (ibid.: 283). Even if the two festivals fit a similar basic framework in their approaches to the format (i.e., presenting premieres of international cinema, with an industry component, and a red carpet), differences in scale, context, and operational resources mean that Cannes offers a reductive benchmark for understanding Edinburgh.[4]

This discrepancy between generalizable frameworks (or how we understand film festivals) and their application to specific events (or how a film festival actually works) presents a challenge for the film festival researcher. If one assumes that every festival strives to be Cannes (or Sundance or Toronto), there is a risk of collapsing the irreducible variability of regional, national, and international festival circuits. It is important to distinguish between the classification of a festival's features (e.g., Mark Peranson's 2009 typology of audience vs. business festivals), and the evaluative benchmarks that either explicitly inform, or implicitly creep into, the discussion. Indeed, most of us probably harbor assumptions about what festival success looks like, and these ideas can exert a reductive pressure on interpretations of festival operations. Another potentially reductive assumption relates to the notion of festival participation and exposes a key fallacy of insider/outsider logic. If we only consider degrees of access to festival space, we lose sight of the breadth of a festival's institutional reach and its connection with potential participants or otherwise interested parties. In other words, what does it really mean to participate in the festival experience?

BK: Diane makes an important point here, and it is one worth exploring at some length for its implications in how we think about film festivals and their place within the broader cinema culture. When used casually, we accept terms like "cinema culture" and "film festival" without bothering to complicate their meanings further. But if we pause to consider what, precisely, we mean by these terms, we recognize that cinema culture actually refers to a very complex web of interdependent parts, one that is far too intricate for a single book chapter to address. For our purposes here, we can recognize that located within that culture are many different constituencies—groups of individuals, firms, governments, and others—that have varying interests and investments in cinema. Viewed this way, film festivals are especially important insofar as they represent a critical site of intersection between these various constituencies.

Many scholars of film festivals refer to these constituencies as the "stakeholders" of festivals. As Ragan Rhyne (2009) shows us, the examination of who or what constitutes the stakeholders of a festival is an important part of the critical work of film festival studies. Here, as an illustration, we might consider the example of the Toronto International Film Festival (TIFF), by any measure one of the world's largest and most important festivals. By considering who or what we mean when we talk about the stakeholders of a festival, we gain insight into the unique nature of the festival's cultural work.[5]

In its 2012 edition, TIFF featured nearly 375 films, selected by a staff of approximately two dozen programmers, supported by a staff of several hundred festival employees. Nearly 300 filmmakers accompanied their films to Toronto, where they would meet members of the 1,200-strong media contingent accredited to cover TIFF that year. An additional 4,000 industry delegates—distributors, government officials, exhibitors, programmers from other festivals, to name but a few—attended the festival that year. When we talk about "festival insiders," we are referring to this group—at its most expansive, perhaps several thousand people—who regularly attend film festivals around the world and personify what we mean when we talk about the "festival circuit." And yet, even a cursory glance reveals how heterogeneous a group that is, with interests that are not always aligned and are sometimes directly in opposition. Marijke de Valck (2007) explores this diversity at greater length, showing us how film festivals use systems of accreditation to differentiate among distinct groups of festival attendees and bring some organizational logic to the festival.

While we do well to recognize the inherent heterogeneity of "festival insiders," narrowing our gaze to focus on the experience of these festival participants runs the risk of missing the forest for the trees. In 2012, they collectively represented approximately 1 percent of the total attendance at TIFF, in a year when more than 400,000 people reportedly attended the festival.[6] The vast majority of people who have direct personal experience with film festivals approach them from the perspective of an audience member, and certainly any discussion of positionality in festival research needs to account for these public audiences.

In light of the proliferation of festivals in recent decades, we are compelled to extend this accounting further, however, to include non-attendees. On its face, it would seem that the absolute prerequisite for meaningful participation within a festival is attendance, and yet upon closer inspection there are numerous ways in which the non-attendee proves to be just as important a stakeholder.

For example, in the case of a large urban festival like TIFF, the scope of its marketing campaigns and the attendant local media coverage means that we can safely assume that even though the majority of Torontonians do not attend any festival events, they are nonetheless *aware* of the festival's existence. As Julian Stringer (2008) suggests, there is a way in which festival marketing works by considering all city residents as potential future attendees of a festival, and thus can be understood as part of a continuing effort to broaden the local audience for a festival.

At the same time, festivals can serve as important sources of local tourism revenue, and many local businesses depend on these events to help drive the local economy. Historically, as Marijke de Valck (2007) has shown, many of the original European festivals were scheduled in such a way as to extend the seasons at popular resorts and tourism destinations. The same remains true in the contemporary festival world, as Claudia Green, Pat Bartholomew, and Suzanne Murrmann (2004) have demonstrated the symbolic and tangible impact of the Tribeca Film Festival in aiding the economic redevelopment of Lower Manhattan in the wake of September 11. For this reason, many festivals—TIFF included—draw support from local governments to help finance their operations (Kredell 2012). Consequently, festivals depend on the (indirect) support of local non-attendees to continue annual operations; these non-attendees are confronted with a decision to make about what the appropriate level of public funding for festivals is when deciding how to cast their vote in local elections.

But beyond the local level, the identity of film festivals within broader cinema culture is also largely determined by the participation—if that is the right word—of non-attendees. When we talk about a "Sundance film," we are doing so with the knowledge that this idea has meaning to a much larger group of people than will ever attend the annual festival in Park City. The prevalence of references to Sundance within broader film culture testifies to the degree that casual cinemagoers and festival insiders alike have seized on the festival as a shared metonym for a certain strain of American independent cinema.

Considered in this way, the diversity of an individual festival's stakeholders (both actual and potential) becomes evident; moreover, such an enumeration should also suggest to us the breadth of research topics awaiting future study.

Industry sectors and a shifting discursive field

DB: While Brendan's observations address who is impacted by the penetration of festival operations into cinema culture, I would like to flip this perspective to look instead at what these diverse functions mean for the festival as an organization. Many festivals have forged institutional stability through the extension of programming activities beyond their annual screening dates. For example, in cities like Berlin, Toronto, and Vancouver, initiatives focused on the cultural and economic revitalization of downtown neighborhoods have provided the festivals with much-needed infrastructure.[7] The provision of dedicated exhibition spaces enables these organizations to build a year-round footprint and to enhance their role in the presentation of art cinema to local audiences. For members of the public audience, the distinctions between art house and festival screenings may not be obvious. Once they have accessed a film, their viewing comprises an endpoint in the commodity chain, regardless of how the screening actually connects to revenue streams.

BK: We are accustomed to thinking about the organization of the film industry into distinct sectors: production, distribution, exhibition. Speaking generally, these distinctions are helpful and productive for cinema studies. Not only has our understanding of the structure and function of the industry as a whole benefited by considering the industry in a systematized way, but scholars have been able to refine methodological approaches to help account for the differences between these various sectors.

However, such an approach proves wanting when we consider the contemporary film festival world. As Dina Iordanova persuasively argues in the foreword to this book and elsewhere (2015), the modern festival sits at the nexus of these three sectors. Appreciating its diversity of function allows us to understand the important role that festivals play within the broader cultural landscape. At the same time, doing so also underscores the necessity of methodological innovation on the part of researchers hoping to understand the complexity of the contemporary festival.

DB: Although the film festival is a form of exhibition, it is important to note the ways in which festivals both converge with and deviate from other theatrical exhibition sites. At the festival, films do not accrue box-office receipts,[8] which would serve as markers of economic profit or relative performance. Not only are the festivals operating as nonprofit organizations, in pursuit of cultural rather than commercial goals, but also the high number of programmed films combined with a low number of screenings per film necessitates a reliance on subsidy, discount, or deferral. The notion of discount applies to the use of sponsorships to support operational needs including shipping, travel, and communications. Another key source of discount comes from the festival's large corps of volunteers (often numbering in the hundreds) who trade their labor for a festival pass.[9]

For the film festival as an organization, attendance figures (which include comps, or free tickets) build prestige by signaling event popularity, while paid admissions contribute operating revenue. Although festivals do tend to publicize overall attendance figures, numbers for individual films are more difficult to ascertain. With accredited guests, who are provided with some degree of complimentary access to screenings, as well as pass holders, who have purchased bulk access rather than individual tickets, it might not even be possible to calculate the revenue generated by specific films; and, even if these data could be presented, the cash receipts from individual screenings would not be meaningful, either as a marker of value for the festival or as an indicator of consumer preference (as compared to weekend "Top 10s" to present aggregated box-office data). What matters instead is the accumulation of symbolic capital, in the form of buzz or prestige that can be converted to economic profit *after* the festival.[10]

For the researcher, the film festival can appear to be a space of flux, as opposed to an endpoint or a singular event. Assessments of value are contingent on perspective, and thus it is important to consider whether one is focused on the public audience, industry stakeholders, sponsors, and government partners, or the festival itself as a cultural institution. At the same time, both value and sectoral positioning raise the relationship between festivals—as a model for comparative appraisal or as a framework for understanding how they interconnect. Festivals often struggle over limited resources, such as public funding and world premieres, in addition to rivalries over calendar position and event prestige. Smaller festivals are able to draw on the global media attention generated by A-list festivals in order to attract local audience attention to their program selections. Generally speaking, there is a tension between collaboration and competition that sustains film festival circuits on regional, national, and international levels. However, although film festivals appear to coalesce into circuits with prints and guests traveling from one event to the next, it is important to acknowledge the contingent nature of these connections.

In two of the seminal articles about how festivals interconnect, both Ragan Rhyne (2009) and Dina Iordanova (2009) reject the notion of a cohesive film festival circuit. Rhyne conceptualizes festivals as a culture industry driven by the material practices of cultural policy, whereas Iordanova draws attention to the operational pressures of supply chain management. Iordanova's model, in particular, lends itself to a discussion of the circulation of films, industry professionals, and even festival labor; and, it is here that the focus may shift from the mechanisms that inform how festivals interconnect to the effects of these interconnections. This shift carries with it a slippage in terminology from the analysis of exhibition sites to distribution networks. For example, Marijke de Valck has referred to the worldwide proliferation of film festivals in terms of "the institutionalization of a non-profit distribution system" (2007: 104), even though there is no formal system in place. Researchers need to consider what terms like distribution, exhibition, and circuit designate—asking whose perspective is represented, and what might be overlooked. Ultimately, film festivals present a complex object of study that is difficult to pin down, leaving researchers with slippery terminology and a shifting discursive field.

Thus far in this chapter, Brendan and I have unpacked some of the ontological complexity and epistemological tangles that await festival researchers. My advice to those heading into this terrain for the first time is to think about how to narrow and frame your topic so that your research maps a focused and manageable position.

Research questions

BK: Part of the allure of studying film festivals derives from the variety of entry points that festivals afford us into the culture of cinema. Given this, we are also faced with the potentially challenging task of identifying how to most effectively devise a methodological strategy for approaching the festival. Put in different terms, the researcher must first decide what sort of research question to ask about film festivals. But before we can begin formulating research questions, however, we should address a series of more fundamental issues: what kinds of questions can researchers of film festivals pose? What are the unique opportunities and challenges that this research presents, and how can researchers develop interesting projects in light of these issues? Given the diversity of avenues for critical inquiry into the film festival, a number of methods are available to us.

At the same time, festivals present particular issues that we must be aware of when conceiving and developing research projects. As we develop our studies, we need to take into account how our own position within the field facilitates certain kinds of research projects while foreclosing on others. This is not to privilege one kind of research over another; the field of film festival studies has benefited both from the contributions of scholars who have been able to draw on their own insight and access to the inner workings of festivals (Czach 2004; Wong 2011) as well as scholars who approach festivals instead as observers or interested researchers (Strandgaard Pedersen and Mazza 2011; Elsaesser 2005). Put simply, we should recognize that there are as many different ways to approach researching festivals as there are festivals themselves.

As a way of thinking about the variety of approaches available to scholars, and the consequences and implications of each, consider the following sample research questions and the issues of methodological diversity that they raise in the study of film festivals.

How did the rise of the film festival movement in postwar Europe affect the development of auteur film criticism during the same time period?

One way of approaching the film festival is to consider it historically, both as a movement in its own right, and also as a way of considering the evolution of film culture more generally. Dorota Ostrowska's chapter in this volume (Chapter 1) serves as a useful illustration of this kind of historical project, which requires the researcher to think carefully about how to muster historical evidence in order to construct an argument. The "archive" of film festival studies can be elusive and incomplete, a challenge especially for researchers coming to the field of festivals for the first time. Invoking Roland Barthes, Daniel Dayan described this as the paradox of the "double festival" (2013 [2000]: 56): a film festival is at once visual—defined by the films that it screens—and written—the sum of the multitude of materials (program notes, festival reviews, press releases, etc.) that are produced by the festival.

Careful historical research requires an attentiveness to the diversity of texts that constitutes the archive of the festival. Given the ephemeral nature of festivals, it is often the case that historical records are incomplete, ad hoc, or simply nonexistent. Even for the most well-established festivals, relatively few historical materials are available in online databases; for older editions, the Festival de Cannes' website lists the festival sections, juries, and award winners for each year, in addition to a collection of film posters.[11] Smaller festivals, which often rely exclusively on volunteer and contract labor and may not have a year-round staff or physical location, present an even more challenging problem for the historical researcher. Informal archives, oral histories, publicity materials, and ephemera become important sources for the researcher in this case, as Ger Zielinski describes in the preceding chapter in this part.

What role do identity-based festivals serve in the formation of alternative public spheres at the local level?

Some of the questions that we want to ask about film festivals are hybrid in nature. Here, we see an example of a research question rooted in a question of cultural theory: what precisely is an "alternative public sphere," and how might that concept help us to understand identity-based film festivals? (This is an issue explored at length in Chapter 5 by Cindy Hing-Yuk Wong in this volume.) On the other hand, this is also an empirical question, one that could be approached ethnographically. Phrased slightly differently, what role does a *specific* identity-based festival serve in the formation of a *particular* alternative public sphere? To answer that question, we would need to develop relationships with the various actors within the festival ecosystem, carefully observing the relationship between festival organizers, stakeholders, community partners, and audience members over a period of time. By gaining an understanding of the investments of each of the different actors and how their interests interrelate, we can in turn perform what Toby Lee (in Chapter 7 in this volume) describes as "ethnographic reading," situating our observation and analysis of festival participants within broader social and cultural frameworks.

While ethnographic accounts of film festivals can be tremendously rich, researchers seeking to conduct such analysis confront a number of challenges. It takes time to develop the kinds of relationships necessary to gain key insight into the workings of a festival, and since festivals typically happen annually, this can mean devoting several years to the study. Researchers must anticipate and consider issues such as this before embarking on such a project.

How do host cities benefit from the presence of international film festivals? What kinds of issues do they confront when deciding how to allocate scarce cultural resources between festivals and fine arts institutions (operas, ballets, etc.)?

A third approach would be to locate film festivals within broader social and political contexts and consider the links between festivals and issues of local, national, and international import. Julian Stringer's study of the film festival in the era of global cities takes this approach, arguing that scholars should "pay as much attention to the spatial logics of the historical and contemporary festival circuit as we do to the films it exhibits" (2001: 138). Such an approach to thinking about festivals opens the field out onto a variety of related discourses—tourism, cultural policy, economics, and cultural geography not least among them. As is implicit in Stringer's formulation above, elevating the study of the networks that envelop film festivals to coequal status with the films that are screened at them leads us down a markedly different methodological path.

In practice, many researchers will employ a methodological approach that blends some combination of the above. In every case, however, we must consider carefully how the methods we choose will help us to best address the research questions we pose. In an era of abundant information, we now have available an incredible richness of primary and secondary literature via university libraries and the Internet, to say nothing of the video releases of many key films. The result is a more fecund environment for new scholarship than ever before.

However, as indicated above, film festivals present challenges for the researcher, particularly when it comes to issues of access and availability. In her discussion of film historiography, Barbara Klinger calls our attention to the dangers of becoming "stuck in synchrony." She means to caution us against focusing inordinate attention upon the moment of a film's initial release at the expense of what she refers to as the film's "diachronic dimension": the cultural life of a film that begins after the moment of its release (1997: 111). Yet film festival researchers face the opposite problem. The unique nature of film festivals is that they describe a particular temporal and spatial junction. When we talk about film festivals and the films that play at them, we are talking about a very specific set of reception contexts; any attempt at recreating these contexts after the fact proves impossible.

As film festivals have proliferated around the globe, it is increasingly the case that researchers are able to attend local festivals. However, unless you live in a city with a major international film festival, it is much less likely that you would have the opportunity to attend one of the world's A-list film festivals. There is no equivalent interlibrary loan or web search for the Berlinale or the Toronto International Film Festival; put simply, there is no substitute for being there.

With that said, such a recognition does not mean that film festival research can only be conducted by people living in Cannes, Venice, Berlin, Toronto, and a handful of other cities around the globe. Indeed, the proliferation of scholarship on festivals in recent years reflects the development of novel and insightful ways of thinking about film festivals by researchers from around the world. The most successful projects are those that begin with an appreciation of the limitations faced by the researcher. A proposed study on the role of sales agents at the Cannes film festival could be fascinating, but without access into the festival such a project would likely suffer from a scarcity of available evidence upon which to construct an argument. It may be unreasonable to expect a student attending her first film festival to secure interviews with festival directors, programmers, or visiting filmmakers. On the other hand, volunteering in the box office at a local film festival often provides a wealth of information to the careful observer. Ultimately, the lesson to developing a good research question is twofold. We should strive to ask questions that are compelling and interesting, while at the same time developing strategies to answer those questions that are robust and accomplishable.

Production of knowledge

DB: Each of Brendan's research questions sets out a potential methodological approach, and also suggests a disciplinary lens or conceptual framework that would align the project with a particular subfield of knowledge production. Often an interdisciplinary endeavor, film festival research can intersect with multiple subject areas such as film studies, communications, or urban studies. This potential interdisciplinarity points to the necessity of attending to the conventions of particular genres of research writing, both in terms of the types of data sources that are consulted and the analytical moves that are undertaken. For example, an ethnographic festival report differs in tone and style from an archival history. Textual analysis differs from audience study. Here, it is once again important to explore issues of position and perspective—a researcher not only must consider how to devise a manageable research question, but also needs to think about how different interests shape how the object of study is framed. This relationship encompasses the researcher, as the research question may privilege a particular interpretation of the data. It also can shape both primary and secondary data, reflecting the multiple stakeholder interests that impact festival operation and film festival space.

For example, film festivals always have some sort of relationship with the public sector. Many festivals operate as nonprofit organizations, which grants independent status as a legal entity, and means that all income is directed to operational objectives. Subsequent registration for charitable status then allows for income tax exemption, and enables the festival to issue tax receipts to donors. For festivals, this business model recognizes their heavy reliance on funding support from public partners, corporate sponsors, and private donors. Depending on the regulations governing nonprofit organizations and/or registered charities in a particular region, the festival may be required to articulate and adhere to an educational or cultural mandate. This type of public service remit differs from the nationalist impulses that sparked the historical emergence of European festivals. What all of this means for the film festival researcher is that there are multiple ways in which the institutional structure of a specific event may have been influenced by its relationship to the state (or province or city)—through direct intervention in founding or operating a festival; via the juridical system that governs nonprofit organizations; or through funding mechanisms used to subsidize festival operations.

From a research perspective, there is a wealth of information available about these contextual factors that shape festival operations. Researchers interested in policy analysis or national cinema can access funding criteria in order to explore the film festival's role in industrial development, canon formation, or national cinema culture. Additional sources of government support for festivals may include national ministries of foreign affairs, trade, and development; state/provincial cultural agencies; or municipal cultural planning boards. As charitable foundations, most festivals are required to publish an annual report, which shows the breakdown of income and expenditures, and also may elaborate on the implementation of the organization's mandate and vision. These data could be used to tease out the nuances of how programming is affected—from priorities to categories to sponsor placement—but it is necessary to be cautious in attributing causality at the risk of oversimplifying the forces exerted by the field's multiple stakeholders. For instance, a national showcase satisfies funding criteria, but also meets the needs of local industry stakeholders, enables audiences to watch indigenous films, and allows the festival programmer to highlight aesthetic trends in international cinema. It is also important to remember that, as a nonprofit organization, the film festival's fiduciary duty is to its Board of Directors and not to its public sector partners.[12]

Beyond this initial step of examining how stakeholder interests can frame or shape your research topic, it is also necessary to turn a critical eye on data sources. What biases or blind spots might be present? How might the data have been impacted by the conditions under which it was produced? In other words, the context of knowledge production carries particular goals or objectives, as well as potential limiting factors. Municipal planners seek to glean different information about the festival than cultural funding agencies. Each festival similarly strives to present a focused brand identity, including a cohesive historical narrative. A healthy dose of skepticism can prove useful. For example, consider how the celebratory festival atmosphere, or the promise of insider gossip, might inflect the tone of a festival review or the account of a festival's seemingly inevitable rise to its present state of glory. Indeed, certain sub-genres of film festival writing invoke the cachet of festival buzz. As a final note, it is important to keep in mind the professional constraints that may impact knowledge production. Festival insiders are often bound by ethical considerations, either as employees who have signed a nondisclosure agreement or as journalists bound by a professional code.

Conclusion: voice and self-reflexivity

BK: In Chapter 6 of this book, Marijke de Valck takes up the work of sociologist Pierre Bourdieu, arguing that we can apply his concepts of field, capital, and habitus to film festival research to better understand the relationships between and among filmmakers, audiences, and festivals themselves. By way of closing this conversation, it is useful to consider how Bourdieu's approach helps us understand not only the interrelations of agents within the field of the festival, but also our own position and relationship to our object of study.

DB: In his own discussion of methodology in *The Rules of Art*, Bourdieu (1996) argued for a rigorous approach to self-reflexivity: The researcher would need to examine his or her own positioning in the field of cultural production, including habitus, in order to fully grasp the forces that shape these relationships. For me, this raises the issue of voice and whether or not the researcher's position should be conveyed explicitly in the text. In the historical development of the genre of film festival writing, the personal voice has emerged (and still persists) as a marker of value even though not all insiders are presenting ethnographic accounts or festival reviews. For example,

Peranson's festival typology straddles style boundaries with a combination of objectively presented data and the frequent use of personalized self-reference. Rather than merely detailing research steps, Peranson's use of first person signals his insider status, presenting his firsthand expertise as the source of his argument. In our encounters with film festival research, it is important to be attuned to the impact of these modes of expression.

BK: If there is one takeaway for the researcher approaching festivals for the first time, it is that there is no "right" way to write about film festivals. As we have indicated, there are a multitude of research methods available to us, each of which helps answer different sets of questions about film festivals. As a result, it is important that we think critically about methodology, as distinct from method. That is, we should determine what research *strategy* will be most effective, and make decisions about which particular methods will be helpful to us as part of that process.

These considerations do not happen in a vacuum, however. Successful festival research requires careful attention to questions of positionality, of access, and of our own relationship to power structures. Simply by writing about festivals, we are implicated in the complex power structure of international cinema. Acknowledging as much should not be considered a weakness; to the contrary, appreciating one's own relationship to the field reflects the nuanced thinking of a scholar who is aware of the complexities of the global festival ecosystem. My advice to my own students, and to those coming to festivals for the first time, is to begin by taking stock of their own position within the field. An audience member attending their first film festival will bring a much different perspective to the proceedings than a programmer or critic who participates within the global festival circuit. Allow this understanding to inform your research and your writing, and your scholarship will in turn benefit.

Notes

1 I came to film festival research as an insider, having worked as a festival programmer, whereas Brendan has not worked at festivals. See our bios for more info.

2 For a foundational discussion of these concepts, see Marvin Harris's (1976) discussion of etic and emic approaches to anthropology. More recently, Geert Hofstede offers a summary of the historical alignments of various social science disciplines along the emic/etic spectrum, while proposing a model for reconciling the two in his "A Case for Comparing Apples with Oranges": "the first (emic) without the second gets stuck in case studies that cannot be generalised, the second without the first in abstractions that cannot be related to real life" (1998: 19). He instead argues that comparative research into apples and oranges requires that we first "possess a fruitology, a theory of fruits" (ibid.: 17).

3 Dina Iordanova examines this debate in a blog post, noting that curator Neil Young has raised the question of whether Cannes, where attendance is predominantly restricted to industry delegates, even qualifies as a festival (as cited in Archibald and Miller 2011: 250).

4 Owen Evans critiques Thomas Elsaesser's view of Cannes as "the template for film festivals the world over, which [...] have largely synchronized their organizational

structures and selection procedures while nonetheless setting different accents to maintain their profile and identity" (Elsaesser 2005: 90). Arguing against what he refers to as the tendency "to use Cannes as a synecdoche for all festivals," Evans considers how local cultural and geopolitical contexts have shaped the programming structure of festivals like Berlin and Karlovy Vary (2007: 27).

5 Throughout this discussion I'll be using the term "stakeholder," which remains the most consistently used term within the field. (In addition to Rhyne 2009, see Getz et al. 2007; Ooi and Strandgaard Pederson 2010; Loist 2011.) However, I would note here that festival researchers would do well to think critically about the terms we employ. In its origins in stakeholder theory (Freeman 1984), "stakeholder" derived its meaning from a contrast with the more narrowly-defined concept of a shareholder. Subsequently, the term has been adopted more broadly beyond the context of management theory, but retains some of its original meaning. Discussing festival stakeholders remains a useful way to identify the various individuals and groups with investment in a festival—from filmmakers to festival organizers to audiences to sponsors. Rhyne describes these as the parties with "particular interests in seeing the [festival] network proliferate" (2009: 9). Yet our theorizing of festivals demands a term that is more diffuse and elastic, so that we might include those people who are not invested in the success of a particular festival per se but are nonetheless affected or served by it. "Constituency" is useful in this regard: its meaning is broad enough to encompass both the aforementioned stakeholder groups as well as those groups whose involvement in a festival is more indirect.

6 This ratio of festival insider to layperson is even greater at festivals that do not enjoy the same level of industry participation as TIFF. Many smaller regional festivals are run by small ad hoc organizations, who often make do without full-time staff and who rely heavily upon volunteer labor to run the festival. Beyond a small local media presence, there is virtually no press or industry participation at these "audience festivals" (to borrow Peranson's term), where the ratio of attendees to insiders could easily approach 500:1.

7 For details about the Berlinale's move to Potsdamer Platz for its fiftieth anniversary, see Jacobsen (2000). Kredell (2012) examines the evolution of municipal cultural policy in Toronto and its culmination in the opening of TIFF's new headquarters, Bell Lightbox. Burgess (2008) discusses the urban policy contexts and real estate development projects associated with the construction of Bell Lightbox and the Vancouver International Film Centre.

8 Distributors tend to defer their economic return and approach the film festival as a marketing platform from which critical acclaim, awards, or positive audience response can be used to launch a subsequent commercial theatrical release. See Peranson's (2009) examination of the power dynamics between different types of festivals, including the rise of sales agents and the economy of festival screening fees.

9 See Loist (2011) for more on the precarious labor conditions of festival workers.

10 For more, see Burgess (2008) and Chapter 6 in this book by Marijke de Valck.

11 In a welcome development, festivals have in recent years begun to place more emphasis on the digitization and availability of their archives. Many festivals—from A-list festivals such as Cannes and Sundance to smaller niche festivals like the Banff Mountain Film Festival and the DC Shorts Festival—have made selected materials available through their websites. Given the variety of texts associated with festivals—and the multiplicity of voices responsible for creating those texts (festival organizers, filmmakers, industry figures, critics, audiences, etc.)—these efforts remain necessarily incomplete.

12 Burgess examines the largely unsuccessful attempt by federal and provincial funding agencies to intervene in the operation of the Montreal World Film Festival by

redirecting funding support toward the launch of the New Montreal FilmFest (2012: 11–14). The result was an overcrowded and confusing fall calendar, with the World Film Festival persevering despite the cuts and the New FilmFest ultimately folding after its inaugural run.

References

Archibald, D. and M. Miller (2011) "The Film Festival Dossier: Introduction," *Screen*, 52(2), pp. 249–252.

Bourdieu, P. (1996) *The Rules of Art: Genesis and Structure of the Literary Field*, trans. S. Emanuel, Cambridge: Polity.

Burgess, D. (2008) *Negotiating Value: A Canadian Perspective on the International Film Festival*, unpublished PhD thesis, Vancouver: Simon Fraser University.

Burgess, D. (2012) "Bridging the Gap: Film Festival Governance, Public Partners and the 'Vexing' Problem of Film Distribution," *Canadian Journal of Film Studies | Revue Canadienne d'Études Cinématographiques*, 21(1), pp. 2–20.

Czach, L. (2004) "Film Festivals, Programming, and the Building of a National Cinema," *The Moving Image*, 4(1), pp. 76–88.

Dayan, D. (2013 [2000]) "Looking for Sundance: The Social Construction of a Film Festival," in D. Iordanova (ed.) *The Film Festivals Reader*, St Andrews: St Andrews Film Studies, pp. 45–58.

De Valck, M. (2007) *Film Festivals: From European Geopolitics to Global Cinephilia*, Amsterdam: Amsterdam University Press.

Elsaesser, T. (2005) *European Cinema: Face to Face With Hollywood*, Amsterdam: Amsterdam University Press.

Evans, O. (2007) "Border Exchanges: The Role of the European Film Festival," *Journal of Contemporary European Studies*, 15(1), pp. 23–33.

Freeman, R. E. (1984) *Strategic Management: A Stakeholder Approach*, Boston, MA: Pitman.

Getz, D., T. Andersson, and M. Larson (2007) "Festival Stakeholder Roles: Concepts and Case Studies," *Event Management*, 10(2), pp. 103–122.

Green, C. G., P. Bartholomew, and S. Murrmann (2004) "New York Restaurant Industry," *Journal of Travel & Tourism Marketing*, 15, pp. 63–79.

Harris, M. (1976) "History and Significance of the Emic/Etic Distinction," *Annual Review of Anthropology*, 5, pp. 329–350.

Hofstede, G. (1998) "A Case for Comparing Apples with Oranges: International Differences in Values," *International Journal of Comparative Sociology*, 39(1), pp. 16–31.

Iordanova, D. (2009) "The Film Festival Circuit," in D. Iordanova and R. Rhyne (eds.) *Film Festival Yearbook 1: The Festival Circuit*, St Andrews: St Andrews Film Studies, pp. 23–39.

Iordanova, D. (2015) "The Film Festival as an Industry Node," *Media Industries*, 1(3), pp. 7–11.

Jacobsen, W. (ed.) (2000) *50 Years Berlinale. Internationale Filmfestspiele Berlin*, Berlin: Nicolai.

Johnson, B. D. (2000) *Brave Films, Wild Nights: 25 Years of Festival Fever*, Toronto: Random House Canada.

Klinger, B. (1997) "Film History Terminable and Interminable: Recovering the Past in Reception Studies," *Screen*, 38(2), pp. 107–128.

Kredell, B. (2012) "T.O. Live With Film: The Toronto International Film Festival and Municipal Cultural Policy in Contemporary Toronto," *Canadian Journal of Film Studies | Revue Canadienne d'Études Cinématographiques*, 21(1), pp. 21–37.

Loist, S. (2011) "Precarious Cultural Work: About the Organization of (Queer) Film Festivals," *Screen*, 52(2), pp. 268–273.

Marshall, W. (2005) *Film Festival Confidential*, Toronto: McArthur & Co.

McGill, H. (2011) "Film Festivals: A View From the Inside," *Screen*, 52(2), pp. 280–285.

Nichols, B. (1994) "Global Image Consumption in the Age of Late Capitalism," *East–West Film Journal*, 8(1), pp. 68–85.

Ooi, C.-S. and J. Strandgaard Pedersen (2010) "City Branding and Film Festivals: Re-Evaluating Stakeholder's Relations," *Place Branding and Public Diplomacy*, 6(4), pp. 316–332.

Peranson, M. (2009) "First You Get the Power, Then You Get the Money: Two Models of Film Festivals," in R. Porton (ed.) *Dekalog 3: On Film Festivals*, London: Wallflower, pp. 23–37.

Porton, R. (ed.) (2009) *Dekalog 3: On Film Festivals*, London: Wallflower.

Rhyne, R. (2009) "Film Festival Circuits and Stakeholders," in D. Iordanova and R. Rhyne (eds.) *Film Festival Yearbook 1. The Festival Circuit*, St Andrews: St Andrews Film Studies, pp. 9–39.

Sarris, A. (1978) "Catch as Catch Cannes: The Moles and the Moths," *The Village Voice*, June 12, pp. 39–40.

Smith, L. (1999) *Party in a Box: The Story of the Sundance Film Festival*, Salt Lake City, UT: Gibbs Smith.

Strandgaard Pedersen, J. and C. Mazza (2011) "International Film Festivals: For the Benefit of Whom?" *Culture Unbound*, 3, pp. 139–165.

Stringer, J. (2001) "Global Cities and International Film Festival Economy," in M. Shiel and T. Fitzmaurice (eds.) *Cinema and the City: Film and Urban Societies in a Global Context*, Oxford: Blackwell, pp. 134–144.

Stringer, J. (2008) "Genre Films and Festival Communities: Lessons From Nottingham, 1991–2000," *Film International*, 6, pp. 53–60.

Turan, K. (2002) *Sundance to Sarajevo: Film Festivals and the World They Made*, Berkeley, CA: University of California Press.

Wong, C. H.-Y. (2011) *Film Festivals: Culture, People, and Power on the Global Screen*, New Brunswick, NJ: Rutgers University Press.

Further reading

Bourdieu, P. (1993) *The Field of Cultural Production: Essays on Art and Literature*, ed. R. Johnson, New York: Columbia University Press. (Bourdieu's foundational collection of essays is essential reading about positionality and power in the cultural field; of particular note, the editor's introduction by Randal Johnson offers a useful primer for readers new to Bourdieu.)

Caldwell, J. (2008) *Production Culture: Industrial Reflexivity and Critical Practice in Film and Television*, Durham, NC: Duke University Press. (Groundbreaking study of the media industries that provides a useful framework for festival researchers, especially those working in the ethnographic tradition.)

Peranson, M. (2009) "First You Get the Power, Then You Get the Money: Two Models of Film Festivals," in R. Porton (ed.) *Dekalog 3. On Film Festivals*, London:

Wallflower, pp. 23–37. (Peranson's essay draws distinctions between the kinds of festivals that exist in the world and the power relations that predominate at those festivals.)

Porton, R. (2009) "Introduction: On Film Festivals," in R. Porton (ed.) *Dekalog 3: On Film Festivals*, London: Wallflower, pp. 1–9. (The introduction to Porton's book grapples with the questions of voice, access, and "embedded-ness" in interesting ways.)

Rhyne, R. (2009) "Film Festival Circuits and Stakeholders," in D. Iordanova and R. Rhyne (eds.) *Film Festival Yearbook 1: The Festival Circuit*, St Andrews: St Andrews Film Studies, pp. 9–39. (Offers a thorough accounting of festival stakeholders and situates our understanding of festival organizational structures within a broader frame of neoliberal governance.)

Part IV

Practice

Introduction

Brendan Kredell

Throughout this book, we have explored the history of film festivals and the variety of theoretical and methodological frameworks that we can employ to help us understand them. In this closing part, we turn to consider the praxis of film festivals. Here, we ask how the lessons learned previously can help us better understand the daily business of film festivals.

There is perhaps no more fertile site in media studies than the contemporary film festival for considering the interaction of theory and practice. Film festivals are the place where the proverbial sausage gets made: filmmakers receive funding for future projects; distributors make decisions about which films to acquire based upon expected future earnings potential; programmers of cinemas and other festivals attend screenings in an effort to scout new films to show; and audiences see new films that they would likely be otherwise unable to view.

And yet while all of this business is being transacted, questions swirl in the background about the influence of globalization on the contemporary media industries, the role of cultural production in the formation of group identity, and the impact of new technologies on existing models of business (to name but a few). Far from being mere academic concerns, festival practitioners must negotiate answers to these complicated questions every day as a condition of maintaining their relevance in a quickly changing world.

In this part, the three authors set out to consider the practical and theoretical implications for these disparate functions of the contemporary film festival. In the first chapter, Roya Rastegar takes up the issue of film festival programming. Drawing on her own diverse experience programming festivals both large and small, she insists upon what she terms the "curatorial potential" of festival programming. By reclaiming the idea of curator-as-caretaker (a connotation that has been lost in the recent popularization of the term), Rastegar offers us a way of thinking about the importance of the festival programmer in broader film culture. Continuing with the theme, Liz Czach explores the "affective labor" of festival programming in the next chapter. Like Rastegar, Czach draws from her own experience as a festival programmer, exploring how the appeal of creative labor is complicated by the intensity of the work, its precariousness, and the positive and negative affect associated with the job.

In the final chapter of this volume, Tamara L. Falicov considers the increasingly important role that festivals play in facilitating the production of motion pictures. In particular, she examines production funds, which have evolved in recent years to play an increasingly important role in the financing of international art cinema. As she demonstrates, the practice and politics of these funds are complex, and any understanding of the contemporary festival ecosystem needs to account for the growing role that these funds play in the production of films for the international festival circuit.

Of course, the constraints of space necessarily limit the survey that this book can offer of contemporary festival practice. As the further reading sections appended to each of these chapters suggest, these authors are participating within much broader conversations about the role of programming and production funds in film festival studies. There are inevitably many aspects of film festival practice that are left unremarked-upon here; for instance, other scholars have previously examined the practice of film festivals from the perspective of organizational studies (see, for example, Rüling and Strandgaard Pedersen 2010), or by situating them within the context of migrant and diasporic community-building (Stewart 2014).

Beyond the academic literature, an entire industry of guidebooks exists: guides for the aspiring filmmaker navigating the festival circuit, for the would-be festival organizer, and even for the potential festival sponsor. Yet while much has already been written about film festival practice, the ever-changing nature of festivals means that much exciting research remains to be done, as we continue to develop our understanding of the evolution of film festivals.

References

Rüling, C.-C. and J. Strandgaard Pedersen (2010) "Film Festival Research From an Organizational Studies Perspective," *Scandinavian Journal of Management*, 26(3), pp. 318–323.

Stewart, M. (2014) "The Ethnocultural Film Festival as Media Happening: French-Maghrebi Film in Marseille," *Interactions: Studies in Communication & Culture*, 5(2), pp. 185–198.

10 Seeing differently

The curatorial potential of film festival programming

Roya Rastegar

Introduction

Before my discussion of the critical practices involved in the curatorial process of film festival programming, I want to first contextualize my own commitments to and background in film festivals. The first festival I curated, in collaboration with fellow doctoral candidate Susy Zepeda, was the Women of Color Film Festival (WOCFF). I had left my investment banking career in London to pursue a doctorate in the History of Consciousness in Santa Cruz. The city on a hill and its occupants felt alien to me, and my academic advisor, Angela Y. Davis, encouraged me to take on the challenge of curating the festival as a way of finding community. A year later, on a panel on the "activist potential of film festivals" at Frameline, San Francisco's LGBT Film Festival, I met Shari Frilot, a senior programmer at the Sundance Film Festival and former director of the MIX New York Experimental Lesbian and Gay Film Festival. As a response to my naïve positioning of community-based festivals in opposition to "mainstream" festivals, Frilot invited me to work for her at the 2006 Sundance Film Festival and gain insight into the relations of independent film production, exhibition, and distribution. One of my committee members, B. Ruby Rich, a feminist cultural critic and longtime beloved member of the independent film scene, encouraged me to accept the offer and complicate my analysis of how films by and representations of women of color circulate within the film industry at large. Off I went over the ivory-rimmed ledge of theory, head first into praxis.

I quickly learned that "mainstream" is relative; Sundance and supporters of independent film are not considered mainstream in relation to the larger film industry. I also learned that championing work solely by "women of color" vastly limited the efficacy of alliances across gender, race, and sexuality, necessary in the face of the larger film industry's biases. As such, both community-based and industry-based festivals are necessary vehicles that can support films that disrupt a dominant order of representation within popular culture. Community-based film festivals are like incubator labs, places that nourish and encourage filmmakers to develop their voice in dialogue with eager audiences from specific communities who are hungry for images and stories that present a different vision of the world (and themselves) than that of a dominant order of representation. Industry-based film festivals, like Sundance, are the gates through which these films and their makers must pass in order to gain larger publics and create cultural shifts on a broad scale. The key here is how the keepers of those gates determine who shall pass, and who shall not. I wanted to be one of those keepers. I worked at the Tribeca Film Festival as a programmer for several years, and continued as a programming associate at Sundance for American narrative feature films. Currently, as the head of programming at the Los Angeles Film Festival, I direct the mission and curatorial process of the festival to recognize and showcase different approaches to storytelling (that tell different kinds of stories).

"Curating" film festivals

The concept of curating has become an increasingly chic way of describing any form of selection that shows off taste. Digital influencers *curate* weekend getaway wardrobes. Nightclubs *curate* guest lists. Bloggers and online sites *curate* content. Fashion collections are *curated* (cf. Williams 2009). But curating is more than simply selecting or arranging a series of objects according to one's taste. From the Latin "to care," one of the first uses of the word curate is found in the eighteenth century. A curate was cleric, a spiritual guide responsible for the care of souls. This connotation of curate and caretaking carries forward today. In a museum context, curators are entrusted with the care of artworks and the artist's vision. Curators mediate between artists and various stakeholders, like museums, galleries, and collectors, to build the framework in which audiences see and engage with artwork in such a way that can resonate within broader cultural, political, and social contexts.

Festival programming generally consists of a two-part process: editorial and curatorial. The editorial aspect of programming requires that a large majority of the thousands and thousands of films submitted for consideration be "edited" out of the selection process in order to hone in on the few hundred submissions that will be debated on. Consider that of the 12,000 short and feature-length films submitted for consideration to the Sundance Film Festival in 2015, barely 3 percent were selected for the festival program.[1] Programmers for industry-based festivals are tasked with identifying a minuscule fraction of films that will be seen by audiences of film professionals who write about, represent, and distribute films. Of those hundred or so films selected for the festival program, still fewer will receive some kind of distribution to be released into the theaters and/or onto DVD or VOD. Since there is no way of systematically tracking, categorizing, cataloguing, and archiving all the films made every year, the thousands of films *not* selected for film festivals are effectively lost without the context and infrastructure provided by the film industry.

The second part of the festival programming process is curatorial. The accessibility of filmmaking technologies over the past decade has meant that more people are telling their stories than ever before. With the thousands of films made every year, festival programmers are the ones who identify groundswells of filmmaking styles and storytelling practices by shining a light on representative films in the festival line-up. But while films by people historically marginalized within the film industry are being made and selected for community-based festivals explicitly designed for specific communities (LGBT, racial or ethnic based festivals, etc.), these films are still not being selected for industry-based film festivals proportional to their rate of production. Many industry-based film festivals have defended the homogeneity of their programs by asserting that there are just not enough films made by women and people of color and that the lack of diversity in the film industry is a universal problem that their festival is not responsible for (cf. Collett-White 2012). The absence of these films, however, is not a reflection of the lack of their production, but a limitation imposed by notions of taste and aesthetics operating within the curatorial process.

Hollywood is the dominant purveyor of films in the world and circulates images and stories that are at best, not reflective, and at worst, grossly misrepresentative of our world's people, cultures, societies, and ways. American film festivals are in a largely unique position to disrupt these dominant images by making space for the contestations, the poly-vocal, the other ways of seeing and being. What distinguishes industry-based film festivals in the US, in relation to, for example, European or other North American festivals, is the wide and long-standing commitment to specifically independent film. Festivals can create spaces in film culture for independent films (films made outside of the studio system and without dependencies on government financing) and different cinematic languages otherwise marginalized within the larger studio systems and prevailing film industries.[2] Festival programmers do not just select films—they actively give shape to film culture.[3] Film festivals facilitate the development of modes of storytelling and cinematic style. The heart of this chapter explicates a curatorial challenge to festival programmers: to see the value and relevance of films that might register our own structures of taste and resonate outside of our personal and professional networks and affiliations.

Festivals attract various stakeholders, each with their own approach to valuing films. Critics judge films based on their technical and narrative mastery, often referencing an established historical canon of cinema. Distributors hunt for films that will attract large audiences and turn a profit in the marketplace. Agents look for new directorial and acting talent to represent. Festivals are generally nonprofits or the exhibitions arm of a parent nonprofit organization and do not make a commission on the films they select. Programmers do not get a cut of the profits when a distributor buys a film and then releases it into theaters or on DVD at a profit or loss. As such, while festival programmers consider the needs of various stakeholders, they are in a unique position to take risks with the films they select, since, unlike other film industry professionals, programmers do not have to account for financial consequences in their decision-making. Festivals can venture to program films not financially "proven," and therefore not on the radar of many industry professionals. In this way, programmers can demonstrate the existence of, and help build, audiences for a certain kind of work.

The curatorial work of de/coding taste

The absences of the voices, stories, reflections, and visions of people who have historically not had the equivalent resources and access to cinematic modes of production have been perpetuated by an independent film culture shaped and sustained by festival curatorial practices. These absences have compelled my work as a scholar and festival curator, and inspired the model of curatorial practice I have honed through my work with industry-based film festivals (and actively engage at the Los Angeles Film Festival). Strongly informed by my cultural activist work with the Women of Color Film Festival, this chapter considers the curatorial practices of film festivals within the relational contexts of taste, aesthetics, ideology, and desire. Cultural theorists and art historians have critically examined the meanings made from and possibilities of curatorial practice within an art context, but film studies rarely shifts the focus away from either a semiotic analysis of films as objects and makers as auteurs, or an analysis of a film's production, to consider the sustained implications for how films are curated, distributed, and exhibited.

Festivals often proclaim they show "the best" cinema, selected by the taste and aesthetic sensibilities of their programmers. It is critical to remember, however, that the concept of "the best" is highly contestable and cannot be taken for granted as universally held. Festival curators value the films that they can recognize as good or high quality in relation to their own knowledge of past films that have garnered acclaim on the festival circuit and more broadly, seen monetary success in the marketplace, and/or are celebrated within a larger canon of established cinema. These "proven" films become the foundation for how professionals define their taste and understanding of a "good" film.

In his groundbreaking text *The Mask of Art: Breaking the Aesthetic Contract*, Clyde Taylor provides a historical foundation from which to examine the ways that the concept of aesthetics is not universal or transcendent across time and culture, but "an eighteenth-century bourgeois construction (taken from aristocratic beginnings) for the control of knowledge, specifically, of the 'beautiful'" (Taylor 1998: 12). Aesthetic reasoning requires that art be seen as separate from its function, essentializing "art for art's sake," in order to mask the ways that "beauty" is tied to moral values and used to reinforce racially charged ideologies and legitimize unjust social structures. Valuations based on aesthetic reasoning and judgments of beauty have been used to inscribe a "mythical notion of inevitable Western superiority" (ibid.: 22) and in doing so, perpetuate an idea of White as intrinsically beautiful, Black as ugly, West as good, and East as evil. Taylor further argues against the notion of a multicultural, varied aesthetics across various cultures and races. He writes:

> the distribution of categories of knowledge among different cultures shows no pattern where they overlap around one category devoted to aesthetic knowledge. Instead, evidence shows that protocols of beauty are integrated within other categories in different societies and often are not isolated in any fashion resembling what Western knowledge has defined as the aesthetic.
>
> (Ibid.: 18)

Rather than argue for the validity of one kind of aesthetic over another, Taylor encourages the reader to dislodge the necessity of aesthetic reasoning and develop new methodologies for engaging cultural expression and art. In his argument against aesthetic reasoning, Taylor asserts: "Whatever is 'lost' by the abandonment of aestheticism would be more than regained in the wider pursuit of cultural liberation" (ibid.: 102).

In *Distinction: A Social Critique of the Judgment of Taste*, Pierre Bourdieu theorizes the ways taste is deeply embedded within and formed through distinctions of class, education, and social position. He writes that "Taste classifies, and it classifies the classifier [...]. Social subjects [...] distinguish themselves by the distinctions they make, between the beautiful and the ugly, the distinguished and the vulgar, in which their position in the objective classifications is expressed or betrayed" (Bourdieu 1984: 6). Bourdieu argues that what is considered "legitimate" culture and art is not defined by some universal and pure form of "taste," but rather by a way of seeing, an "'eye' [that] is a product of history reproduced by education." Valuations of taste are based on distinctions belonging to particular economic, educational, and cultural class formations.[4] Bourdieu describes the consumption of art as "a stage in a process of communication, that is, an act of deciphering, decoding, which presupposes practical or explicit mastery of a cipher or code." In order to be able to value and recognize art, one relies on "the capacity to see (*voir*) [which] is a function of the knowledge (*savoir*)." Ultimately, Bourdieu writes, "A work of art has meaning and interest only for someone who possesses the cultural competence, that is, the code, into which it is encoded" (1984: 2).

A shared ideological framework is at work during the programming process, fortified by shared backgrounds and affiliations between the programmers and the films (and by extension, the filmmakers), which then is reinforced by similarly invested stakeholders (critics and distributors) in their reception of films. As such, while festival programmers are not the ones making films, they create meaningful discourses around film culture and society through the films they select and curate. Audiences at the festival take in these meanings, and articulate them to broader publics (film journalists), contextualize them within a longer cinematic tradition (critics), and gauge whether audiences outside the festival circuit will pay to see the films (distributors). Since aesthetic valuations of films selected at festivals—first by programmers, and then by critics, agents, distributors, etc.—are not attributed to a distinct ideological framework, but considered reflective of the comprehensive state of independent film, festival curators not only evaluate, they also define which films, stories, and characters are considered "good."

In his classic essay "Encoding, Decoding," Stuart Hall provides useful tools, which he uses in his analysis of televisual communication, reception, and infrastructure, to consider the kinds of meanings festivals make, and their role in shifting critical discourse. Festivals, through their curatorial influence and significant filtering role, have become akin to the broadcasting institutions Hall discusses in his essay with respect to television production. Hall argues how codes can become so naturalized that they are not seen as constructed codes, but as the very thing they represent:

> Certain codes may, of course, be so widely distributed in a specific language community or culture, and be learned at so early an age, that they appear not to be constructed—the effect of an articulation between sign and referent—but to be "naturally" given. [...]. This has the (ideological) effect of concealing the practices of coding which are present.
>
> (Hall 1993: 95)

Further, Hall notes that what the process of naturalization represents is not reality itself, but "the degree of habituation produced when there is a fundamental alignment and reciprocity—an achieved equivalence—between the encoding and decoding sides of an exchange of meanings" (ibid.). When the ideological investments and personal affiliations of those encoding (programmers) align with those decoding (audiences), the festival becomes a closed circuit of making meaning that reinforces a dominant order of aesthetic and taste.

Festivals have been critical sites for reinforcing what Hall refers to as a "dominant cultural order" around beauty and stories in relation to the formation of national identity, establishing who belongs and who does not; whose expressions of selfhood and humanity are validated and whose are not; and who has access to the structures of cultural influence, or not (Hall 1993: 98–99).[5] After all, festivals began as wartime machines to legitimize (what we now recognize as) propaganda as art, despite the widely held understanding of festivals as cinephilic havens.[6] The art of film and its exhibition cannot be separated from its politics. The curatorial challenge for film festivals is to navigate the tension between established registers of knowing and reading film, and exploring different ways of seeing.

Missions and stakes: community and industry festivals

It is impossible to provide a clear-cut, universal guide to programming because the curatorial process of evaluating films varies greatly according to a festival's mission and size. Festivals organized around the film industry are programmed and organized according to a different set of resources, expectations, and goals than community-based festivals; yet, the commitment to a clearly articulated mission is necessary for guiding the curatorial process of all festivals. Since there are thousands of festivals in the world, it is critical for film festivals to establish a clear and distinct mission that can effectively guide the festival's selection process. There are three key questions at the heart of any festival's mission: What are the stakes and investments behind organizing a film festival? What is the goal of the festival's film selection? Who is the festival's core audience? A festival's audience cannot be "everyone," and concretely understanding who the audience is, is necessary for accomplishing the festival's mission. When theaters are empty, the audiences a festival purports to serve have been misunderstood.

The mission of the most important film festival for American independent film, the Sundance Film Festival, has been to connect independent filmmakers who have the ideas and the guts with Hollywood's financial and technical resources. As Sundance accomplished this mission through the early 1990s, the festival's leadership began to clearly message another part of the Institute's mission: to focus on innovative forms of storytelling found within independent film. Sundance's mission has been so effective, that it has made "independent film" synonymous with film festivals—so much so, that some festivals think that by virtue of being a film festival, the films they screen are independent. This has contributed to a widespread misrecognition of what constitutes independent filmmaking. A lack of clarity around what independent film means to larger film culture and the role of festivals in relation to independent work causes a number of contradictions in programming approaches.

Industry-based festivals are geared toward selecting a wide range of films that critics, agents, and distributors have not yet seen, in an effort to connect these films and their talent with broader audiences (through film reviews, representation with a talent agency for future work, and theatrical and/or video-on-demand distribution). As I will discuss through my work with the Women of Color Film Festival later, community-based festivals, often structured around race, gender, nationality, sexuality, or genre, offer spaces where people otherwise marginalized within the larger film industry can share cultural representations and reflections with like-minded people.

For a festival whose mission is discovering emerging talent, the primary role of programmers is to select films that have not yet premiered in the world from "blind" submissions, films submitted directly through the submission process without connection to agencies, distributors, and established production companies. Often low-paid or volunteer, screeners are the first group of evaluators for blind submissions and vital to the festival programming process. Screeners need explicit direction (aligned with the festival's mission) when evaluating films with written and/or numerical evaluations that detail their observations on: the film's visual style, formal qualities, narrative structure, content (synopsis from beginning to end), analysis of the film's originality, and the screener's overall impressions. Programmers monitor screener coverage for the interplay between numerical scores and written evaluations. Programmers further scout films at other festivals and meet with distributors, agents, and other professionals to identify suitable films that are already making their rounds within industry circles.

In the case of films making their world premieres at a festival, the programming notes, or "film capsules," are one of the first-ever pieces of writing on the film (since it has yet to be seen by critics, or even publicists). Programming notes create a bridge between the filmmaker and the audience. These notes contextualize the film's importance and how it was selected among so many others. Film journalists and critics reference these programming notes. Since many independent films do not continue on to find broad distribution, festival catalogs mark the primary discussions around film culture at a given time, and for many independent films, serve as the only trace that these films ever existed. In this way, festivals can be seen not only as gate-keepers shaping the future of film culture, but also an archive of its history.

Elaborating on my earlier curatorial work provides the reader insights into my current approaches to curating industry-based festivals.[7] The Santa Cruz Women of Color Film Festival (WOCFF) was created in 1991 as a two- to three-day event programmed and organized by women of color graduate students at the University of California. The mission of the festival is to create a space for women of color to engage each other about cinematic representations of race and gender, specifically those films that are made by women of color. The festival aims to unsettle conventional academic paradigms by providing another model for producing knowledge. The exhibition and programming strategies of the festival's organizers reflect these goals.

The call for submissions is directed to women of color filmmakers around the nation, and requires a director's statement on each film. As a highly contestable term, the call frames "woman of color" as a political category and identity formation that implicitly calls forth dialogues around political visions and struggles like prison abolition, welfare reform, native and indigenous sovereignty struggles, resistance around violence against women, immigration, antiwar, border impositions, sex work, and other struggles facing people of color and immigrant communities.[8] The submissions total between 30 and 60 films—mostly short in length—and are reviewed in relation to the director's statement.

The WOCFF's curating/programming practices actively negotiate the power of the selection process, the instability of the category "women of color" as a sole identity marker, and Western/Anglo valuations of quality and aesthetic merit. Festival curators deliberately do not judge the films as "good" or "bad." Instead, they consider the work the film is trying to do, as articulated in the filmmaker's statement, and films on the basis of both aesthetic merit and the maker's investments and purpose. They felt it important to show work with both conventionally "low" and "high" production values, factors that spoke more to the "knowledge or the training and resources" than to the overall intent of the film. This shifted the focus from determining the "best" film (the festival also presents no competitive prizes) and onto the overall work that women of color are doing through film from a grassroots, self-trained documentarian to an industry-driven film student. Some films submitted were objectionable to some and/or boring to others, and some films were very low production quality or viewed as not political enough. Yet the relevance and importance of all the films was acknowledged because of the range of perspectives offered, beyond the individual agreement or taste of the festival curators. As such, rejecting films was a rarity, and the number of days the festival lasted was often directly determined by the number of sub-missions received. This was a deliberate way for the curatorial team to mediate their position of power to choose whose work would be present and whose work would be absent. The work of programming in this context became not about selecting the films, but arranging them into programs that would enable unexpected connections.

Conventional cinematic venues have been the spaces where many of the festival's participants and audiences have seen grossly misrepresented images and biased narratives about themselves. The exhibition structure of a festival impacts which audiences attend, how they watch the films, and what kinds of engagements they make with each other before and after screenings. Rather than screening all the films in distinct programs within a conventional screen-ing room or theater hall, the organizers of the WOCFF experimented with screenings in dining halls, gymnasiums, community centers off campus, outdoor courts, resource centers on campus, or living rooms, enabling audi-ences to build a different relationship to the screen by creating their own exhibition spaces. British film curator June Givanni argues that creating the contexts for "new social viewing experiences" is a critical part of enfranchis-ing people of color audiences so that they can be connected with, and support the continued production of, independent films that are made foremost for them (Givanni 2004: 65).

Organizers I interviewed explicitly detailed how they used the festival event as a strategic vehicle for mobilizing university resources to fund travel and hospitality for the filmmakers and other key participants of the festival. This meant that throughout the festival, there were many opportunities for artists, activists, and community organizers from around the world to engage with academic discourse and scholarship. While at times tense and uncom-fortable, this resulted in many of the academic participants and festival organ-izers being actively challenged on the arrangement of the festival's program, the use of inaccessible theoretical language to describe and discuss artist and activist work, and on the presence (or absence) of certain communities in the audience. The festival's shifting and open exhibition structure and program-ming strategies allows for what writer, filmmaker, and film scholar Toni Cade Bambara calls "an authenticating audience" (Massiah 2014)—an audience that is vocal about what they like and want (or not) from cultural works and the way they are programmed and exhibited. In this way, the WOCFF facilitates a collective spectatorship among participants toward a feminist of color political project of recognizing difference and building coalition.

The WOCFF carries the possibility of illuminating the complexities of identity and experience by putting forth potentially transformative connections that are questioned, contested, and revised. These connections are less likely in festivals that sideline work by queer, gender nonconforming, and women of color directors as the "alternative" or "other" portion of the program. Over its 20-year history, the WOCFF has prompted a critical interrogation of the university as an elite space of knowledge appropriation; compelled feminist scholars to create knowledge that is relevant, resonant, and urgent; and facilitated ongoing coalitions between feminists from different positions around a more socially, economically, and politically just world.

Seeing differently

An essential part of the curatorial process of festival work is building a programming team that is highly attuned to their own and each other's weaknesses, tastes, and proclivities when watching films. There are many approaches to programming a festival, depending on one's investments. Programming intellectually, according to what one already knows, relies on a prior order of knowledge of a canon of established films that have been selected for other festivals, won awards, been bought and successfully distributed, etc. This would in turn create a program reflective of the dominant film industry and culture. In the next part of this chapter, I outline my approach to developing a curatorial practice that calls for programmers to be open to seeing and feeling something differently, and acknowledging the limits of one's own sensibilities and taste in order to make space for films that fall outside of individual registers of knowledge.

In *Camera Lucida: Reflections on Photography*, literary theorist Roland Barthes describes two different modes of viewing and engaging with photography, the "studium" and "punctum," that have been formative to how I have learned to look at films when programming. The "studium" is an intellectual engagement, a "polite interest" that conveys taste ("I like/I don't like") based on the viewer's expertise, reading the code, utilizing a lettered knowledge to discern whether one approves or disapproves, agrees or disagrees with the artist's intent. The studium is an "order of liking, not of loving; it mobilizes a half desire, a demi-volition; it is the same sort of vague, slippery, irresponsible interest one takes in the people, the entertainments, the books, the clothes one finds 'all right'" (Barthes 1981: 26–27).

The punctum is a way of reading that disrupts the studium. Barthes writes: "This time it is not I who seek it out [...] [the punctum] is this element which rises from the scene, shoots out of it like an arrow, and pierces me." The punctum is not a conscious way of reading art, but "that accident which pricks me (bruises me, is poignant to me)" (ibid.). The punctum is an aberrant detail that wounds the viewer, unexpectedly triggered, often without rationale. The punctum cannot be classified, articulated, or encoded. "What I can name cannot really prick me." Barthes writes, "The incapacity to name is a good symptom of disturbance" (ibid.: 55). The act of naming enables the viewer to know and this articulated knowledge reflects an existing order of knowledge. The incapacity to name signals the possibility of another kind of response outside of preset frameworks of good/bad, right/wrong, beautiful/ugly.

Since my investments in festivals and film programming are to unsettle dominant paradigms for valuing film, my approach to programming is not based on my expertise of film canons or market successes. Shaped by my work as an activist scholar organizing the Women of Color Film Festival, my approach to programming is not through what I know, but rather, an adventure toward what I do not even know I do not know. I want to learn better how I have been taught to see, and explore the possibilities of seeing differently. As such, programming is not an intellectual exercise for me, steeped in a studied analysis of aesthetics and narrative approaches that constitute a canon of acclaimed and successful films. Films that do not engage established registers of quality, and have the potential to disrupt naturalized or dominant codes, may approach aesthetic or narrative differently, and as such, may not be legible (and even considered to be failures) to those looking for films that exemplify cinema's conventions.

Programming for larger festivals is physically and emotionally taxing. The most immediate surprise for new programmers is the amount of labor and patience required to actually sit down and—with wide-open eyes and mind—watch eight to ten films a day, eventually covering more than four or five hundred films within a four-month time frame. Many of these films are in a rough stage of development with scenes missing, unmixed sound and color, and temporary musical scores. Most often, a programmer is the first person to see a film outside the filmmaking team itself. Watching films within a vacuum, without audience members, critics, or friends to gauge one's reactions elicits feelings of exhaustion, loneliness, and insecurity. Immersed in this vulnerable state, a programmer is particularly prone to be pierced by emotional triggers. The curatorial work occurs when these triggers are activated and engaged (rather than dismissed or ignored) as a focal point for engaging the film, so that desires and revulsions are not displaced onto a judgment of the film's "quality" or a viewer's "taste."[9] From my perspective of doing this work for the past decade, these intense conditions afford one the opportunity to destabilize one's own structures of taste, suspend expertise, ward off what we *think* we know—what our intellect dictates our taste to determine as "good." Watching film after film, I wait to be caught off guard, taken aback by a mode of storytelling, a character, an emotion that triggers some deeply personal place informed by where I come from, what I desire, and how I have learned to see.

Filmmakers bring more than their film prints with them into the physical space of a festival. They bring their posse—networks of directors, writers, producers, and actors. A film can literally grow the space of the theater with its entourage and create excitement around the film, visible for the industry to better see its value. Two years after Lee Daniels' film *Precious* world-premiered at Sundance in 2009, the film received two Oscars. It is no coincidence that after *Precious*'s success in the marketplace and Oscar nominations, industry professionals attending the 2011 edition of Sundance were highly interested in films written and directed by filmmakers of color about young women of color negotiating sexuality and gender identity within their communities (*Circumstance, Gun Hill Road, Pariah*). The next year, Ava DuVernay became the first African American person to win the US Directing Award for her film *Middle of Nowhere*. A few years later, in 2015, DuVernay's film *Selma* was nominated for an Oscar.

Separately, these films can be seen as lifeboats for discrete communities floating on the margins of film culture. But placed in relation to one another, these films are more than their niche appeal or box-office earnings. They are the crest of a waxing filmmaking movement.[10] This physical presence compounds over the years to shift the constitution of festival audiences and build momentum for different kinds of films—and for a needed expansion of film culture. Festival programming is not just about selecting films, but also creating exhibition spaces that compel networks of filmmakers and audiences for their work that do not just represent difference—or rather, one's idea of difference—but are shaped by and through difference.

To curate films is to care for the films, their makers, and viewers, to guide their meanings and consequences within culture and society. Festivals create and expand taste, cinematic sensibilities, and ways of storytelling as a way to dynamically make and remake our aesthetic, social, and cultural values through the stories brought to screen about who we are, where we came from, and what we want. Over the past decade, there has been a massive emergence of digital technologies for telling and watching stories, engaged greatly by makers and audiences who have been historically disenfranchised or alienated from the means of cinematic production and exhibition. Within this new order of cultural expression and engagement, the resonance of film can remain vibrant and vital only if the gatekeepers of film wholeheartedly take up a curatorial practice and usher through the independent visions that steward the next generations of storytellers and future of our world.

Notes

1 Of the 12,166 submissions received for consideration to the 2015 Sundance Film Festival, 4,105 were feature-length films and 8,061 were short films. Of the feature film submissions, 2,016 were from the United States and 2,089 were international. Press Release from the Sundance Institute, "Sundance Institute Announces Films in U.S. and World Competitions, Next < = > for 2015 Sundance Film Festival." December 3, 2014, www.sundance.org/blogs/news/us-world-and-next-films-announced-for-2015-festival.

2 Every film that does *not* come out of Hollywood is not by default independent. International films, which are largely supported by state funding, are not independent. Films produced by the "indie" arms of studios are also not independent. Independent filmmaking is not an oppositional formation—it is a relational distinction. Independent films are made when the filmmakers or producers on the film are themselves the bearer of the risk, without infrastructural funding or support that can absorb or profit from the film's failure (or success). Risk breeds bold choices, and ultimately this is what sets independent film apart from an "independent film aesthetic."

3 For example, while gay and lesbian films and makers have been the focus of LGBT film festivals since the early 1970s, it was when these films were recognized on a larger platform like Sundance and proclaimed as a filmmaking movement noteworthy among other American independent films that they were able to "break out" and inspire pop culture at large, consequently inspiring a shift in popular opinions and social mores around gay and lesbian people since the early 1990s. A panel at the 1992 Sundance Film Festival was dedicated to "New Queer Cinema" and moderated by B. Ruby Rich. The festival catalog that year also featured two articles on LGBT film, one by Bill Oliver on the funding and exhibition of gay film, and the other on "New Queer Cinema" by B. Ruby Rich that gestured not only to the films that make up this new wave of film, but also to the exclusionary parameters of filmmaking practices (video work largely excluded) and accessibility of these practices (namely, for women and lesbians).

4 Bourdieu writes:

> Whereas the ideology of charisma regards taste in legitimate culture as a gift of nature, scientific observation shows that cultural needs are the product of upbringing and education: surveys establish that all cultural practices (museum visits, concert-going, reading etc.), and preferences in literature, painting or music, are closely linked to educational level (measured by qualifications or length of schooling) and secondarily to social origin.
>
> (1984: 1)

5 For more on film festivals and nation-making, see Felicia Chan's essay where she provocatively asks "do nations create cinema or does cinema create nations?" (Chan 2011: 255).

6 The first film festival was started in Venice by Mussolini, and after the jury awarded the grand prize to *Olympia*, the US, France, and the UK stormed off to found Cannes. For more on the European roots of film festivals, see Marijke de Valck's *Film Festivals: From European Geopolitics to Global Cinephilia* (2007). Later, American film festivals were established by the federal government to train its citizenry. Based on original research, my study on the origins of American film festivals is forthcoming.

7 The insights about the Women of Color Film Festival are based not only on my experience, but also on extensive archival research and interviews with 32 former participants.

8 UC Santa Cruz has been a longtime hub for feminist of color scholarship, grounded in a humanities-based research center, The Research Cluster for the Study of Women of Color in Collaboration and Conflict. This is further articulated in the work of The Santa Cruz Feminist of Color Collective.

9 I once worked with a screener who had rated very lowly a documentary about assisted suicide. The film's approach was not to focus on the ethics of assisted suicide, but rather to consider the interior process and emotions of doctors who help patients end their lives. Upon reading the screener's coverage of the film, I was able to ascertain that the documentary in and of itself was not "bad" enough to warrant a one-out-of-five rating. Rather, the style of the film, the way it was

organized, and the intensity of the interviews featured were all noted by the screener—as was her general belief that assisted suicides were unethical in all cases, hence her low score. Without the written comments, I would not have been able to have a discussion with the screener about the value of the film in a way that exceeded the moral constraints of the film's subject.

10 Ava DuVernay is known not only for her deft directorial hand, but also for founding AFFRM, the African American Film Festival Releasing Movement, a distribution company whose approach to building audiences for Black films has been at the forefront of a formidable voice in independent film. See my article on DuVernay and AFFRM (Rastegar 2012).

References

Barthes, R. (1981) *Camera Lucida: Reflections on Photography*, transl. R. Howard, New York: Macmillan.

Bourdieu, P. (1984) *Distinction: A Social Critique of the Judgement of Taste*, transl. R. Nice, Cambridge, MA: Harvard University Press.

Chan, F. (2011) "The International Film Festival and the Making of a National Cinema," *Screen*, 52(2), pp. 253–260.

Collet-White, M. (2012) "Regret But No Surprise Cannes Lacks Women Directors," *Reuters*, May 17, US, www.reuters.com/article/2012/05/17/entertainment-us-cannes-women-idUSBRE84F0UD20120517 (August 3, 2015).

De Valck, M. (2007) *Film Festivals. From European Geopolitics to Global Cinephilia.* Amsterdam: Amsterdam University Press.

Givanni, J. (2004) "A Curator's Conundrum: Programming 'Black Film' in 1980s–1990s Britain," *The Moving Image*, 4(1), pp. 60–75.

Hall, S. (1993 [1980]) "Encoding, Decoding," in S. During (ed.) *The Cultural Studies Reader*, London: Routledge, pp. 95–103.

Massiah, L. (2014) "The Authenticating Audience," *The Feminist Wire*, November 18. www.thefeministwire.com/2014/11/authenticating-audience/ (July 24, 2015).

Rastegar, R. (2012) "*Middle of Nowhere* and the Black Independent Film Movement," *Huffington Post*, November 10, www.huffingtonpost.com/roya-rastegar/middle-of-nowhere_b_1953337.html (August 3, 2015).

Taylor, C. R. (1998) *The Mask of Art: Breaking the Aesthetic Contract—Film and Literature*, Bloomington, IN: Indiana University Press.

Williams, A. (2009) "On the Tip of Creative Tongues: The Word 'Curate' No Longer Belongs to the Museum Crowd," *New York Times*, October 2, p. ST1.

Further reading

Alloway, L. (1996) "The Great Curatorial Dim-Out," in R. Greenberg, S. Nairne, and B. Ferguson (eds.) *Thinking About Exhibitions*, London: Routledge, pp. 221–230. (Analysis on the position of art curators between artists, museums, dealers, and audiences, with an emphasis on the educative role of curatorial practice.)

González, J. (2008) *Subject to Display: Reframing Race in Contemporary Installation Art*, Cambridge, MA: MIT Press. (Critiques how curatorial practice and installation have reified racial identity within visual culture.)

Graham, B. and S. Cook (2010) *Rethinking Curating: Art after New Media*, Cambridge, MA: MIT Press. (Considers how new media work is challenging and changing the very concept of curatorial practice.)

Lorde, A. (1984) "Uses of the Erotic: The Erotic as Power" in *Sister Outsider: Essays and Speeches*, Berkeley, CA: Crossing Press, pp. 53–59. (Classic theorization of the erotic as a form of valid knowledge.)

O'Neill, P. (2012) *The Culture of Curating and the Curating of Culture(s)*, Cambridge, MA: MIT Press. (Rumination on the authorial role that curators are taking in the art world.)

The Santa Cruz Feminist of Color Collective (2014) "Building on 'the Edge of Each Other's Battles': A Feminist of Color Multidimensional Lens," *Hypatia*, 29(1), pp. 23–40. (Lends further context into the mission of the Santa Cruz Women of Color Film Festival.)

11 Affective labor and the work of film festival programming

Liz Czach

From 1995 to 2005 I was a film programmer at the Toronto International Film Festival (TIFF)—one of the most prestigious film festivals in the world. Along with a co-programmer or two, I would help select the Canadian films that would screen at the festival that year. In many respects this was a dream job. I got paid to watch movies and discuss them with my film–obsessed colleagues. I met filmmakers, producers, actors, and other members of the creative teams. I traveled to other festivals and cities to preview films. My programming decisions and the films I advocated helped shape national film culture. During the festival I introduced films and facilitated question-and-answer periods, I attended parties and dinners, and I accompanied celebrities down the red carpet. The months of hard preparatory work melted away in the euphoria of those fast-paced adrenaline-filled ten days; it was all very exciting and yes, at times, glamorous.

Programming is one of the most desirable and sought-after positions at a festival. Given the idealization of programming as an occupation, it is unsurprising that during the 11 years I worked at TIFF I was frequently asked by volunteers, interns, junior staff, programming assistants, and others how I became a programmer, as many of them yearned for the opportunity to do the same. More than a decade after leaving the festival I am still asked if I miss working there. And in some respects, I do. As an unrepentant cinephile who will watch almost anything (a good quality for a film programmer) I loved being able to screen hundreds of films and see what young as well as seasoned filmmakers were up to. It was an amazing privilege to have an insider's view on the film productions of the last year and to meet so many talented and interesting people. There is little doubt that film programming can be an exciting and fulfilling job, but the romanticized view of programming as hobnobbing with celebrities and leisurely screening films obfuscates the fact that despite all the perks and privileges, it is still a job.

In this chapter I propose that one productive way to understand the work of film programming is as a form of affective labor: examining the positive forms of affect that festival work can entail—that is, the pleasure and excitement experienced during the festival—alongside the lesser-known affective states of despair, disappointment, and anger that need to be managed as a consequence of films being rejected from the festival. Employing Carolyn Ellis' understanding of autoethnography as "research, writing, story, and method that connect the autobiographical and personal to the cultural, social, and political" (Ellis 2004: xix), I draw upon my experience of working at TIFF as an autoethnographic case study to examine film programming as affective labor.

Beginning in the 2000s, critical labor scholars have examined working in the creative industries to argue for the immaterial, affective, and precarious aspects of creative labor. Groundbreaking work such as Mark Deuze's *Media Work* (2007) as well as David Hesmondhalgh and Sarah Baker's *Creative Labour* (2011) have investigated the emotional, financial, and physical toll that working a precarious dream job can have on cultural workers. Their studies have primarily addressed workers in the music, film, and television production industries, but their findings correlate strongly with my experiences working as a film programmer. Skadi Loist has addressed the precarious nature of festival work arguing that:

> Despite the (supposedly) prestigious status of film festival labour, most people working for festivals find themselves in insecure working conditions. The festival organizations are often precarious entities themselves, struggling for funding and usually operating on a bare minimum, with only very few full-time and year-round employees, some seasonal staff, in low-pay or entry-level positions, and supported by interns and volunteers. This is true for most festivals (even at A-list events such as Berlin, Cannes and Venice).
>
> (Loist 2011: 268–269)

The result of this precariousness is that workers accept "the low pay, project-based temporary employment and a lack of career objectives, benefits or retirement plans" in order to work at jobs that give them more freedom "regarding time frames, mobility and being able to work for something they believe in" (ibid.: 270). But living and working precariously, as an increasingly number of labor scholars are pointing out, not only has financial repercussions but also affective consequences. Feelings of despair, anxiety, stress, and depression are common among creative workers who have uncertain work conditions, are often juggling multiple contracts to make ends meet, or feel exhausted from constantly hustling to find their next job. It is precisely the combination of low pay, long hours, and insecurity that leads many cultural workers to "burn out" physically and emotionally. The degree of precariousness a festival faces varies given the differences in government funding, corporate sponsorship, donations, volunteers, etc. that any specific festival can generate (ibid.: 271–273). Likewise, individuals can have very different experiences of precariousness within the same organization. At a glance, my work conditions had all the hallmarks of such uncertainty: a short-term contract (roughly four months) that was signed year to year without any guarantee of recurrence and no benefits. The nature of film programming means that films have to be screened in a very short time frame and screening films for 12-plus hours daily is common during the busiest times. As a programmer I was paid a set salary per contract rather than an hourly wage. Early in my programming career, a fellow TIFF programmer noted that if we calculated the hours we worked against our salary, we were making less than minimum wage. My salary did improve significantly over the years I worked there (increasing almost three-fold) as the festival aimed to address some of the key issues of insecurity and exploitation. And despite the outward appearance of precarity, I experienced the job as a fairly stable, dependable work environment—my contract was always renewed (until I decided to leave) and, as I have noted, my salary increased from year to year. But all of this should be framed by the caveat that during my second year at TIFF I returned to pursue graduate studies and, since the contract ran from May to September, I approached my work at TIFF as an ideal summer job. Paid teaching assistant-ships and lecturing provided income the rest of the year and I did not have to scramble for additional contracts. Obviously, the degree to which any festival employee may experience his or her job as precarious differs considering individual circumstances. And while I may not have experienced the precarious work conditions that many cultural workers face, there are strong resonances with my film programming work as a form of affective labor that arises from the specific tasks involved in the job.

Before I proceed, it would be helpful to review what film programming is. The *raison d'être* of any film festival is ostensibly to screen films. What a festival shows is winnowed down from a larger pool of entries and the final selection of films is referred to as the film program. Film programming, Peter Bosma argues, refers to "the phenomenon of selecting films and presenting them on a big screen, to a paying audience, whether at a film theatre, film festival or film archive" (2015: 1). Jeffrey Ruoff's collection of essays, *Coming Soon to a Festival Near You: Programming Film Festivals* (2012) similarly discusses programming solely in terms of selecting films for festivals and the final line-up. While the final selection of films shown in a festival is correctly referred to as the festival program this does not accurately reflect the *process* of film programming. An understanding of programming at this final stage—as what transpires over ten days during the festival—fails to account for the fact that the bulk of the "work" of programming actually takes places in the months before the festival starts. As a noun, a "program" refers to a discrete object, a schedule or list of films, but as a verb, "programming" concerns the action of selecting and—critically to my argument—*rejecting* films. Thus, I want to sharpen the current use of the term "film programming" to draw more attention to the other half of the equation when discussing film selection—that is, when films are being selected, other films are being rejected. Because film programmers engage with the selection/rejection process they are seen as powerful "gatekeepers" and influential power brokers "making" or "breaking" careers through their choices. The ability to influence film culture is one of the aspects that makes film programming appealing. As Roya Rastegar puts it in her contribution to this volume (Chapter 10), "Festival programmers do not just select films—they actively give shape to film culture" (page 183). Elsewhere I have written about the role film programming plays in canon formation and national film culture (Czach 2004), but my interest here lies less in the politics and aesthetics of programming decisions per se and more with the idea of film festival programming as work. Recognizing film programming as a process of *selection and rejection* offers an entry point into a discussion of the affective labor required to perform these two distinct but interrelated functions. To put it succinctly, accepting films (and the associated consequences, the festival screenings, visiting guests, etc.) is a pleasurable form of labor whereas rejecting films (and dealing with disappointed filmmakers and producers) is not—and a programmer does both. In outlining both the enjoyable facets of film programming alongside the negative repercussions of a programmer's decisions, my objective is to provide a fuller understanding of the affective labor involved in the work of film programming.

Film programming as a dream job

Film programming understood solely as the watching, selecting, and presenting of films is perceived as exciting and glamorous. In part, film programming, like other forms of cultural labor, is alluring because it is considered pleasurable and appears to primarily generate positive affects. There is no denying, for example, the incredible feeling that a programmer experiences phoning a filmmaker, producer, or distributor to inform him or her that a submitted film has been selected for the festival, or the exhilaration that is felt standing with a director in a theater thundering with applause after a well-received screening. Many audience members at film festival screenings have experienced moments of intense positive affect, and can attest to being swept up in the outpouring of heightened emotion. Terms such as "buzz" or "hype" attempt to capture the fleeting but powerful tidal wave of positive affect that a festival can create. Of course, the films themselves engender affective responses, but the festival context works to intensify those reactions. A fan's sighting of a star, for example, can generate a positive emotion of excitement, waiting in line for a film a sense of anticipation, and so on. Film buyers at TIFF often speak about halving the public audience's response to a film to get a sense of how an audience might respond to the same film at a local cinema. A measure of a festival's success is how well it can generate affective responses from a public audience both in the experience of the film screenings as well as in the experience of the festival itself. The glamour and hype that the public, film industry, and casual onlookers experience when engaging with the festival undoubtedly influences the idea of programming as desirable work.

In opposition to work that might be considered drudgery, dehumanizing, or alienated in Marxist terms, film festival work—like other creative labor—has the potential to be humanizing and self-actualizing. Film festival work is alluring because it promises to be rewarding as one maximizes one's intellectual or creative potential (and within the infrastructure of the festival, programming is considered one of the most highly regarded positions). In working as a film programmer I had, in many ways, successfully found rewarding work. In his book, *How to Find Fulfilling Work*, philosopher Roman Krznaric describes this as a recent phenomenon. He writes:

> The desire for fulfilling work—a job that provides a deep sense of purpose, and reflects our values, passions and personality—is a modern invention. [...] For centuries, most inhabitants of the Western world were too busy struggling to meet their subsistence needs to worry about whether they had an exciting career that used their talents and nurtured their wellbeing. But today, the spread of material prosperity has freed our minds to expect much more from the adventure of life.
>
> (Krznaric 2013: 7)

In many respects, programming provided just such a sense of purpose. Admittedly a festival like TIFF is a huge event with hundreds of screenings and almost two dozen programmers covering different regions and genres, so the influence of any individual programmer can vary, but there is great satisfaction in playing a role in bringing films, filmmakers, and audiences together. I had what many would consider an exciting career that brought me in contact with creative people.[1]

In 2012, the Arts and Life section of *The National Post*, one of Canada's national newspapers, ran a series entitled "I Want Your Job" which featured a number of people employed in the creative industries: a costume designer, a record company A&R (artist and repertoire) representative, and the programmer of TIFF's Midnight Madness section Colin Geddes (Leong 2012). In each case, the interviewees outlined the career path that led them to their dream job. That the series features a TIFF film programmer is unsurprising. Working at a large international film festival such as Cannes, Berlin, Venice, or Toronto can be an influential and prestigious job. Working at TIFF I met directors, producers, actors, and other talent who had poured their heart and soul into their films. I learned to deal with distributors, funders, and government officials. I wrote program notes; participated in press conferences; and was interviewed for radio, television, newspaper, and magazine stories. A nod to the influence the decisions my co-programmers and I exerted was noted in a magazine article that placed us among the most influential people in the Canadian film industry.[2] There is great satisfaction in having a film you championed receive the accolades you think it deserves, or seeing a program note that you took particular pride in crafting appear in the catalog.

In addition to the well-reported hype and glamour, a festival can also generate negative affects. Whereas the public audiences at TIFF are known for their overly enthusiastic responses to screenings, many films at Cannes have been subject to unrestrained hostility—openly and vocally booed—while outraged critics, buyers, and others dramatically exit the theater to the sound of their seats slapping shut. In these cases, an audience or a critic may wonder why a film was selected, i.e., why it was not rejected, and this brings into sharper focus the dual role of the programmer. I would argue, however, that during the festival a programmer's role is overwhelmingly perceived positively as the "selecting and presenting" of films. Generally, film festivals are discrete events that unfold over a short time frame. In Toronto's case the festival runs for ten days in early September every year, and while there is some understanding on the part of the public and industry that months of work went into the planning and staging of the event, the awareness of this work involved is mostly forgotten in the exhilarating chaos of festival itself (its positive affect). The months of preplanning are intentionally rendered invisible. Like a well-edited film adhering to the rules of continuity editing, a film festival doesn't explicitly foreground how it is put together—it doesn't show its seams. Festivals conceal their processes, make their edits unobtrusive, and hope to unspool flawlessly. The idea of film programming as what transpires over ten days during the festival fails to account for the labor that goes into planning and executing a festival, and the majority of the film programming labor is not selection, but rejection.

Film programming as work

In the aforementioned "I Want Your Job" article, Colin Geddes, the Midnight Madness programmer at TIFF, succinctly outlines two rarely discussed aspects of film programming: (1) the large number of films that need to be screened; and (2) the process of rejecting films. He states:

> Anytime, people hear about [my job], they say, "That must be so good." It is good, however, the downside is you have to watch a lot of bad films. For the ten films that I watch for Midnight Madness, I will watch around two hundred other films, 75% are not very good. Then I have to engage in conversations with the directors and producers. You have to tell a mother why her child is ugly and will never succeed—in the most diplomatic way. Or it's like speed-dating. When you reject a film, you say: "You're funny, you're smart but it's me, not you." They'll come back next week and say, "Oh, I've changed my hair colour, my vocal chords are enhanced by the Czechoslovakian philharmonic." And you have to do it again.
>
> (Leong 2012)

In this section, I want to elaborate on these two aspects: first, that the bulk of film programming work occurs in the months leading up to the festival; and second, the emotional labor involved in managing the rejection process.

One of the most appealing aspects of film programming is the idea of watching films for a living. Film programming at a major international film festival sounds like an ideal and enviable job—one gets paid to watch films. Screening films as a function of programming is unlike watching films for one's amusement. The films that are available at a festival, on television or a pay-per-view service, at a movie theater or at a rental store, have been vetted—these films have been chosen by a festival and/or a distributor before making their way to an audience. Programmers are this vetting process for a festival. They are the so-called gatekeepers. In practice this means watching plenty of films that never make it to a public audience and often don't get distributed. As Geddes puts it, "75% are not very good." A programmer does not spend his or her days watching stupendous films but wading through many hours of mostly mediocre work to stumble upon the rare outstanding film and, more often than we care to admit, being subjected to some truly horrendous work. A programmer must contend with not only the quality of the work but also the sheer volume.

Unlike catching the latest blockbuster at the multiplex, attending a screening at the local art house theater (if you are lucky enough to have the latter where you live), or even watching something on Netflix, film programmers do not have the luxury of leisurely absorbing films. One of the unavoidable necessities of the jobs is that programmers must watch a lot of films in a very short period of time. A-list festivals aggressively vie for new films and premieres, consequently films stale-date very rapidly on the festival circuit. To remain competitive film festivals must respond quickly to the newest and most recently completed films. For programmers this means a fairly small window of opportunity to watch all eligible films. For example, let's assume a film is completed in the fall. It then would most likely aim to find a berth at Sundance (January), Rotterdam (January/February) or Berlin (February). If the film isn't programmed in any of these festivals, it is assumed that the film has been passed over and is now considered, for lack of a better expression, "damaged goods." The implicit understanding is that at least one of these festivals would have picked up the film if it were programmable. Thus programmers are more attentive to recently completed films and not films that have been languishing on the circuit. Festivals and programmers want films that they get first crack at, so to speak. Newness on the festival circuit is measured in months, not years. As a consequence, film programmers do not have the luxury of spreading out their programming duties across a calendar year; a film completed in the fall will most likely not be under consideration for a festival that runs the next fall (such as TIFF in September). More often than not, programmers are squeezing all their viewing into a few precious months. In practice this translates into viewing marathons that easily exceed the eight-hour workday. Yet unlike binge watching television shows, where it matters little if the viewer can recall what happened in a specific episode, being attentive and thoughtful after many hours of viewing is a necessary programming skill. Programmers become habituated to judiciously watching copious volumes of moving image material, but this is not to suggest that programmers are infallible. They get tired, they pass over good films, and they might critically appraise the last film of the day more harshly than the first. Programming can be exhausting and it easily feels, say after a 12-hour day, more like a chore than a pleasurable activity. The upshot of these long hours and wading through hundreds of films in search of that undiscovered gem is that the lion's share of a programmer's job is actually rejecting films and excluding them from participating at the festival.

Programming statistics for the 2013 Toronto International Film Festival highlight the degree to which the work of programming at a well-known festival is predominantly about excluding films from presentation. A "fact sheet" available to media and on the TIFF website outlines various statistics pertaining to the films shown at the festival.[3] Among the numbers are figures indicating how many world premieres the festival presented and how many countries were represented as well as numbers pertaining to film submissions and acceptances. So in 2013, 4,892 films were submitted to the festival and 366 were accepted. Spinning the numbers from a different perspective (not included in the fact sheet), filmmakers had an approximately 7 percent chance of getting a film into TIFF. Put yet another way, film programmers rejected 93 percent of the films they screened. It is these films and this work that goes unaccounted for in the prevailing understanding of film festival programming. It is perhaps more accurate to say that film programming is not so much about the selection of films for inclusion in a festival as it is the rejection of them.[4]

Managing the negative affect of rejection

In her influential sociological study, *The Managed Heart* (2003 [1983]), Arlie Hochschild introduced the concept of workers who perform emotional labor. Her study looked specifically at flight attendants, but she acknowledges that "most of us have jobs that require some handling of other people's feelings and our own, and in this sense we are all partly flight attendants" (Hochschild 2003: 11). I would argue that a case can be made for film festival programming as a form of affective labor that is taxing. Hochschild describes service workers who are required, as part of their job, to display particular emotions as well as to influence the emotional state of others. Programming is a form of service work and requires the management of one's emotions and the emotions of the client—the filmmaker. Most film programmers care deeply about film and became programmers as a way to express their cinephilia. Film programmers are meant to love their job, be passionate about film, and be invested in the work they are screening. But how do they manage these feelings with the experience of having to reject countless filmmakers and their films? When the vast majority of your programming work is about dashing filmmakers' hopes and rejecting films, it can be, to say the least, dispiriting. The seemingly endless cycle of rejection takes an emotional toll on even the most thick-skinned person. The ability to control and manage the negative affect of film programming can vary widely depending on circumstances. As one of the top film festivals in the world, a berth at TIFF is highly sought after. The festival propagates a narrative in which the presentation of a film at the festival can be the breakthrough moment in a filmmaker's career— making a rejection all the more crushing. Furthermore, my ability to escape the "fall-out" from programming decisions was complicated by the fact that I was a programmer of Canadian film living in one the largest centers of English-Canadian film production, Toronto, and more specifically in the "arts district" of the city. Running into rejected filmmakers on walks in the neighborhood and at social and professional functions resulted in innumerable uncomfortable situations. This is the flipside to programming at a prestigious festival—the sheer volume of hopeful filmmakers vying for a spot. Rejecting dozens of films year after year takes an emotional toll and often leads to burnout. The glamour, glitz, and euphoria of the festival never feels so distant as during the period in which the rejection notices go out.

Coping with the negative consequences of rejection is one of the less visible and certainly unglamorous parts of programming. Taking phone calls from irate directors, producers, and distributors is draining. Each iteration of a festival creates scores of rejected filmmakers, so mitigating the disappointment is a necessary function of the job. One of the ways of coping with the rejection is to depersonalize the interaction and keep a distance. Hesmondhalgh and Baker describe the British production team of *Show Us Your Talent* experiencing a similar process of emotional labor when they had to inform parties they wouldn't be participating on the show. Understandably, the "[r]ejected parties were often upset and sometimes angry" (Hesmondhalgh and Baker 2008: 108). The producers, however, didn't give particular reasons for the rejection. Instead, by "tying their responses to production conventions, workers are able to maintain an emotional distance while simultaneously managing the caller's emotional response to the situation" (ibid.: 109). A similar strategy is employed in festivals via the depersonalized film festival rejection letter, or these days email, that tends to follow a fairly standard template:

> We are fortunate to always have a large number of entries submitted to the festival each year. The overall quality is typically quite high, making our selection process a perpetually difficult and challenging one.

> We were working up to the very last minute hoping to find a spot for all the films that we were interested in showing, but in the end, had to make some very difficult decisions. I am sorry to say that we were unable to fit your film into our program.

> Unfortunately, we're forced to make tough choices between an over-abundance of intriguing topics and we're being pulled more strongly in other directions for our limited slots.

There are so few slots in our program and so many deserving films, that we are forced to make many difficult decisions.[5]

These quotes show a remarkable consistency. Festivals and programmers shy away from any specific critique of the film and overwhelmingly rely on the standard equation of too many films and too few slots. Of course, this formulation is true—there are simply more films than screening slots, but this does little to manage the disappointment the filmmakers experience. The depersonalized email cannot be employed effectively when the programmer knows the filmmaker or when the filmmaker or producer has reached out to the programmers. It is in the personal interactions that emotional labor of rejection is felt most acutely and hardest to manage. Filmmakers are understandably disappointed, but they can also be very angry. Trying to manage their emotions and keeping your own emotions in check can be trying, particularly if the filmmaker is abusive or unreasonable. Although a more personalized response might seem like the better approach, in my experience getting into the particulars of why a film wasn't selected does more harm than good. Giving feedback on a film in progress may help a filmmaker shape the final outcome, but providing a critique on a finished film achieves little. Filmmakers might go back and do some more editing or tweak their soundtracks, but the problems are always bigger than a few small adjustments and the film ends up being rejected all over again. Given the vast amount of labor that goes into rejecting films and knowing that few are accepted—there's only so much good news that can be delivered—it is unavoidable that there can be power struggles among festival staff as to who actually gets to invite a film.

In some cases, festivals do not even send rejection letters or emails, leaving the filmmakers who submitted films in an unnerving state of limbo. This lack of communication can, on the one hand, be chalked up to poor communication practices, or on the other, to simple avoidance of the unenviable process of rejection. Either way, it is unprofessional and disrespectful. An email—even a curt and detached one—is better than nothing at all. Going a step further some festivals have deviated from the standard dry correspondence to use the rejection letter as an opportunity to attempt to mitigate or, as Hochschild would argue, manage the disappointment. The following is part of a letter sent out in 2013, it reads:

As filmmakers ourselves, [Festival Name] programmers are keenly aware of how disappointing a letter like this can be. After all is said and done, we owe each and every one of you a debt of gratitude. This year, we were inspired to see the dedication to originality that still exists in an industry that seems evermore helplessly engulfed by the Hollywood machine. The stories you dared to tell, the gorgeous landscapes and moods you captured, and the risks you took in style and execution challenge us to achieve more in the years to come, both as programmers and as filmmakers. We saw your willingness to tramp into the wilderness, set props on fire, send your cameras downriver, destroy your own apartments, and stay up all night to catch the light when it is just perfect, all for the sake of the bigger picture. As a result, your work was able to transport us to the distant future, the forgotten past, and worlds most people could not even imagine. Whether you screen at [Festival Name] is ultimately irrelevant; you are vital to the health and spirit of this industry, and the most important thing is that you never let anyone else deter you from your work.

Yours in cinema,
[Festival Name] Programming Team[6]

This letter makes a concerted effort to cushion the inevitable disappointment of rejection. To effectively do this, the programmers distance themselves from their role as gatekeepers and align themselves as kindred spirits—as fellow filmmakers. Positioning themselves as filmmakers, not programmers, permits them to occupy a space as a potentially fellow rejectee, rather than the powerbrokers that are making the decisions. After this rhetorical move, the letter proceeds to acknowledge the disappointment and offer solace while going on to downplay the significance of the rejection. At first blush, this letter successfully eases the reader's frustration. It focuses on the passion, commitment, and dedication of the filmmaker—acknowledging these as positive qualities that the festival celebrates. Yet, despite the positive affect that has been generated, the film is still rejected. When the letter declares, "whether you screen at [Festival Name] is ultimately irrelevant," it veers toward the disingenuous. Declaring the irrelevance of their event is a bankrupt statement. Of course, it matters if your film is selected or not. If the festival was truly irrelevant there would be no point in it taking place and filmmakers would not bother submitting their films. Furthermore, the letter's directive that the filmmaker follow his or her dreams and not "let anyone else deter you from your work" is craftily composed to inspire the filmmaker while simultaneously rejecting them. That is, do not let this letter be read as rejection but rather as a rousing call to continue making films despite the fact that we do not want them. This slyly composed letter exhibits an astute understanding the powerful negative affects of rejection and the emotional work of trying to manage those feelings.

Conclusion

Several years after I had left the festival I ran into Piers Handling, then director of TIFF (now CEO), during the intermission of a performance at the Canadian Opera Company. Handling was having a conversation with an arts reporter from *The Toronto Star* and reintroduced me to him (although I knew him from my programming days). The latter, always on the lookout for some kind of TIFF scandal story, asked if I had been "forced out." "No," I replied. "I burned out." His question suggested that the only way one would leave a desirable programming position would be through force rather than choice. There had been acrimonious departures from the festival, so the question was not without foundation, but after more than a decade of the ups and downs of festival programming I needed to stop. My dream job was becoming less fun and more like work. The long hours of watching films was one part of the job I had grown weary of and the years of cumulative rejection had caught up with me. I no longer wanted to be a gatekeeper. I wanted someone else to weed out the weaker films. As a programmer of one thin slice of the festival pie (to use a clichéd metaphor) I was missing out on the bigger picture of international cinema. I was keen to return to attending the festival to watch films rather than having to work during the festival and missing out.

Since leaving the TIFF programming team in 2005, I return yearly to attend the festival to catch up with friends, former colleagues, and watch films. In 2013, I was invited back to TIFF as a member of the Canadian feature film jury. Along with three co-jurors, I was tasked with selecting the best Canadian feature film and best Canadian first feature made the previous year. Over the course of the festival's ten days, the jury watched 30 eligible films to select the two winning films. Following this, I agreed to participate as a panel member of Canada's Top Ten, a TIFF initiative that selects the top ten films produced in the country in the previous year. So I watched approximately an additional 40 more films. Although a jury chooses winners from a smaller pool of films than a programmer, the process of selecting some films once again means rejecting (if in a somewhat less explicit fashion) others. For better or for worse, this jury duty took me back to my programming days at TIFF. Positively, I recalled how much I enjoyed the access I had to seeing so many films, but I also recalled sitting through hours upon hours, days upon days, of films that exist somewhere on a continuum from great to merely watchable and sometimes outright painful. This is not an indication of the Canadian film industry per se as most film programmers will attest to this being a fundamental function of film programming. After a few weeks of watching many, many films, I remembered all too well that film programming is work.

Notes

1 It should be noted that Krznaric's advice about seeking fulfilling work is aimed at a financially secure middle-class reader who can pursue "the great dream [that] is to trade up from money to meaning" (2013: 7). The idea that a job "was worth far more than a pay check" (ibid.: 8) may ring hollow for precariously employed and poorly paid cultural workers.

2 "The Players: The 30 Most Important People in Canadian Film," *Shift*, September 1998: 39.

3 This is available on their website under the TIFF media releases section and while the fact sheet obviously varies from year to year the high number of rejections is a recurrent feature. The fact sheet for 2015 is available at: https://s3.amazonaws. com/presscontent.tiff.net/docs/Z4G078_2015_Festival_Fact_Sheet_8874233_1444 314942.pdf (August 27, 2015).

4 I keenly recall the word 'rejection' penciled in day after day in the day planner of a festival staffer whose job it was to send out rejection letters to filmmakers.
5 These quotes are drawn from rejection emails a friend generously shared with me. Further examples are available on the website graphicsandbeer.com. See the page "Film Festival Rejection" where a number of rejection letters are reproduced. http://graphicsandbeer.com/war-film-preproduction-tutorials/festival-rejection (July 30, 2015).
6 This letter was shared with me by a friend.

References

Bosma, P. (2015) *Film Programming: Curating For Cinemas, Festivals, Archives*, London, New York: Wallflower.

Czach, L. (2004) "Film Festivals, Programming, and the Building of a National Cinema," *The Moving Image*, 4(1), pp. 76–88.

Deuze, M. (2007) *Media Work*, Cambridge, UK and Malden, MA: Polity.

Ellis, C. (2004) *The Ethnographic I: A Methodological Novel about Autoethnography*, Walnut Creek, CA: AltaMira.

Hesmondhalgh, D. and S. Baker (2008) "Creative Work and Emotional Labour in the Television Industry," *Theory, Culture & Society*, 25(7–8), pp. 97–118.

Hesmondhalgh, D. and S. Baker (2011) *Creative Labour: Media Work in Three Cultural Industries*, New York and Abingdon: Routledge.

Hochschild, A. R. (2003 [1983]) *The Managed Heart: Commercialization of Human Feeling*. Berkeley and Los Angeles, CA: University of California Press.

Krznaric, R. (2013) *How to Find Fulfilling Work*, New York: Picador.

Leong, M. (2012) "I Want Your Job: TIFF Programmer Colin Geddes," *National Post*, January 19, http://news.nationalpost.com/health/i-want-your-job-tiff-programmer-colin-geddes (July 30, 2015).

Loist, S. (2011) "Precarious Cultural Work: About the Organization of (Queer) Film Festivals," *Screen*, 52(2), pp. 268–273.

Ruoff, J. (ed.) (2012) *Coming Soon to a Festival Near You: Programming Film Festivals*, St Andrews: St Andrews Film Books.

Further reading

Bosma, P. (2015) *Film Programming: Curating For Cinemas, Festivals, Archives*, London and New York: Wallflower. (A discussion of film curating in different exhibition contexts including film festivals.)

Czach, L. (2004) "Film Festivals, Programming, and the Building of a National Cinema," *The Moving Image*, 4(1), pp. 76–88. (An examination of the role that film festivals can play in the canon formation of a national cinema.)

De Valck, M. (2007) *Film Festivals: From European Geopolitics to Global Cinephilia*, Amsterdam: Amsterdam University Press. (A groundbreaking study of the rise and proliferation of European film festivals and the film festival circuit.)

Gann, J. (2012) *Behind the Screens: Programmers Reveal How Film Festivals Really Work*, Washington: ReelPlan. (Interviews with film programmers from a wide range of festivals regarding their programming choices and practices.)

12 The "festival film"

Film festival funds as cultural intermediaries

Tamara L. Falicov

In a darkened movie theater, the Thai film *Uncle Boonmee Who Can Recall His Past Lives* (Apichatpong Weerasethakul, 2010) ends. Before the house lights slowly fade on, the film aficionados remain in their seats through the credits and view what has become an all-too-familiar sight in the realm of low-budget world cinema: multiple logos listing various film funds, many sponsored by European film festivals, are dotting the screen, from which the filmmakers received support to develop, produce, or post-produce their films. In this particular case, they see fund "brands" which we might deem "endorsements of quality" with the Hubert Bals Fund (International Film Festival Rotterdam), World Cinema Fund (Berlin International Film Festival), plus the French Film Institute's (CNC) Fonds Sud (now called *aide aux cinémas du monde* or World Cinema Support) which recognized Weerasethakul's potential to make an award-winning film. And in 2010, win it did, as the first Asian film since 1997 to win the *Palme d'Or* award at the Cannes film festival.

Multiple funds have become invaluable stamps of approval for the directors, film curators, and for the funding bodies themselves who might award funds to a project if they note that the filmmaker is a prior grant recipient of one of many funds associated with film festivals. These film funds serve various functions; one is that at the most basic level, they provide a crucial avenue of film funding for directors from emerging film cultures that may not have state film funds at their disposal, let alone private investors. Listing these funds at the end of their film might also serve as a "ticket" to gain access to exhibition venues and distribution channels associated within and outside of these first-tier film festivals. Films funded by these festivals also have the potential to be an exciting "discovery" for European and other film festival programmers (Stringer 2001: 134–135) who then can "claim them" in part and they often request that the director premiere their partially funded film. As SooJeong Ahn points out, film festivals are increasingly acting as "cultural intermediaries" (2011: 111–112) in helping to shape the kinds of films they think will show promise and demonstrate a particular story, or aesthetic, or combination of the two. The filmmaker recipients do not always comply with the request to premiere their film at the "funding" festival, and in some cases the films are not ultimately selected, but becoming a grantee helps them gain access to the inner track of the film festival circuit.

This chapter will examine the phenomenon of film festival funds which stem from support initiatives of various international film festivals principally throughout Europe, some in the United States, and some in East Asia and the Middle East, aimed at assisting filmmakers from the "Global South" or the "developing world."[1] The term Global South, according to cultural theorist Siba Grovogui, implies "a symbolic designation of former colonial entities engaged in political projects of decolonization toward the realization of a postcolonial international order" (Grovogui 2010) and implies that these countries are emerging economies that are still wrestling with the legacies of colonialism.

This essay will illustrate what the film funds are for, and some of the debates circulating about whether they help or hinder professional development efforts in various underserved parts of the globe. At the crux of this discussion is the end product: what kind of film is typically selected for financial/development/exhibition/distribution support to be nurtured by, and ultimately exhibited (and in some cases distributed by) film festivals?

Since the 1990s there has been a proliferation of film festival initiatives that help make film festivals a site to produce and ultimately sell films at the level of pre-production (training initiatives for newer directors, residencies, and seminars), and production and post-production initiatives (film funds, co-production markets, and post-production competitions). Given that there is a preponderance of these programs within festivals currently, I will discuss these initiatives more generally with the majority of the examples being extracted from the Latin American region, given this author's area of expertise.

By orchestrating fund competitions for Global South filmmakers such as the World Cinema Fund at Berlin, the Hubert Bals Fund at Rotterdam, or the Asian Cinema Fund at Busan, or training programs such as the Cannes Residence Program, the Berlinale Talents (renamed in 2014 from Berlinale Talent Campus), or the *Produire au Sud* workshop at the Festival des 3 Continents in Nantes, France, this is changing the face of film festivals by adding the needed scaffolding to foster the film festival space as a place for (pre-)production, including script development and networking, but also deepening transnational collaboration, financial exchange, and deal making for transnational film production. Film festivals are, more than ever, acting as a broker between international producers, between seasoned veteran producers and newer Global South director-producers, and between newly minted film school directors and film festival curators throughout Europe and other parts of the world.

This relatively recent phenomenon demonstrates the many ways in which film festivals now function apart from simply exhibiting films. They are now more active players in developing new projects by having a hand in adjudicating film pitches, helping fund them, and then launching said films via premieres and hopefully on to future critical and financial acclaim. In fact, many of these high profile film festivals manage to create multiple initiatives to help shepherd promising films by Global South filmmakers through different phases of the filmmaking cycle from the initial script writing/development process, through the production phase, and into the post-production and then distribution phase. Hypothetically, one could imagine a fully funded film produced solely within the confines of one or more film festivals (though, at this point, the funding amount from each initiative is still quite low). We'll begin with a historical overview of these funds and then generally describe the debates surrounding them.

Historical overview of film festival funds

Large, celebrated film festivals such as Cannes, Venice, Toronto, Sundance, and Berlin often have film markets or industry spaces where stakeholders, in Ragan Rhyne's words (including filmmakers and studios, journalists and press agents, professionals and programmers, local cultural councils and supranational agencies, tourist boards, cinephiles, and the like) (Rhyne 2009: 9) come to support their country or region's filmmaking, or they have a stake in investing in and buying films. These agents are part of a deeply interwoven tapestry of transnational funding modules which have become the industry standard for most filmmakers in Europe, Asia, and the Global South since the 1990s.

With shifts in the global economy to a neoliberal model of finance, countries without state funding often seek out financing in other countries, making co-production a commonplace, and in some cases, essential, funding scheme for filmmakers around the globe (with the exception of the large studios in the United States, India, Hong Kong, and other countries with a robust film industry sustained by private-sector investment). Darrell W. Davis and Emilie Y. Yeh have argued that film festivals "have moved beyond their traditional role as gatekeepers in the art of cinema and ventured onto a new international field of transactions in film co-production, investment, promotion and exhibition" (Davis and Yeh 2008: 140). Transnational co-financing and co-production have become dominant trends in the global market, thus making film funding initiatives an exemplary model of how film festivals position themselves within a global economy (Stringer 2001: 142).

Marijke de Valck's research on the history and theory of film festivals shows that the role of film festival funds is increasingly to elevate their "cultural prestige" when festivals "produce" films from the developing world (De Valck 2007: 106) with the aim of assisting with the production of a film culture in these underserved parts of the world, but also for film festival curators to have a chance to screen these new works. Moreover, film festivals, with their more independent, "art house" form of filmmaking (in contrast to the typically mainstream Hollywood circuit of multiplex cinema circulation) created a privileged space for film directors and producers to hopefully sell their work in a specialty marketplace that recognizes a smaller, niche market-based potential.

Thus, one way for film festivals to solidify their brand is to help fund a particular kind of "festival film" that fits the profile of their festival.

These funding bodies become "cultural intermediaries" that help shape the distinctive look of the festival. This term, which comes out of sociological literature, assigns an important role to institutional players, which in this case are film fund administrators who mediate the selection process in subjective ways. David Hesmondhalgh prefers to use the term "creative manager" which he defines as brokers or mediators between the interests of owners and executives (e.g., the World Cinema Fund) and those of creative personnel, who will want to achieve success and/or build their reputation by producing original, innovative and/or accomplished works (Hesmondhalgh 2013: 78).

Each fund supports different aspects of the production process (script development, production, post-production), and in some cases, filmmakers compete for and win multiple grants from various (and in some cases the same) funds for different stages of the production cycle (for example, a script development grant from Sundance, a residency grant from Cannes; see Ostrowska 2010 for more on this topic), a production grant from Hubert Bals (see Steinhart 2006; Falicov 2010; and Ross 2011, for more on this topic), and a Tribeca Film Institute Latin America Media Arts Fund grant. (See Table 12.1 at the end of the chapter detailing a selection of notable film festival funds and their characteristics.)

If the objective of these film festival fund managers is to facilitate the creation of new works by Global South filmmakers that might adhere to a kind of cinema that would be "a good fit" for a (typically European) film festival, then we must interrogate what kind of "festival film" is being produced with the help of these festival funds. As Thomas Elsaesser observes, the "festival film" also signifies films "made to measure" and "made to order" to such an extent that filmmakers could even "internalize" and "target" a certain film festival or festival circuit schedule for their work (Elsaesser 2005: 88). But how might we approximate the definition of a "festival film" and what are the practices and initiatives by which festival funds act as "cultural intermediaries"? What are the criteria of "festival films" and do they vary by film festival funding mechanism? Finally, how are these festival films produced differently in Europe, as they might be in the United States or elsewhere?

Definitions of the "festival film"

Gilles Jacob, former president of the Cannes film festival, playfully described the supposed origins of the "festival film" in a 2013 newspaper column beginning with Plato, who after all, "claimed his cave was the world's first movie theater." He points out that while the festival film over time was defined as films marked by "excess" in some cases, and "internalization of expressions" [by actors] in others, that ultimately, the "festival film [term] fell by the wayside and we returned to making the best films possible" (Jacob 2013). This nonsensical piece does not so much elucidate the origins of the term, but points to the fact that "festival film" can be seen as contentious as it has adopted meanings for different constituencies. For example, film critic Jonathan Rosenbaum notes that the industry used to brand a festival film as "a film destined to be seen by professionals, specialists, or cultists but not by the general public because some of these professionals decide it won't or it can't be sufficiently profitable to warrant distribution" (Rosenbaum 2002: 161). Others, such as film scholar Rick Altman, take a more neutral approach and aim to classify it. In his book *Film/Genre* he notes that "festival films are defined by their exhibition rather than by their textural characteristics" (Altman 1999: 91).

Julian Stringer, in his 2003 dissertation, approximates a working definition of the term "festival film" by, in his words, considering two ways of thinking about it as an "identifiable generic product." He states that:

> On the one hand, the term festival film is often used simply as a means to classify films exhibited *at* festivals. On the other hand, it works on occasion to identify titles assumed to be produced *for* festivals. Examination of both of these usages reveals much about the production of cultural hierarchies of taste on an institutional and an international scale.
>
> (Stringer 2003: 143)

As mentioned previously, this chapter will focus on Stringer's latter definition of festival films. Marijke de Valck rightly observes that festival funds add "a whole new layer of meaning to the label "festival film," as these films are not only predominantly produced for the festival circuit, but also partially by (and with the cultural approval of) the festival circuit" (2007: 181). These kinds of "festival films" produced by and for film festivals constitute a very small number of films that screen at film festivals, and are by no means the vast majority of films that screen there. It is this group of "festival films," groomed to premiere at film festivals which partially (or totally) fund them, that will be examined here.

As pointed out by Rick Altman, the film festival is indeed a genre unto itself, but given the multiple varieties of niche film festivals (documentary, human rights, women's, disability, queer, comedy, shorts, animation, Jewish, etc.) a multitude of diversity can be found in the film festival world. But in terms of the large film festivals that program world cinema in competition, we might dub those typical "art cinema festival films." There are many factors that influence whether a film concept is considered film festival material. For one, the narrative is often of the "art house" variety, which we might define as a film with particular aesthetic and narrative conventions for an educated audience and from a higher socioeconomic class stratum. Given that there are so many iterations of what a festival film might look like, perhaps we could approach a working definition in terms of what a festival film is not. For example, they are generally not fast-paced action genre films with large budgets, high production values, and familiar narratives. These genre films are made with a much larger swath of (younger, male) moviegoers in mind and are, theoretically, purely for entertainment. These fast-paced thrillers, spectacles and the like are not usually what filmmakers are trying to achieve for the art house theater (or film festival) setting. That said, there are festival films that are entertaining.

Rosalind Galt and Karl Schoonover, in their theorizations of the definition of art cinema, also prove instructive. They consider art cinema to have the following typical, but not essential features:

> overt engagement with the aesthetic, unrestrained formalism, and a mode of narration that is pleasurable but loosened from classical structures and distanced from its representations. By classical standards, the art film might be seen as too slow or excessive in its visual style, use of color, or characterization.
>
> (Galt and Schoonover 2010: 6)

David Andrews, in his study of how art cinema might be categorized, does not see describing formal characteristics of art cinema as a way to define it, but instead favors a definition of "art cinema that credits its high art potential" (Andrews 2013: 34). He goes on to point out the importance of film festivals (and film studies within academia) in furthering the prestige of art house cinema that circulates in festivals. To that end, he observes that the definition of the festival film has the same unrestricted and ever-changing tendencies as the art film. It can include many diverse films from around the world, with their respective established auteurs; it is always changing, never static (ibid.: 172–190).

Cindy Wong outlines a number of aesthetic and narrative tropes in her book on film festivals that help to describe how one might define a "festival film." In this thoughtful typology, she observes tropes such as films typically "serious" in tone; there is an austerity and oftentimes minimalist aesthetics within the mise-en-scène, and many of these films have open narratives (Wong 2001: 75–77). A significant number of the films are character portraits and the narratives linger on "small moments" rather than spectacle (ibid.: 78–79). Finally, most of these films attempt to achieve realism by employing non-actors so as to achieve, in Wong's words, a sense of "everydayness" (ibid.: 82–83).

Other factors that play into the definition are how much importance can be attributed to the role of the auteur in ascribing whether a film might be defined as a "festival film" or not. In Jean Ma's study of Taiwanese auteur Tsai Ming-liang, she notes that "the reassertion of authorial presence demands to be understood in the broader context of a globalized commercial industry in which the auteur has become reified as a marketing category" (Ma 2010: 346). In other words, she, along with film scholar Timothy Corrigan, points out that auteurs are no longer seen as romantic, modernist figures of subjective authorship, but rather a "critical concept bound to distribution and marketing aims that identify and address the potential cult status of an auteur" (Corrigan 1991: 103). These auteur cinema festival films are made by celebrated directors that oftentimes are selected for inclusion (and many times for premieres) due to the value-added prestige factor these filmmakers—with their "signature styles"—bring to these festivals, despite the shortcomings a specific film might have. This continuity in a "brand" of auteur by festival programmers has thus created strong links between specific auteurs and important film festivals. For example, the Argentine filmmaker Pablo Trapero tends to premiere all of his films at the Toronto International Film Festival (Sanchez 2014).

Finally, among other concerns, the question of traditional, mainstream genres as linked or delinked to festival films always prefigures in a discussion of whether a film fits the "film festival" designation. If genre films usually are construed to be more formulaic, popular, and predictable, then one might say that festival films, on the whole, are not considered genre films. But Wong astutely points out that there are always exceptions to the rule, and that some genre films have played at festivals and indeed have won awards (Wong 2011: 71–72). So these definitions are never clear-cut, and some creative festival films are typically hybrid genre and art house films, such as the Paraguayan film, *7 Boxes*/*7 cajas* (Juan Carlos Maneglia and Tana Schémbori, 2012) which, as a mixture of thriller and a film festival "new discovery" spoken in Jopará (a mixture of Spanish and Guaraní), won the prestigious "industry award" at the *Cine en Construcción* post-production competition at the San Sebastian International Film Festival. It later played in film festivals and art houses in the United States, though in Paraguay, it played in mainstream cinemas (the few that exist in the capital city), breaking box-office records there (Falicov 2013).

Finally, there are different films that might be selected for inclusion such as low-budget Filipino films, or Spanish horror films that are not of the "art house" variety, but are more commercial and/or cult in nature. Film festival programmers include these perhaps for the kitsch factor, the fact that they are not accessible in mainstream movie theaters and they might also be selected because they are part of a trend, a cult following, or some type of niche market that film programmers have identified. And finally, there are commercial blockbuster films that top festivals such as Cannes and Sundance screen due to pressure from Hollywood and so-called indie studios (The Weinstein Company, etc.) in their never-ending quest to remain relevant to the global film industry (Rosenbaum 2002: 145).

The development of film funds

Historically, most European film festival funds developed as a former colonial power's legacy to dispense development aid through the form of cultural funding to the developing world. Carol Lancaster traces the beginnings of European foreign aid to the 1920s, when French and British governments shifted their notions that colonies had to be self-financing to the idea that both private and public funds could be used to improve impoverished conditions through funds for expanding infrastructure, health services, and education in their territories (Lancaster 2007: 27). Later this aid became part of the Cold War phenomenon, as a bulwark against Communism, but in the case of funding from the Netherlands, Germany, Spain, France, and other countries, the concept came from an earlier colonial period. European film finance funds are taxpayer-funded initiatives often funneled through the Ministry of Foreign Affairs. For example, the Hubert Bals Fund of the International Film Festival Rotterdam was founded in 1988 after Huub Bals, the director of the festival, lobbied the Dutch government for development funds to support filmmakers from the developing world. He died a few months later, not knowing the fate of what he dubbed the "Tarkovsky Fund." Thus, the Hubert Bals Fund was created posthumously and named in his honor. Therefore the discourse around this fund, as one financed by government development aid, along with a large NGO, a foundation grant, and funds from the national lottery, is that it is considered development aid money to support filmmakers in emerging film cultures "expressing and preserving their cultural diversity" (Bhalotra 2007). This fund was also instituted as a response to what cultural activists have argued is the "homogenizing" power of Hollywood industrial cinema, a rallying cry that surfaced in the late 1960s and continued into the 1980s. (See, for example, the seminal McBride Report in 1980 in which UNESCO decried the one-way flow of communication from the United States to the rest of the world, stating that it threatened cultural diversity, national sovereignty, cultural identity, and the right to communicate.) Steven Neale has also pointed out how the dominance of Hollywood, and the specter it raised of an invasion of American mass culture, played a key motivating factor in efforts by liberal-democratic European governments to subsidize and shore up national art cinemas within their own borders (Neale 1981: 30–31).

In the Asian context, there were other motivating factors for the creation of film funds. In the case of the Asian Cinema Fund and the Asian Film Market initiatives that are part of the Busan International Film Festival, scholar SooJeong Ahn (who was employed at the film festival between 1998 and 2002) casts the development of these funds as a strategy that Busan developed to help launch the financing and incubation of more Asian films that would be destined for the global marketplace after circulating at the film festival circuit; a way of being proactive rather than "relying on being discovered by the West in their film festivals" (Ahn 2011: 104).

In the case of private-sector funding initiatives in US film festivals such as the Tribeca Film Institute (TFI) Latin American Media Arts Fund, founded in 2009, one might speculate—given the corporate funding model—that this might shape the kinds of films selected for funding support. However, the jury is composed of independent film professionals and Latin American film curators, so in this sense, there is not a correlation, but the rationale for why these companies decided to contribute funding toward independent filmmaking in Latin America comes from a different ideological place than the European funding model. Corporations such as Bloomberg News and Heineken have their specific corporate strategies for why they have sponsored the TFI Latin American Media Arts Fund. In the case of Bloomberg, who is the main (or in Tribeca's language, the "presenting") sponsor, their decision to support the Media Arts Fund coincided with the opening of their offices in Brazil, Chile, and Mexico. Therefore, an effort to cultivate stronger cultural bonds with the region through cinema and media may have justified the investment. In the case of Heineken, according to the fund manager, José Rodríguez, the Dutch beer company signed on to a three-year contract "to further their efforts to market their brand within the Latino community" (Rodríguez 2014). More recently, the TFI has initiated a series of feature-length fiction and documentary film funds sponsored by the Mexican Chamber of the Film Industry (Canacine) whose current president, Alejandro Ramírez, is also the CEO of Cinepolis, the largest theater exhibition chain in Mexico. Another sponsor is Mexico's answer to Netflix, called MovieCity. According to José Rodríguez, members of Canacine and MovieCity are interested in funding Latin American and US Latino/a filmmakers to help them break into the United States and hopefully the international market (Rodríguez 2013).

Implications of funding "festival films"

In recent decades, with the proliferation of film festivals throughout the globe, the involvement of the International Federation of Film Producers Associations (FIAPF) has increased in importance. Their mandate is to represent the common economic, legal, and regulatory interests of their member film and TV production industries, which stretch across five continents. Their main concerns deal with compliance with copyright and intellectual property (IP) issues as it relates to film piracy. They also concern themselves with ensuring IP compliance in the realm of film festivals, and have created a ranking system for film festivals around the world. Each film festival, if they are interested in being classified for "A-list" status, must undergo an accreditation process.

According to film scholar Minerva Campos, the ability to host world and international premieres at film festivals helps ensure and maintain the ranking of the top film festivals. She found that film festivals such as Cannes, Berlin, and Mar del Plata had to program a minimum of 14 world premieres in order to maintain their A-list status (Campos 2012: 92). These premieres help further a festival's stature as a "main player" in the field. Thus, there is a never-ending quest on the part of programmers and other staff members to continually find sources of premieres.

One method to help foster new, fresh material with potential for world premieres in the future is to develop a film funding initiative or host a co-production market/forum whereby the film festival becomes a participant in funding and later promoting and premiering cinema it helps produce. Campos argues that post-production initiatives are part of the "premieres" pipelines that festivals such as San Sebastian know will give them first look on the projects that they helped to finance (ibid.).

One of the implications of this pressure to find new material to satisfy the A-list designation is that Global South filmmakers may then opt to premiere their works at major European film festivals, thus relegating second- and third-tier works to film festivals in their home countries (De Valck 2007: 71). Manthia Diawara states this as a case in point when he asserts that "the best African films are screened at […] European and American film festivals […] filmmakers no longer look to FESPACO [the Pan-African Film Festival in Ouagadougou, Burkina Faso] for the premiere of their films" (Diawara 1994: 386).

Another implication of these film funds is that there is an inherent power dynamic that lies between the European/Asian/North American funders and those from the Global South seeking funds to begin or complete a project. Scholars have examined this relationship as one of neocolonialism (Halle 2010), and one of filmmakers having the "burden of representation" (Branston 2000) to write storylines about marginalization for the benefit of wealthy viewers or what has been deemed "poverty porn (*pornomiseria*)" (Ross 2011: 262). Others have cataloged instances where producers have been asked to make their films look more "authentic" (e.g., "more African") and examine a kind of "global art house aesthetic" that Global South filmmakers may conform to (Bartlet 2000). Finally, these funds might begin to create what Miriam Ross calls a "favoured group of filmmakers" after she observed that from 2005 to 2009, 7 of 20 film projects received funding both from the Hubert Bals Fund and the World Cinema Fund. Moreover, in one instance, the Chilean film *Lucia* (Niles Atallah, 2011) was given funding from Hubert Bals, Cine en Construcción, and the Global Film Initiative (the latter fund is now suspended) (Ross 2010: 132–133).

The criteria that Hubert Bals employs, according to its annual report, is that it looks for "the artistic quality and authenticity of the film" and, among other more standard criteria (country of production, nationality, gender, feasibility of the project both financially and artistically), there is another category, which is "the extent to which the project can contribute to strengthening the local film climate" (Hubert Bals Fund Annual Report, 2011–2012). Though these categories certainly fall within the mission to help developing countries with fomenting local film culture and infrastructure, it could be argued that it is part of a discourse of development that "advanced industrialized countries" filmmakers need not concern themselves with. This observation merely points out how development aid discourses permeate funding in ways that might be limiting or reductive in narrative content to filmmakers from the Global South. This is another example of the issue of filmmakers having to potentially demonstrate "authenticity," or what scholar Kuan-Hsing Chen has decried what he perceives as a "global nativism" where "exotic images of natives and national local histories and signs are employed as selling points in world cinema" (Chen quoted in Ma 2010: 340) that can be found, regardless of how a filmmaker might define it, in the considerations for funding in arguably the most venerated of all film festival funds, the Hubert Bals Fund.

Whether filmmakers are "kowtowing" to what funders may expect from "world cinema" may not ever be proven. There are precedents in history of the relationships that artists enjoyed before the Renaissance period whereby there were parameters for art creation, approval, and funding—in other words, a potentially fraught or complicated relationship between artists and their funders. However, it is important to consider what Brazilian filmmaker and visual artist Arthur Omar has observed: that festival films comprise a "genre that are especially made according to their own rules and traditions in order to win prizes at festivals. The film festival genre of films is immediately recognizable as festival films by juries, critics, and audiences alike" (cited in Wollen 2002: 9). In other words, most festival films, regardless of funding, conform to specific rules, practices, aesthetics, and traditions to be selected.

Film fund practices: what to consider before applying

In order to facilitate access to European film funds and (hopefully) later a market for their finished works, filmmakers from the Global South apply for these funds. Each of these funds have different requirements that vary by which countries are eligible to apply, what materials are needed for the application, and regulations about what procedures filmmakers need to conform to if they are awarded funds. (See Table 12.1 at the end of the chapter for specific information about a select number of funds.) And, each of these funds have their own distinctive type of film that they screen at their festival. In interviews with Brazilian producer Andrea Giusti about her decision to apply for specific festival funds or not, she stated "[g]iven that each fund associated with film festivals has a particular kind of film they are looking for, producers seriously decide if it is worth their while to apply, especially because the funds are so low" (Giusti 2011).

Moreover, in the case of many of these festival production funds, they are aimed at cultivating newer directors from Global South countries, rather than veterans. Thus, if a film director has made more than two films and has begun to gain recognition in the festival circuit, they will not necessarily want to take the time to apply for these smaller grants, and moreover, they will most likely not be selected by funders such as the Hubert Bals and World Cinema Fund given their seniority and potential to access private sources of funding. The anecdote of Argentine director Pablo Trapero was discussed by Marianne Bhalotra (then fund manager of the Hubert Bals Fund), where his trajectory went from winning a Hubert Bals script development grant, to later, a Hubert Bals production grant, and then later was encouraged to apply for CineMart with his film *Born and Bred/Nacido y criado* (2006) which he needed to fund and did so, after attending (Bhalotra 2007).

In the case of the World Cinema Fund (WCF) at the Berlin International Film Festival, it stipulates that filmmakers partner with a German producer in addition to their local one. According to French film producer Marc Irmer, this is actually quite valuable for both parties because it not only facilitates access for the filmmaker in question, but also is helpful for European producers who wish to have access to cash flow from national film institutes that may offer credits or later subsidies. In other words, it is a two–way street for

Europeans to gain access to state funding schemes in Latin America (Irmer 2011). Clearly, Latin Americans benefit by having access to a potentially lucrative and prestigious European market, but what is not often discussed is the financial support that Europeans also potentially gain access to.

Many of these funds have application processes, which are time-consuming and complex. There are also funds that limit which countries may apply given that they target countries that are in the most dire economic straits. So how are countries defined as "developing" versus "industrialized"? In the case of the Hubert Bals Fund, as part of the application process, filmmakers must ensure that their country of origin is on a list drawn up by the Organisation for Economic Co-operation and Development (OECD) that categorizes a country's level of development aid given based on each country's per capita gross domestic product (GDP).

There are four categories, and using the Latin American region as an example of the differences in levels of development, in the "least developed countries" category, the only Latin American/Caribbean country represented is Haiti. In the third quadrant, labeled "Lower Middle Income Countries and Territories," countries such as Belize, Bolivia, El Salvador, Guatemala, Guyana, Honduras, and Paraguay are listed. The remainder of the Latin American countries is considered to be "Upper Middle Income Countries and Territories" and include Argentina, Brazil, Chile, Mexico, Costa Rica, Cuba, Ecuador, and others.[2]

In order for readers to better understand the processes by which director-producers from the Global South experience applying for these film festival funds, here is a broad theoretical, step-by-step outline of how applicants prepare to apply for funds and what steps they must consider in weighing their options. This is not an exhaustive schema, but designed to give readers a sense of what is involved in applying for film financing for (generally) low-budget projects.

1   Which country does the filmmaker hail from, or what is their country of origin? Is their country eligible for a particular fund based on geography? Given the variation in definition of the various funds, it is incumbent on the filmmaker to be savvy in learning what fund might be available to their specific project/country of origin.

2   What films has the director made in the past? Do they have a track record? Were any awards won or festivals attended for short or feature-length films? If it is their first feature, or documentary, this will determine which funds are available. There are fewer funds open to documentary projects, despite typically being less expensive in general. Some film funds are more open to newer directors, such as World Cinema Fund, which are generally small awards.

3   At what stage is the film project? If it is in the pre-production, or script development stage, it is possible to apply for funds such as the script development fund at Sundance or Hubert Bals. There are funds for

production and post-production stages, and all require different forms of documentation.

4   What are the parameters of each fund's application? Does an arrangement with a European producer need to be established before applying for funds? In what language must one apply? Does it have to be submitted in English? French?

5   If the project is selected for funding, when can you expect the funding? Is it disbursed based on completing the film in stages and sending over that proof? Will it be possible to conform to the timeline?

6   After the film is completed, is the applicant required to present the film at the festival that awarded funding as a courtesy "first look"? In the case of post-production funding, might distribution rights for a European country be relinquished as a stipulation?

7   What are the odds that your film project will be selected for the fund you're applying to? For example, the Hubert Bals Fund typically accepts 7 percent of submitted applications.

This is just a sampling of the kinds of questions that filmmakers and producers must consider upon applying for various film funds associated with festivals and other initiatives. Table 12.1 describes a sampling of film fund initiatives associated with various international film festivals and gives Global South filmmakers a sense of the various opportunities available, along with their prerequisites for them to begin a project or complete one.

Conclusion

In recent decades, film festivals have made film pre-production, production, and post-production funding an added resource for filmmakers. As this chapter has shown, there are multiple reasons why some film festivals (typically Western, but including some Asian and Middle Eastern) choose to help foster filmmaking from the Global South. Though this opportunity might present itself as welcome for some, it also might have some larger implications, such as reinforcing a power dynamic between Northern gatekeepers and cultural arbiters and Global South filmmakers in terms of what films might be selected for these specific funds. These expanded film finance and training functions also help film festivals stay relevant, novel, and in business.

To add a level of training, and funding for script development, production or post-production funding, keeps film festivals such as Berlin, Rotterdam, San Sebastian and others uniquely positioned to shape, shepherd, and select the film projects that could potentially hit the film festival circuit by storm, thus lending prestige to the festival that "initiated" or "discovered" it. By creating hubs, or networks of film producers, new directors, and other agents associated with film markets, film festivals are now truly entrenched in the business of (ideally) creating the perfect "festival film"— from the bottom up.

Table 12.1 Select characteristics of notable film funds

Fund and Festival	Year fund est.	Application language	Which part of the filmmaking process is supported?	What kind of funding is available?	Who can apply?	Specific requirements
Hubert Bals Fund International Film Festival Rotterdam (IFFR)	1989	English	Script and project development; post-production of feature-length films.	Up to €10,000 for script and project development; up to €20,000 for post-production.	Filmmakers and producers from countries on the OECD's Development Assistance Committee (DAC) list; the country of development and production should also be on the DAC-list.	World premiere of the completed film should take place at IFFR. Distribution rights to the film for the Netherlands, Belgium, and Luxembourg become the property of the IFFR.
Sundance Labs Sundance Film Festival	1990	English, Spanish, French, Portuguese, or Russian	Feature-length screenplay development through collaboration with creative advisors.	Air travel, accommodations and meals at Sundance Resort for the duration of the Lab.	Current regions of focus are: Eastern Europe, Southeast Asia, Northern Africa, and Central America though filmmakers from other regions may also be considered.	The lab is for a writer/director or writer–director team working on a first or second feature film. A completed script (written in or translated into English) is required with the application.
Cannes Cinéfondation Residence Program Cannes Film Festival	2000	English or French	Script and project development for feature-length fiction films, animation excluded.	Accommodations in Paris for the 4½-month residence session, €800 per month stipend, free access to Paris cinemas.	Filmmakers from any nation may apply. All candidates must be fluent in English or French.	Applicants are evaluated on the strength of their previous work (short or feature films) and must submit a screenplay in development or short treatment of the work they will develop during residency.

Festival	Year	Language	Focus	Support offered	Eligibility	Notes
Cine en Construcción San Sebastián International Film Festival (Spain) and Cinélatino Latin American Film Festival Toulouse (France)	2002	Basque, Castilian, Portuguese, or English	Post-production of feature-length films (sound mixing, color correction, special effects, etc.).	In San Sebastián, the winning project receives post-production services from partner companies as well as theatrical distribution and advertising in Spain. In Toulouse, the winning film receives post-production services, and Cine+TV network purchases broadcast rights to the winning film for €15,000.	Filmmakers from Latin America whose films have been shot but have not completed post-production.	Submitted films are jointly screened by organizers from both festivals. Six films are chosen to compete in each festival, and these are screened for professionals (producers, distributors, exhibitors, buyers, festival programmers, etc.) only. Upon completion winning films are screened with the *Instituto Cervantes* touring exhibition.
Open Doors Co-production Lab Locarno International Film Festival	2003	English	Film development, production, and post-production of feature-length films.	Airfare, accommodations and meals for the Co-production Lab held during the festival. The top project to emerge from the Lab receives a €40,000 production grant.	Varies by year. Past editions have highlighted projects from Cuba and Argentina, countries in the Mekong, the Maghreb, Southeast Asia, the Middle East, Latin America, Greater China, central Asia, India, sub-Saharan Africa and the South Caucasus.	Locarno focuses on a different world region each year and selects 12 projects from that region to participate in the Lab, which is designed to connect film professionals from the selected region with potential partners.

Table 12.1 Continued

Fund and Festival	Year fund est.	Application language	Which part of the filmmaking process is supported?	What kind of funding is available?	Who can apply?	Specific requirements
World Cinema Fund Berlin International Film Festival	2004	English	Feature-length fictional and documentary film production.	Up to €100,000 per project, funding may not exceed 50% of total production costs.	Filmmakers from Africa, Latin America, Central America and the Caribbean, the Middle East, Central Asia, Southeast Asia, and the Caucasus region.	German production company is required. A screenplay in English or French (or, in the case of documentary, an extended treatment) is a required component of the application.
RAWI Middle East Screenwriters Lab Sundance Film Festival	2005	English	Feature-length screenplay development through collaboration with creative advisors.	Travel, accommodations and meals for the duration of the Lab, which takes place in Jordan.	Emerging Middle Eastern screenwriters, co-writers, or writers/directors. Only Arab screenwriters/ filmmakers are eligible, regardless of country of residence.	The lab is for screenwriters working on a first or second feature film. A completed script (written in or translated into English) is required with the application.
Asian Cinema Fund Busan International Film Festival	2007	English	Feature-length fiction film script development and post-production; feature-length documentary production or post-production.	$10,000 for script development. $10,000 or $5,000 for documentary (post-) production. The post-production award for fiction includes airfare, accommodations, facility use and post-production labor in Korea.	Eligible applicants must be Asian nationals, or be either of Asian heritage or be a non-Asian residing in an Asian country. A full list of eligible countries is available on the fund's webpage.	All work must be original (resubmissions are ineligible) and intended for theatrical release. Applicants must reside in Asia and submitted projects should contain Asian characters, stories, themes, and settings.

Program	Year	Language	Funding Type	Award Amounts	Eligibility	Notes
Tribeca Film Institute Latin American Media Fund Tribeca Film Festival	2009	English	Production or post-production of feature-length animation, documentary and/or hybrid films.	Up to $10,000 per project.	Filmmakers from the Caribbean, Mexico, Central and South America.	Films should be story-driven with no existing US or Latin American distribution in place.
Doha Film Institute Grants Initiative Doha Film Festival: for filmmakers from the Middle East and North Africa	2010	English or Arabic	Development, production, and post-production funding for short and feature-length films. Narrative, documentary, experimental, and essay films are eligible.	For short films of all kinds, awards range from $2,500 to $15,000. For feature-length films of all kinds, development funding awards range from $5,000 to $20,000. Production and post-production awards for feature-length projects range from $15,000 to $100,000.	Filmmakers from the Middle East and North Africa (MENA). First-generation descendants of nationals of MENA countries are also eligible to apply.	Funds are for filmmakers working on their first or second films. For production and post-production funding, a production company must also be attached to the project.
Doha Film Institute Grants Initiative Doha Film Festival: for filmmakers from OECD developing countries	2010	English or Arabic	Production and post-production of feature-length narratives. Documentaries are eligible by invitation only.	$50,000 to $100,000 for narrative production and $30,000 to $75,000 for narrative post-production. $30,000 to $75,000 for documentary production and $20,000 to $50,000 for documentary post-production.	Filmmakers from countries on the OECD's Development Assistance Committee (DAC) list.	Funds are for filmmakers working on their first or second films. A producer and production company must be attached to the project.

Table 12.1 Continued

Fund and Festival	Year fund est.	Application language	Which part of the filmmaking process is supported?	What kind of funding is available?	Who can apply?	Specific requirements
SANAD Fund Abu Dhabi Film Festival	2010	English or Arabic	Development and post-production of feature-length documentaries and narratives.	Up to $20,000 per project for development and up to $60,000 per project for post-production.	Filmmakers from Algeria, Bahrain, Comoros Islands, Djibouti, Egypt, Iraq, Jordan, Kuwait, Lebanon, Libya, Mauritania, Morocco, Oman, Palestine, Qatar, Saudi Arabia, Somalia, Sudan, Syria, Tunisia, UAE, and Yemen.	The director of the project must be a national of one of the eligible countries and a production company from at least one of the eligible countries must also be attached to the project.
Mumbai Mantra Sundance Institute Screenwriters Lab Sundance Film Festival	2011	English	Feature-length screenplay development through collaboration with creative advisors.	Travel, accommodations, and meals for the duration of the Lab, which takes place in India.	Indians, people of Indian origin, or filmmakers who have mixed heritage (i.e. one Indian parent).	The Lab is for screenwriters working on a first or second feature film. Shortlisted applicants must provide a completed screenplay.

Sources: filmfestivalrotterdam.com; tribecafilminstitute.org; sundance.org; film.jo; mumbaimantra.com; sansebastianfestival.com and cinelatino.com.fr; berlinale.de; festival-cannes.com; pardolive.ch; acf.biff.kr; dohafilminstitute.com; abudhabifilmfestival.ae.

Acknowledgments

The author wishes to thank Courtney Aspen Sanchez for her research assistance in compiling Table 12.1 on film festival funding as well as editorial help. Additionally, thanks go to the co-editors for their astute advice, and to producer Marc Irmer for his feedback on the step-by-step schema.

Notes

1 The term "Global South" gained cultural currency at the end of the Cold War, when the moniker "Third World" was no longer used, since this no longer had any relevancy. The latter term assumed that there was a First World (capitalist industrialized societies), Second World (socialist bloc countries), and Third World, a consortium comprising some newly independent (ex-colonial) countries, formed a movement of nonaligned countries in 1955 at the historic Bandung conference in Indonesia.
2 Browse from www.oecd.org/dac/stats/daclist.htm for the latest configuration countries and their status based on GDP (January 20, 2014).

References

Ahn, S. (2011) *The Pusan International Film Festival, South Korean Cinema and Globalization*, Hong Kong: Hong Kong University Press.

Altman, R. (1999) *Film/Genre*, London: BFI.

Andrews, D. (2013) *Theorizing Art Cinemas: Foreign, Cult, Avant-Garde, and Beyond*, Austin, TX: University of Texas Press.

Bartlet, O. (2000) *African Cinema: Decolonizing the Gaze*, London: Zed Books.

Bhalotra, M. (2007) Hubert Bals Fund manager, personal interview, January 28.

Branston, G. (2000) *Cinema and Cultural Modernity*, Buckingham: Open University Press.

Campos, M. (2012) "Reconfiguración de flujos en el circuito internacional de festivales: el programa 'Cine en construcción'," *Secuencias: Revista de Historia del Cine*, 35, pp. 84–102.

Corrigan, T. (1991) *A Cinema Without Walls: Movies and Culture After Vietnam*, New Brunswick, NJ: Rutgers University Press.

Davis, D. W. and E. Y. Yeh (2008) *East Asian Screen Industries*, London: British Film Institute/Palgrave.

De Valck, M. (2007) *Film Festivals: From European Geopolitics to a Global Cinephilia*, Amsterdam: Amsterdam University Press.

Diawara, M. (1994) "On Tracking World Cinema: African Cinema at Film Festivals," *Public Culture*, 6(2), pp. 385–396.

Elsaesser, T. (2005) *European Cinema: Face to Face With Hollywood*, Amsterdam: Amsterdam University Press.

Falicov, T. L. (2010) "Migrating South to North: The Role of Film Festivals in Shaping and Funding Global South Video," in G. Elmer, C. H. Davis, J. Marchessault, and J. McCullough (eds.) *Locating Migrating Media*, Lanham, MD: Lexington Books, pp. 3–22.

Falicov, T. L. (2013) "'Cine en construcción'/'Films in Progress': How Spanish and Latin American film-makers negotiate the construction of a globalized art-house aesthetic," *Transnational Cinemas*, 4(2), pp. 253–271.

FIAPF (International Federation of Film Producers Associations) www.fiapf.org/.

Galt, R. and K. Schoonover (2010) "Introduction: The Impurity of Art Cinema," in R. Galt and K. Schoonover (eds.) *Global Art Cinema: New Theories and Histories*, Oxford: Oxford University Press, pp. 1–27.

Giusti, A. (2011) Film producer, personal interview, September 22.

Grovogui, S. N. (2010) "The Global South: A Global Metaphor, not an Etymology" *Global Studies Review*, 6(3), www.globality-gmu.net/archives/2271 (August 19, 2015).

Halle, R. (2010) "Offering Tales They Want to Hear: Transnational European Film Funding As Neo-Colonialism," in R. Galt and K. Schoonover (eds.) *Global Art Cinema: New Theories and Histories*, Oxford: Oxford University Press, pp. 303–319.

Hesmondhalgh, D. (2013) *Cultural Industries*, 3rd edition, London: Sage.

Hubert Bals Fund Annual Report, 2011–2012, https://acceptatie.iffr.com/sites/default/files/content/jaarverslag_hbf_2011-2012.pdf (November 6, 2015).

Irmer, M. (2011) Producer, Dolce Vita Films, personal interview, February. 27.

Jacob, G. (2013) "Cannes: Festival de Films ou Films de Festival?" *Le Huffington Post*, December 5, www.huffingtonpost.fr/gilles-jacob/festival-de-cannes_b_3252457.html?utm_hp_ref=fr-culture (June 16, 2014).

Lancaster, C. (2007) *Foreign Aid: Diplomacy, Development, Domestic Politics*, Chicago, IL: University of Chicago Press.

Ma, J. (2010) "Tsai Ming-Liang's Haunted Movie Theater," in R. Galt and K. Schoonover (eds.) *Global Art Cinema: New Theories and Histories*, Oxford: Oxford University Press, pp. 334–350.

McBride Report (1980) *Many Voices One World, Towards a New, More Just and More Efficient World Information and Communication Order*, Paris: UNESCO.

Neale, S. (1981) "Art Cinema as Institution," *Screen*, 22(1), pp. 11–39.

Ostrowska, D. (2010) "International Film Festivals as Producers of World Cinema," *Cinéma & Cie: International Film Studies Journal*, 10(14/15), pp. 145–150.

Rhyne, R. (2009) "Film Festival Circuits and Stakeholders," in D. Iordanova and R. Rhyne (eds.) *Film Festival Yearbook 1*, St Andrews: St Andrews Film Studies, pp. 9–39.

Rodríguez, J. (2013) Tribeca Film Festival Latin American Media Fund manager, email correspondence, December 12.

Rodríguez, J. (2014) Email correspondence, June 2.

Rosenbaum, J. (2002): *Movie Wars: How Hollywood and the Media Conspire to Limit What Films We Can See*, Chicago, IL: Chicago Review Press.

Ross, M. (2010) *South American Cinematic Culture: Policy, Production, Distribution and Exhibition*, Newcastle Upon Tyne: Cambridge Scholars Publishing.

Ross, M. (2011) "The Film Festival as Producer: Latin American Film and Rotterdam's Hubert Bals Fund," *Screen*, 52(2), pp. 261–267.

Sanchez, D. (2014) Latin America film programmer for the Toronto Film Festival, email correspondence, May 30.

Steinhart, D. (2006) "Fostering International Cinema: The Rotterdam Film Festival, CineMart, and the Hubert Bals Fund," *Mediascape: A Journal of the Critical Studies Program at the UCLA School of Film, TV, and Digital Media*, 2, pp. 1–13.

Stringer, J. (2001) "Global Cities and the International Film Festival Economy," in M. Shiel and T. Fitzmaurice (eds.) *Cinema and the City: Film and Urban Societies in a Global Context*, London: Blackwell, pp. 134–144.

Stringer, J. (2003) *Regarding Film Festivals*, Indiana University, ProQuest, UMI Dissertations Publishing.

Wollen, P. (2002) *Paris Hollywood: Writings on Film*, New York: Verso.

Wong, C. H.-Y. (2011) *Film Festivals: Culture, People, and Power on the Global Screen*, New Brunswick, NJ: Rutgers University Press.

Further reading

De Valck, M. (2013) "Sites of Initiation: Film Training Programs at Film Festivals," in M. Hjort (ed.) *The Education of the Filmmaker in Europe, Australia, and Asia*, New York: Palgrave Macmillan, pp. 127–145. (This text is very helpful in delineating the various film training initiatives offered by film festivals that exceeded the scope of this essay.)

Falicov, T. L. (2010) "Migrating South to North: The Role of Film Festivals in Shaping and Funding Global South Video," in G. Elmer, C. H. Davis, J. Marchessault, and J. McCullough (eds.) *Locating Migrating Media*, Lanham, MD: Lexington Books, pp. 3–22. (This essay delves more into depth about the implications of when Northern film festivals help to fund South filmmakers.)

Galt, R. and K. Schoonover (eds.) (2010) *Global Art Cinema: New Theories and Histories*, Oxford: Oxford University Press. (A definitive anthology in describing the definition of art house cinema that relates to "festival filmmaking.")

Ross, M. (2011) "The Film Festival as Producer: Latin American Film and Rotterdam's Hubert Bals Fund," *Screen*, 52(2), pp. 261–267. (This piece is a deeper look into the politics of film festival funds for Latin American filmmakers.)

Steinhart, D. (2006) "Fostering International Cinema: The Rotterdam Film Festival, CineMart, and the Hubert Bals Fund," *Mediascape: A Journal of the Critical Studies Program at the UCLA School of Film, TV, and Digital Media*, 2, pp. 1–13. (The in-depth discussion of the Rotterdam film festival's CineMart is instructive here.)

Index

Page numbers in *italics* denote tables, those in **bold** denote figures.